OXFORD STUDENT TEXTS

Series Editor: Steven Croft

John Webster
The White Devil

Edited by Jackie Moore

Oxford University Press

OXFORD

UNIVERSITY PRESS

Great Clarendon Street, Oxford OX2 6DP

Oxford University Press is a department of the University of Oxford.
It furthers the University's objective of excellence in research, scholarship,
and education by publishing worldwide in

Oxford   New York

Auckland   Cape Town   Dar es Salaam   Hong Kong   Karachi
Kuala Lumpur   Madrid   Melbourne   Mexico City   Nairobi
New Delhi   Shanghai   Taipei   Toronto

With offices in

Argentina   Austria   Brazil   Chile   Czech Republic   France   Greece
Guatemala   Hungary   Italy   Japan   South Korea   Poland   Portugal
Singapore   Switzerland   Thailand   Turkey   Ukraine   Vietnam

Oxford is a registered trade mark of Oxford University Press
in the UK and in certain other countries

British Library Cataloguing in Publication Data

Data available

ISBN: 978-0-19-8310747

10 9 8 7 6 5 4 3 2 1

Typeset in India by TNQ

Printed in China by Printplus

Paper used in the production of this book is a natural, recyclable product made
from wood grown in sustainable forests. The manufacturing process conforms
to the environmental regulations of the country of orgin.

The publishers would like to thank the following for permission to reproduce photographs:

Page 4: National Galleries of Scotland; page 11: Luminarium; page 198: Photographers
Direct; page 209: Victoria and Albert Museum; page 214: English School/The
Bridgeman Art Library/Getty Images; page 225: Mary Evans Picture Library; page 245:
Pope Sixtus V (1520–90) (engraving), Italian School, (16th century) (after)/Private
Collection/Ken Welsh/The Bridgeman Art Library; page 252: Donald
Cooper/Photostage

Illustrations Page 6: Martin Cottam; page 230: Q2A Media

Contents

Acknowledgements

The text of the play is taken from *John Webster: The Duchess of Malfi and Other Plays*, edited by René Weis (Oxford World's Classics, 1998). The extract from the *Authorized Version of the Bible* (*The King James Bible*), the rights in which are vested in the Crown, is reproduced by permission of the Crown's Patentee, Cambridge University Press.

Acknowledgements from Jackie Moore

I would like to thank Steven Croft for his encouragement and warm support. I am hugely indebted to Jan Doorly for her sensitive interventions and for her insightful editing. I am grateful to my friend and colleague Paul Dean for our long and fruitful discussions and last, but not least, I would like to thank all at OUP who have helped with this text.

Editors

Steven Croft, the series editor, holds degrees from Leeds and Sheffield universities. He has taught at secondary and tertiary level and headed the Department of English and Humanities in a tertiary college. He has 25 years' examining experience at A level and is currently a Principal Examiner for English. He has written several books on teaching English at A level, and his publications for Oxford University Press include *Exploring Literature*, *Success in AQA Language and Literature* and *Exploring Language and Literature*.

Jackie Moore read English Language and Literature at the University of Manchester with Elizabethan and Jacobean drama as a special option. She was later awarded her doctorate in English Literature with Philosophy. After lecturing in literature in higher education, she moved to the secondary sector, becoming head of an English department. She is now an educational consultant and Senior Examiner in English Literature for national and international examinations, and is the author of several books on A level literature.

Foreword

Oxford Student Texts, under the founding editorship of Victor Lee, have established a reputation for presenting literary texts to students in both a scholarly and an accessible way. The new editions aim to build on this successful approach. They have been written to help students, particularly those studying English literature for AS or A level, to develop an increased understanding of their texts. Each volume in the series, which covers a selection of key poetry and drama texts, consists of four main sections which link together to provide an integrated approach to the study of the text.

The first part provides important background information about the writer, his or her times and the factors that played an important part in shaping the work. This discussion sets the work in context and explores some key contextual factors.

This section is followed by the poetry or play itself. The text is presented without accompanying notes so that students can engage with it on their own terms without the influence of secondary ideas. To encourage this approach, the Notes are placed in the third section, immediately following the text. The Notes provide explanations of particular words, phrases, images, allusions and so forth, to help students gain a full understanding of the text. They also raise questions or highlight particular issues or ideas which are important to consider when arriving at interpretations.

The fourth section, Interpretations, goes on to discuss a range of issues in more detail. This involves an examination of the influence of contextual factors as well as looking at such aspects as language and style, and various critical views or interpretations. A range of activities for students to carry out, together with discussions as to how these might be approached, are integrated into this section.

At the end of each volume there is a selection of Essay Questions, a Further Reading list and, where appropriate, a Glossary.

We hope you enjoy reading this text and working with these supporting materials, and wish you every success in your studies.

Steven Croft   *Series Editor*

John Webster in Context

The life of John Webster

John Webster was born between 1578 and 1580, probably in the parish of St Sepulchre, Clerkenwell, just to the north of London's city walls. He lived a stone's throw from Smithfield Market, where his father established the family business. It was a centre of trade and commerce teeming with life, especially during the annual Bartholomew Fair; traders bellowed, bullied and bargained. Diverse customers thronging the narrow ways were sweet-talked and seduced into buying various goods, always aware of the menace of pickpockets, cutpurses and drunks. A life could be lost for a couple of pence. The adjacent cattle yards, awash with blood, mud and detritus, stank foully.

Such closeness to the daily drama of life and death must have nourished the imagination of the future dramatist, helping him to create his characters and the sense of a real society outside the court that is evoked in *The White Devil* by Monticelso's *black book* (IV.i).

Webster's family became prosperous; his father, a member of the prestigious Guild of Merchant Taylors, made his money out of a successful coach-building business. With his son he made and sold coaches, also hiring them out as stage props, so Webster would have had early contact with the theatre. He probably attended the Merchant Taylors' School, going on to study at the Inns of Court, as most wealthy young men of the age did. Webster is likely to have studied law, and again this experience was relevant to his future career as a dramatist.

Luke Wilson, in *Theaters of Intention: Drama and the Law in Early Modern England* (see Further Reading, page 263), explains the close links between the law and the stage. Students of law and aspiring actors alike studied rhetoric (the effective and persuasive use of language); lawyers and actors learned similar techniques to persuade their audiences, whether these audiences were legal or theatrical. Trainee lawyers and those destined for the theatre frequently staged performances together. Whether or not Webster ever practised the legal profession, he attained the legal expertise that allowed him to shape great scenes such as Bracciano's and Isabella's divorce (II.i), and Vittoria's trial scene (III.ii).

Webster began by writing plays in collaboration with other dramatists. The diary of Philip Henslowe – an important man of the theatre, a shareholder in the company known originally as The Admiral's Men – records that Webster was paid to write plays for theatrical production along with other writers such as Thomas Dekker, Thomas Heywood, Michael Drayton and Thomas Middleton. Young writers had the opportunity to develop their professional skills in this way, and Webster soon began to write independently, with his Induction to a revised version of John Marston's play *The Malcontent* in about 1604. He then collaborated on *Westward Ho* and other plays. In 1611–1612 the first of his two great plays, *The White Devil*, was produced, followed in 1613–1614 by *The Duchess of Malfi*. Webster was married in 1606 and died some time after 1625, probably in 1633 or 1634.

Webster's society

In 1603 the Tudor queen, Elizabeth I, was succeeded by the Stuart monarch James I, who was already King James VI of Scotland, thereby uniting for the first time the crowns of England and Scotland.

Although James I was a strong, educated and cultured king, there were problems in his reign, some of which may be reflected in *The White Devil*. The new king brought to his English throne the aggressive approach that had been necessary to maintain control of the ambitious Scottish feudal lords. James expressed his beliefs about monarchy in *True Lawe of Free Monarchies*,

1598, proclaiming the divine right of kings and the absolute power of the monarch on earth, who could 'make and unmake' his subjects. The English nobles were naturally concerned when he succeeded to the throne, believing that a king should rule with the consent of the lords and the agreement of his people.

James strengthened his power by appointing allies as members of the policy-making Privy Council, and by promoting favourites such as Robert Carr (Earl of Somerset) and George Villiers (Duke of Buckingham). These concerns may be indirectly presented in *The White Devil* with the plight of the less privileged courtiers such as Flamineo and Lodovico as they fall out of favour. The dangers of absolute power are presented through Francisco, with his tyrannous rule on behalf of the state, and Monticelso, who wields the corrupt power of the Catholic Church.

Scandals connected with sex and marriage were frequent at court. Throughout his life James was rumoured to have love affairs with male courtiers. In 1605 Lady Penelope Rich – one of the most famous beauties at court – was divorced, admitting adultery after a scandalous affair with Baron Mountjoy. James refused to allow divorcees to remarry and banished the couple from court, but they married privately, and she died disgraced in 1607.

Lady Arabella Stuart, the king's cousin who herself was regarded as having claims to the throne, married in secret without his permission in 1610 and tried to escape to France with her husband, only to be snatched and imprisoned by the king to prevent her producing heirs who might threaten the succession of his son. And there was great public interest in the case of the Countess of Essex, who in 1613 gained a divorce from her husband on the grounds of his impotence, in order to marry the Earl of Somerset.

Issues related to patriarchy and women's roles are reflected through Vittoria and the other female characters in *The White Devil*.

Lady Arabella Stuart, cousin of King James I, was punished for
marrying without his permission

Religion presented another problem. Although Elizabeth I
had carried on the reforms of her father, Henry VIII, and
strengthened English Protestantism, James I was married to
Anne of Denmark, who was rumoured to have converted to
Catholicism. He also appointed Catholic sympathizers to
important posts so Catholics felt more optimistic of tolerance,
while Protestants felt threatened. The Catholic-led Gunpowder
Plot of 1605, which planned to blow up the Houses of
Parliament while the king and his family were in attendance, was
only the most prominent of many conspiracies aimed at
restoring a Catholic monarch to the throne. Protestants in the
first audiences for *The White Devil* would enjoy the attack on
Roman Catholic corruption evident in the words and deeds of
Monticelso, and the parodies of Catholic religious observances,
such as the sacrament administered to the dying Bracciano in
V.iii.

Webster's theatre

London theatre was flourishing in Webster's time. Three major acting companies secured royal patronage when James I became king. He was patron of The King's Men, the company for whom Shakespeare wrote; this leading group had built the Globe Theatre in Southwark in 1599 for summer performances, and played in winter at the indoor Blackfriars Theatre. The other adult companies were Prince Henry's Men (whose most famous writer had been Christopher Marlowe) and Queen Anne's Men, who played at the Curtain at Shoreditch and the Red Bull at Clerkenwell. There was also a children's company, the Children of Paul's, who later merged with an adult group becoming Lady Elizabeth's Men.

The outdoor theatres could accommodate an audience of 3,000, and some also hosted bear-baiting and other activities. Their audience would be from a mixture of social backgrounds, but attendance at the indoor Blackfriars Theatre was more expensive and exclusive, and its audience was mostly well educated and upper class.

These theatres and acting companies were provided with a stream of plays by great writers including Thomas Dekker, John Ford, Thomas Heywood, Ben Jonson, John Marston, Thomas Middleton, William Rowley, William Shakespeare, Cyril Tourneur and Webster himself. His first play, *The White Devil*, had a bad start; when performed by Queen Anne's Men at the Red Bull it was poorly received. When he wrote his preface to the play (see page 13), Webster blamed its initial failure on the weather, a 'dull' winter's day; on the 'open and black' theatre; and on the audience, whom he said resembled 'those ignorant asses' who prefer 'new books' to 'good books'. His next play, *The Duchess of Malfi*, fared better as it was performed by the leading company, The King's Men, at the superior Blackfriars Theatre. Webster was finally assured of an intelligent and sympathetic audience, who greatly approved of his play.

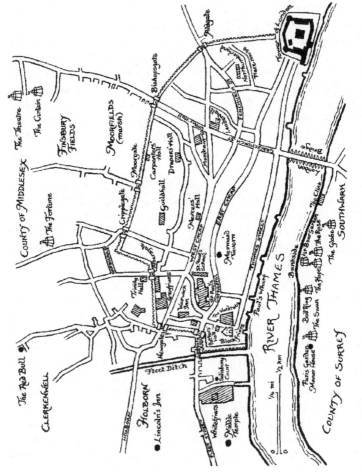

Webster's London: theatres and related venues around the city in 1600

Webster's tragedy and *The White Devil*

Webster's approach to tragedy is a complex blend of different types of drama drawn from classical Greek theatre, the Roman writer Seneca, and contemporary English drama.

In his preface to *The White Devil*, Webster claims that a play 'observing all the critical laws' traditionally associated with the Greek philosopher Aristotle's ideal of tragedy would not suit the Red Bull audience. Nevertheless, the play conforms to some of those 'laws': the characters are of noble status; the plot is strong and exposes the qualities of the characters; there are commentators who help the audience interpret events, and who relate those that happen off-stage (in place of the traditional messengers and chorus); sudden reversals of fortune occur; and there is masterly use of dramatic irony.

The revenge tradition comes indirectly from Senecan tragedy, which often included bloody revenge and then the death of the revenger. Seneca is also associated with *sententiae*, or moral sayings, which Webster echoes, and a stoical acceptance of the disasters inflicted by fate.

In the 1580s, with Thomas Kyd's hugely successful play *The Spanish Tragedy*, English revenge drama found its formula. The setting is Italian or Spanish; there is evidence of political and legal corruption; violence occurs and there are one or more revengers, with poisoning being one of the prevalent murder methods; there may be ghosts and other supernatural trappings; and finally, the rule of law will be established with the death of the revenger. Webster adopts many of these features in *The White Devil*. In *The Malcontent* (acted in 1604), Marston added another significant ingredient: a central character who is profoundly discontented and who, although perhaps participating in the action, will offer a detached and cynical perspective on events. Shakespeare had perfected this character type with the depth of psychological insight evident in *Hamlet*, written a few years before; it is clearly echoed in Webster's play, although deployed differently.

7

Another influence was the English tradition of morality plays, which had remained strong since medieval times. Here a central character, representing humankind, would be tempted by good and bad advice from angels and counsellors. To achieve salvation, he must choose the right path. Webster's drama integrates this tradition obliquely. For example, Gasparo and Antonelli act as 'Good Counsel' to the banished Lodovico in the first scene. Francisco and Monticelso might be seen as bad angels to Camillo in II.i, while in IV.iii Francisco features as the bad angel tempting Lodovico into losing his soul through murderous revenge, then Monticelso appears to represent the good angel by warning him against the idea.

These features suggest a moral, Christian framework to the play, although this is generally hard to discern. Webster also includes references that imply human destiny rests entirely on chance. At the very beginning of the play, Lodovico describes Fortune (traditionally represented as a blindfolded goddess arbitrarily doling out triumph or disaster) as *a right whore* (I.i.4). References to the Wheel of Fortune (see page 225) recall the medieval belief that individuals would rise only to fall again helplessly as the wheel turned. Flamineo expresses this idea when he likens *Fate* to a *spaniel* that cannot be beaten off (V.vi.179). Related to this is the genre of *de casibus* tragedy (named after a work by the fourteenth-century Florentine author Giovanni Boccaccio), which shows famous people suffering a catastrophic reversal at the height of their happiness and power. Bracciano refers to this as he is dying, commenting that while lesser men can die a peaceful, natural death, *horror waits on princes* (V.iii.34).

There is also the influence of English 'domestic tragedies' such as the anonymous *Arden of Faversham* (1592), based on a notorious murder of a husband by his wife and her lover. These plays raised on a smaller scale the concerns in Webster's play: considerations about relations between the sexes, the clash between public and private matters, and the failure of law to protect citizens.

Webster adjusted all the tragic perspectives of his play by adding a dash of the humour found in the 'city comedies' of the time, with their all-round appeal. He will have learned in his collaboration with Dekker about the need for tight plotting and how humour could be obtained through the gulling of naïve and unsophisticated citizens such as Camillo.

All these influences are evident in *The White Devil*, and Webster's inventive genius complicates an apparently linear plot with a complex spatial structure using framing, repetitions and echoes, so that the play is rich in ambiguity and multiple perspectives.

Sources for *The White Devil*

The White Devil is based on real events that took place in Rome in the 1580s. Vittoria Accoramboni, much admired for her beauty and accomplishments, was the wife of Francesco Peretti (called Camillo in the play), nephew to a cardinal who was in line to be the next pope. She had many admirers including the Duke of Bracciano, who was married to Isabella de Medici, a member of the supremely powerful Medici family of Florence. Isabella and Vittoria's husband were both murdered – probably on the orders of the duke and of Vittoria's ambitious brother, respectively – and the two lovers married shortly afterwards. Great scandal ensued, and Vittoria was briefly imprisoned.

When her first husband's uncle became pope, he vowed vengeance on the pair, and they fled to Venice. Bracciano died of natural causes, leaving his property to Vittoria but his duchy to the son he had by Isabella; soon afterwards, Vittoria was murdered, apparently in a quarrel over the division of property with one of Bracciano's relatives.

Webster and Jacobean tragedy

Tragedy raises profound questions about humanity's place in a hostile universe; such issues are universal and not tied to any specific period. So what is specifically 'Jacobean' in Webster's drama?

The name derives from *Jacobus*, the Latin version of James, the king's name. This establishes a precise historical, political and social framework for *The White Devil*. As discussed earlier, topics relating to the kingship of James I and to the court are reflected in this play through the issues of power, patronage, law, religion and gender.

The term 'Jacobean tragedy' has come to be associated with a dark view of the world where there are no moral certainties to support humankind, and where violence and injustice are common. Characters struggle to find their way through this world and to attain some human dignity in the face of suffering. To contain such huge topics, Webster employs a complex style of patterning and framing, using vivid language to evoke this darkness, and bold characterization. Flamineo is the central commentator in *The White Devil*, and through him Webster suggests a cynical and world-weary vision, shocking in its fatalism, but also a grisly humour: Flamineo speaks of being murdered by one who *tickles you to death, makes you die laughing* (V.iii.203), and as he lies dying, says *I have caught/An everlasting cold. I have lost my voice/Most irrecoverably* (V.vi.272–274).

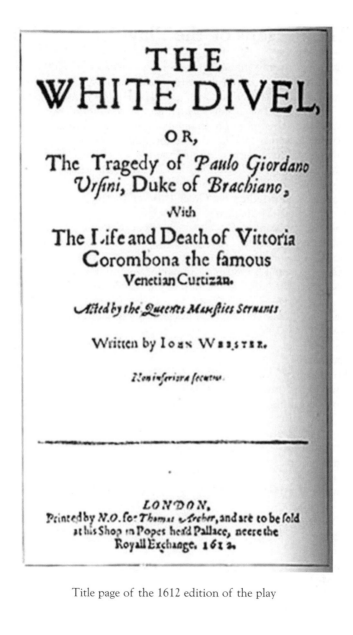

THE
WHITE DIVEL,

OR,

The Tragedy of *Paulo Giordano*
Urſini, Duke of *Brachiano*,

With

The Life and Death of Vittoria
Corombona the famous
Venetian Curtizan.

Acted by the Queenes Maiesties Seruants.

Written by IOAN WEBSTER.

Non inferiora secutus.

LONDON,
Printed by N.O. for Thomas Archer, and are to be sold
at his Shop in Popes head Pallace, neere the
Royall Exchange. 1612.

Title page of the 1612 edition of the play

The Persons of the Play

Vittoria Corombona, *a Venetian lady, married to Camillo and sister of Flamineo; later marries Bracciano*

Bracciano, *Duke of Bracciano, otherwise Paulo Giordano Orsini; married to Isabella de Medici, and later Vittoria*

Flamineo, *secretary to Bracciano and brother of Vittoria*

Cornelia, *mother to Vittoria, Flamineo and Marcello*

Zanche, *a Moor and servant to Vittoria*

Camillo, *husband of Vittoria and related to Monticelso*

Hortensio, *of Bracciano's household*

Francisco de Medici, *the Great Duke of Florence; later disguised as the Moor Mulinassar*

Isabella, *first wife of Bracciano and sister of Francisco*

Giovanni, *Bracciano's son by Isabella*

Jaques, *a Moor and servant to Giovanni*

Marcello, *younger brother of Flamineo, and of Francisco's household*

Lodovico, *an Italian count in love with Isabella; later conspires against Bracciano*

Gasparo, *friend of Lodovico; later conspires with Francisco*

Antonelli, *friend of Lodovico*

Carlo } *of Bracciano's household, secretly in league with Francisco*
Pedro }

Monticelso, *a cardinal; later Pope Paul IV*

Aragon, *a cardinal*

Doctor Julio, *a quack and conjurer*

Ambassadors	Armourer
Attendants	Cardinals
Chancellor	Conclavist
Conjurer	Courtiers
Lawyer	Matron of the House of Convertites
Officers and Guards	Physicians
Page	Register
Servants	
Christophero	Ferneze
Guid-Antonio	

To the Reader

In publishing this tragedy, I do but challenge to myself that liberty which other men have ta'en before me; not that I affect praise by it, for *nos haec novimus esse nihil*, only since it was acted in so dull a time of winter, presented in so open and black a theatre, that it wanted (that which is the only grace and setting out of a tragedy) a full and understanding auditory; and that since that time I have noted, most of the people that come to that playhouse resemble those ignorant asses (who visiting stationers' shops, their use is not to inquire for good books, but new books) I present it to the general view with this confidence:

> *Nec rhonchos metues, maligniorum,*
> *Nec scombris tunicas, dabis, molestas.*

If it be objected this is no true dramatic poem, I shall easily confess it; *non potes in nugas dicere plura meas: ipse ego quam dixi.* Willingly, and not ignorantly, in this kind have I faulted; for should a man present to such an auditory the most sententious tragedy that ever was written, observing all the critical laws, as height of style, and gravity of person, enrich it with the sententious *Chorus*, and as it were lifen death, in the passionate and weighty *Nuntius*; yet after all this divine rapture, O *dura messorum ilia*, the breath that comes from the uncapable multitude is able to poison it, and ere it be acted, let the author resolve to fix to every scene this of Horace:

> *Haec hodie porcis comedenda relinques.*

To those who report I was a long time in finishing this tragedy, I confess I do not write with a goose-quill,

winged with two feathers; and if they will needs make it   30
my fault, I must answer them with that of Euripides to
Alcestides, a tragic writer: Alcestides objecting that
Euripides had only in three days composed three verses,
whereas himself had written three hundred, 'Thou tell'st
truth,' quoth he, 'but here's the difference: thine shall   35
only be read for three days, whereas mine shall continue
three ages.'

Detraction is the sworn friend to ignorance. For
mine own part I have ever truly cherished my good
opinion of other men's worthy labours, especially of   40
that full and heightened style of Master Chapman, the
laboured and understanding works of Master Jonson;
the no less worthy composures of the both worthily
excellent Master Beaumont, and Master Fletcher; and
lastly (without wrong last to be named) the right happy   45
and copious industry of Master Shakespeare, Master
Dekker, and Master Heywood, wishing what I write may
be read by their light: protesting that, in the strength of
mine own judgement, I know them so worthy, that
though I rest silent in my own work, yet to most of   50
theirs I dare (without flattery) fix that of Martial:

non norunt, haec monumenta mori.

Act I Scene I

Noble men would be banished.

Enter Count Lodovico, Antonelli and Gasparo

LODOVICO Banished? *E shocking first word. Sin or crime unferred*

ANTONELLI   It grieved me much to hear the sentence.

LODOVICO Ha, ha, O Democritus thy gods
That govern the whole world! Courtly reward, *feels a sense of*
And punishment! Fortune's a right whore. *injustice or*
If she give aught, she deals it in small parcels, *corruption* 5
That she may take away all at one swoop.
This 'tis to have great enemies, God quite them:
Your wolf no longer seems to be a wolf *wealth never not*
Than when she's hungry. *recognised vs riches.*

GASPARO   You term those enemies
Are men of princely rank.

LODOVICO   O I pray for them.   10
The violent thunder is adored by those
Are pashed in pieces by it.

ANTONELLI   Come, my lord,
You are justly doomed; look but a little back
Into your former life: you have in three years *wasted all*
Ruined the noblest earldom. *into nones*

GASPARO   Your followers   15
Have swallowed you like mummia, and being sick
With such unnatural and horrid physic
Vomit you up i'th' kennel. *gutter*

ANTONELLI   All the damnable degrees
Of drinkings have you staggered through; one citizen
Is lord of two fair manors, called you master   20
Only for caviare.

GASPARO   Those noblemen
Which were invited to your prodigal feasts,
Wherein the phoenix scarce could scape your throats,

Laugh at your misery, as foredeeming you
An idle meteor which drawn forth the earth   25
Would be soon lost i'th' air.

ANTONELLI   Jest upon you,
And say you were begotten in an earthquake,
You have ruined such fair lordships.

LODOVICO   Very good;
This well goes with two buckets, I must tend
The pouring out of either.

GASPARO   Worse than these,   30
You have acted certain murders here in Rome,
Bloody and full of horror.

LODOVICO   Las they were flea-bitings:
Why took they not my head then?

GASPARO   O my lord,
The law doth sometimes mediate, thinks it good
Not ever to steep violent sins in blood;   35
This gentle penance may both end your crimes,
And in th'example better these bad times.

LODOVICO   So; but I wonder then some great men scape
This banishment; there's Paulo Giordano Orsini,
The Duke of Bracciano, now lives in Rome,   40
And by close panderism seeks to prostitute
The honour of Vittoria Corombona,
Vittoria, she that might have got my pardon
For one kiss to the duke.

ANTONELLI   Have a full man within you.
We see that trees bear no such pleasant fruit   45
There where they grew first, as where they are new set.
Perfumes the more they are chafed the more they
    render
Their pleasing scents, and so affliction
Expresseth virtue, fully, whether true,
Or else adulterate.

play concerned not
interior ...

LODOVICO   Leave your <u>painted comforts</u>.   50
  I'll make Italian cut-works in their guts
  If ever I return.
GASPARO   O sir.
LODOVICO   I am patient.
  I have seen some ready to be executed
  Give pleasant looks, and money, and grown familiar
  With the knave hangman; so do I – I thank them,   55
  And would account them nobly merciful
  Would they dispatch me quickly.
ANTONELLI   Fare you well,
  We shall find time, I doubt not, to repeal
  Your banishment.
    A sennet sounds
LODOVICO   I am ever bound to you.
  This is the world's alms (pray make use of it):
  Great men sell sheep, thus to be cut in pieces,   60
  When first they have shorn them bare and sold their
    fleeces.
    Exeunt

Almost like
a prologue

Act I Scene II

  Enter Bracciano, Camillo, Flamineo, Vittoria
  Corombona, [and Attendants carrying torches]
BRACCIANO *[to Vittoria]*   Your best of rest.
VITTORIA   Unto my lord the Duke,
  The best of welcome. *[To Attendants]* More lights,
    attend the duke.
    [Exeunt Camillo and Vittoria]
BRACCIANO   Flamineo.

 17

FLAMINEO   My lord.

BRACCIANO   Quite lost, Flamineo.

FLAMINEO   Pursue your noble wishes; I am prompt
As lightning to your service. O my lord!   5
(*Whispers*) The fair Vittoria, my happy sister,
Shall give you present audience. – Gentlemen,
Let the caroche go on, and 'tis his pleasure
You put out all your torches and depart.
    [*Exeunt Attendants*]

BRACCIANO   Are we so happy?

FLAMINEO   Can't be otherwise?   10
Observed you not tonight, my honoured lord
Which way soe'er you went she threw her eyes?
I have dealt already with her chambermaid
Zanche the Moor, and she is wondrous proud
To be the agent for so high a spirit.   15

BRACCIANO   We are happy above thought, because
'bove merit.

FLAMINEO   'Bove merit! We may now talk freely! 'Bove
merit! What is't you doubt? Her coyness? That's but
the superficies of lust most women have. Yet why   20
should ladies blush to hear that named, which they do
not fear to handle? O they are politic; they know our
desire is increased by the difficulty of enjoying, where
a satiety is a blunt, weary and drowsy passion. If the
buttery-hatch at court stood continually open there   25
would be nothing so passionate crowding, nor hot suit
after the beverage.

BRACCIANO   O but her jealous husband.

FLAMINEO   Hang him, a gilder that hath his brains
perished with quicksilver is not more cold in the liver.   30
The great barriers moulted not more feathers than he
hath shed hairs, by the confession of his doctor. An
Irish gamester that will play himself naked, and then

wage all downward at hazard, is not more venturous.
So unable to please a woman that like a Dutch doublet   35
all his back is shrunk into his breeches.
Shroud you within this closet, good my lord;
Some trick now must be thought on to divide
My brother-in-law from his fair bedfellow.

BRACCIANO   O should she fail to come –   40

FLAMINEO   I must not have your lordship thus unwisely
amorous: I myself have loved a lady and pursued her
with a great deal of under-age protestation, whom
some three or four gallants that have enjoyed would
with all their hearts have been glad to have been rid of.   45
'Tis just like a summer bird-cage in a garden: the birds
that are without despair to get in, and the birds that are
within despair and are in a consumption for fear they
shall never get out. Away, away, my lord.
    [*Enter Camillo. Exit Bracciano*]
[*Aside*] See here he comes; this fellow by his apparel   50
Some men would judge a politician;
But call his wit in question, you shall find it
Merely an ass in's foot-cloth. [*To Camillo*] How now,
    brother,
What, travelling to bed to your kind wife?

CAMILLO   I assure you, brother, no. My voyage lies   55
More northerly, in a far colder clime;
I do not well remember, I protest,
When I last lay with her.

FLAMINEO   Strange you should lose your count.

CAMILLO   We never lay together but ere morning
There grew a flaw between us.

FLAMINEO   'Thad been your part   60
To have made up that flaw.

CAMILLO   True, but she loathes
I should be seen in't.

FLAMINEO Why sir, what's the matter?
CAMILLO The Duke your master visits me; I thank him,
And I perceive how like an earnest bowler
He very passionately leans that way 65
He should have his bowl run.
FLAMINEO I hope you do not think –
CAMILLO That noblemen bowl booty? 'Faith, his cheek
Hath a most excellent bias; it would fain
Jump with my mistress.
FLAMINEO Will you be an ass
Despite your Aristotle, or a cuckold 70
Contrary to your ephemerides
Which shows you under what a smiling planet
You were first swaddled?
CAMILLO Pew wew, sir, tell not me
Of planets nor of ephemerides;
A man may be made cuckold in the daytime 75
When the stars' eyes are out.
FLAMINEO Sir, God boy you,
I do commit you to your pitiful pillow
Stuffed with horn-shavings.
CAMILLO Brother.
FLAMINEO God refuse me,
Might I advise you now your only course
Were to lock up your wife.
CAMILLO 'Twere very good. 80
FLAMINEO Bar her the sight of revels.
CAMILLO Excellent.
FLAMINEO Let her not go to church, but like a hound
In lyam at your heels.
CAMILLO 'Twere for her honour.
FLAMINEO And so you should be certain in one
fortnight,
Despite her chastity or innocence, 85

To be cuckolded, which yet is in suspense:
This is my counsel and I ask no fee for't.

CAMILLO   Come, you know not where my nightcap
wrings me.

FLAMINEO   Wear it i'th' old fashion, let your large ears   90
come through, it will be more easy. Nay, I will be bitter.
Bar your wife of her entertainment! women are more
willingly and more gloriously chaste, when they are least
restrained of their liberty. It seems you would be a fine
capricious mathematically jealous coxcomb, take the   95
height of your own horns with a Jacob's staff afore they
are up. These politic enclosures for paltry mutton makes
more rebellion in the flesh than all the provocative
electuaries doctors have uttered since last Jubilee.

CAMILLO   This doth not physic me.   100

FLAMINEO   It seems you are jealous. I'll show you the
error of it by a familiar example. I have seen a pair of
spectacles fashioned with such perspective art that, lay
down but one twelvepence o'th' board, 'twill appear
as if there were twenty; now should you wear a pair of   105
these spectacles, and see your wife tying her shoe, you
would imagine twenty hands were taking up of your
wife's clothes, and this would put you into a horrible
causeless fury.

CAMILLO   The fault there, sir, is not in the eye-sight.   110

FLAMINEO   True, but they that have the yellow jaundice
think all objects they look on to be yellow. Jealousy is
worser: her fits present to a man, like so many bubbles
in a basin of water, twenty several crabbed faces; many
times makes his own shadow his cuckold-maker.   115

    Enter [Vittoria] Corombona

See she comes; what reason have you to be jealous of
this creature? What an ignorant ass or flattering knave
might he be counted, that should write sonnets to her

eyes, or call her brow the snow of Ida, or ivory of Corinth, or compare her hair to the blackbird's bill, when 'tis liker the blackbird's feather. This is all: be wise, I will make you friends and you shall go to bed together. Marry, look you, it shall not be your seeking, do you stand upon that by any means; walk you aloof, I would not have you seen in't. Sister, [*whispers to Vittoria*] my lord attends you in the banqueting-house – [*aloud*] your husband is wondrous discontented.   120   125

VITTORIA   I did nothing to displease him; I carved to him at supper-time.

FLAMINEO   [*whispers to Vittoria*] You need not have carved him in faith, they say he is a capon already. I must now seemingly fall out with you. [*Aloud*] Shall a gentleman so well descended as Camillo – [*aside*] a lousy slave that within this twenty years rode with the blackguard in the Duke's carriage 'mongst spits and dripping-pans –   130   135

CAMILLO   [*aside*] Now he begins to tickle her.

FLAMINEO   [*aloud*] An excellent scholar, [*aside*] one that hath a head filled with calf's brains without any sage in them, [*aloud*] come crouching in the hams to you for a night's lodging? [*aside*] that hath an itch in's hams, which like the fire at the glass-house hath not gone out this seven years. [*Aloud*] Is he not a courtly gentleman? [*Aside*] When he wears white satin one would take him by his black muzzle to be no other creature than a maggot. [*Aloud*] You are a goodly foil, I confess, well set out, [*aside*] but covered with a false stone, yon counterfeit diamond.   140   145

CAMILLO   [*aside*] He will make her know what is in me.

FLAMINEO   Come, my lord attends you; thou shalt go to bed to my lord –   150

CAMILLO   [*aside*] Now he comes to't.

FLAMINEO   With a relish as curious as a vintner going
to taste new wine. [*To Camillo*] I am opening your case
hard.   155

CAMILLO   [*aside*] A virtuous brother, o'my credit.

FLAMINEO   He will give thee a ring with a philosopher's
stone in it.

CAMILLO   [*aside*] Indeed I am studying alchemy.

FLAMINEO   Thou shalt lie in a bed stuffed with turtles'   160
feathers, swoon in perfumed linen like the fellow was
smothered in roses; so perfect shall be thy happiness,
that as men at sea think land and trees and ships go
that way they go, so both heaven and earth shall seem
to go your voyage. Shalt meet him, 'tis fix'd, with nails   165
of diamonds to inevitable necessity.

VITTORIA   [*aside to Flamineo*] How shall's rid him hence?

FLAMINEO   [*aside to Vittoria*] I will put breeze in's tail,
set him gadding presently. [*To Camillo*] I have almost
wrought her to it, I find her coming; but, might I   170
advise you now, for this night I would not lie with her:
I would cross her humour to make her more humble.

CAMILLO   Shall I, shall I?

FLAMINEO   It will show in you a supremacy of
judgement.   175

CAMILLO   True, and a mind differing from the
tumultuary opinion, for *quae negata grata.*

FLAMINEO   Right: you are the adamant shall draw her
to you, though you keep distance off.

CAMILLO   A philosophical reason.   180

FLAMINEO   Walk by her i'the nobleman's fashion, and
tell her you will lie with her at the end of the progress.

CAMILLO   Vittoria, I cannot be induced, or as a man
would say incited –

VITTORIA   To do what, sir?   185

CAMILLO   To lie with you tonight; your silkworm useth

23

to fast every third day, and the next following spins
the better. Tomorrow at night I am for you.

VITTORIA   You'll spin a fair thread, trust to't.

FLAMINEO   [*aside to Camillo*] But do you hear, I shall   190
have you steal to her chamber about midnight.

CAMILLO   Do you think so? Why, look you, brother,
because you shall not think I'll gull you, take the key,
lock me into the chamber, and say you shall be sure
of me.   195

FLAMINEO   In troth I will, I'll be your gaoler once.
But have you ne'er a false door?

CAMILLO   A pox on't, as I am a Christian. Tell me
tomorrow how scurvily she takes my unkind parting.

FLAMINEO   I will.   200

CAMILLO   Didst thou not mark the jest of the
silkworm? Good-night. In faith, I will use this trick
often.

FLAMINEO   Do, do, do.

Exit Camillo

So now you are safe. Ha, ha, ha, thou entanglest   205
thyself in thine own work like a silkworm. Come,
sister, darkness hides your blush. Women are like
cursed dogs: civility keeps them tied all daytime, but
they are let loose at midnight; then they do most good
or most mischief.   210

Enter Bracciano

My lord, my lord.

BRACCIANO   Give credit: I could wish time would stand
still
And never end this interview, this hour,
But all delight doth itself soon'st devour.

*Zanche brings out a carpet, spreads it and lays on it
two fair cushions. Enter Cornelia [behind listening]*

Let me into your bosom, happy lady,   215

Pour out instead of eloquence my vows;
Loose me not, madam, for if you forgo me   */ desperate.*
I am lost eternally.

VITTORIA   Sir, in the way of pity
I wish you heart-whole.

BRACCIANO   You are a sweet physician.

VITTORIA Sure, sir, a loathèd cruelty in ladies   220
Is as to doctors many funerals:
It takes away their credit.

BRACCIANO   Excellent creature.
We call the cruel fair, what name for you
That are so merciful?

ZANCHE   See now they close.

FLAMINEO   Most happy union.   225

CORNELIA   [*aside*] My fears are fall'n upon me. O my
    heart!   *Pimp*
My son the pander! Now I find our house
Sinking to ruin. Earthquakes leave behind,
Where they have tyrannized, iron, or lead, or stone,
But, woe to ruin, violent lust leaves none.   230

BRACCIANO   What value is this jewel?

VITTORIA   'Tis the ornament
Of a weak fortune.

BRACCIANO   In sooth I'll have it; nay, I will but change
My jewel for your jewel.

FLAMINEO [*aside*]   Excellent,
His jewel for her jewel; well put in, Duke.   235

BRACCIANO Nay, let me see you wear it.

VITTORIA   Here, sir?

BRACCIANO   Nay lower, you shall wear my jewel lower.

FLAMINEO   [*aside*] That's better; she must wear his
    jewel lower.

VITTORIA   To pass away the time, I'll tell your grace
A dream I had last night.

Poisonas, is
well b deey with
out of graveyards.

BRACCIANO   Most wishedly.   240

VITTORIA   A foolish idle dream:
  Methought I walked about the mid of night
  Into a churchyard, where a goodly yew-tree
  Spread her large root in ground; under that yew,
  As I sat sadly leaning on a grave,   245
  Chequered with cross-sticks, there came stealing in
  Your duchess and my husband; one of them
  A pickaxe bore, th'other a rusty spade,
  And in rough terms they gan to challenge me
  About this yew.

BRACCIANO   That tree.

VITTORIA   This harmless yew.   250
  They told me my intent was to root up
  That well-grown yew, and plant i'th' stead of it
  A withered blackthorn, and for that they vowed
  To bury me alive; my husband straight
  With pickaxe gan to dig, and your fell duchess   255
  With shovel, like a Fury, voided out
  The earth and scattered bones. Lord, how methought
  I trembled, and yet for all this terror
  I could not pray.

FLAMINEO [*aside*]   No, the devil was in your dream.   260

VITTORIA   When to my rescue there arose methought
  A whirlwind, which let fall a massy arm
  From that strong plant,
  And both were struck dead by that sacred yew
  In that base shallow grave that was their due.   265

FLAMINEO [*aside*]   Excellent devil.
  She hath taught him in a dream
  To make away his duchess and her husband.

BRACCIANO   Sweetly shall I interpret this your dream:
  You are lodged within his arms who shall protect you   270
  From all the fevers of a jealous husband,

26   *She is planting the idea of killing them*
  in Bracciano's mind not Flamineo knows.

corruption of one.

From the poor envy of our phlegmatic duchess.
I'll seat you above law and above scandal,
Give to your thoughts the invention of delight
And the fruition; nor shall government   275
Divide me from you longer than a care
To keep you great: you shall to me at once
Be dukedom, health, wife, children, friends and all.

CORNELIA [*coming forward*]   Woe to light hearts: they still
    forerun our fall.

FLAMINEO   What Fury raised thee up? Away, away!   280
    Exit Zanche

CORNELIA   What make you here, my lord, this dead of
    night?
Never dropped mildew on a flower here
Till now.

FLAMINEO   I pray will you go to bed then,
Lest you be blasted?

CORNELIA   O that this fair garden   285
Had with all poisoned herbs of Thessaly
At first been planted, made a nursery
For witchcraft; rather than a burial plot
For both your honours.

VITTORIA   Dearest mother, hear me.

CORNELIA   O thou dost make my brow bend to the
    earth   290
Sooner than nature. See the curse of children!
In life they keep us frequently in tears,
And in the cold grave leave us in pale fears.

BRACCIANO   Come, come, I will not hear you.

VITTORIA   Dear my lord.   295

CORNELIA   Where is thy Duchess now, adulterous
    Duke?
Thou little dreamed'st this night she is come to Rome.

FLAMINEO   How? come to Rome?

cornelia represents the Christian moral viewpoint

VITTORIA   The Duchess –
BRACCIANO   She had been better –
CORNELIA   The lives of princes should like dials move,
Whose regular example is so strong,   300
They make the times by them go right or wrong.
FLAMINEO   So, have you done?
CORNELIA   Unfortunate Camillo.
VITTORIA [*kneels*]   I do protest if any chaste denial,
If anything but blood could have allayed
His long suit to me –
CORNELIA [*kneels*]   I will join with thee,   305
    To the most woeful end e'er mother kneeled:
    If thou dishonour thus thy husband's bed,
    Be thy life short as are the funeral tears
    In great men's.
BRACCIANO   Fie, fie, the woman's mad.
CORNELIA   Be thy act Judas-like: betray in kissing.   310
    May'st thou be envied during his short breath,
    And pitied like a wretch after his death.
VITTORIA   O me accursed!
    Exit Vittoria
FLAMINEO [*to Cornelia*]   Are you out of your wits?
    [*To Bracciano*]
    My lord,
    I'll fetch her back again.
BRACCIANO   No, I'll to bed.   315
    Send Doctor Julio to me presently.
    Uncharitable woman, thy rash tongue
    Hath raised a fearful and prodigious storm;
    Be thou the cause of all ensuing harm.
    Exit Bracciano
FLAMINEO   Now, you that stand so much upon your
    honour,   320
    Is this a fitting time o'night, think you,

To send a duke home without e'er a man?
I would fain know where lies the mass of wealth
Which you have hoarded for my maintenance,
That I may bear my beard out of the level   325
Of my lord's stirrup.
CORNELIA   What? Because we are poor,
Shall we be vicious?
FLAMINEO   Pray what means have you
To keep me from the galleys, or the gallows?
My father proved himself a gentleman,
Sold all's land, and like a fortunate fellow,   330
Died ere the money was spent. You brought me up,
At Padua, I confess, where I protest
For want of means – the university judge me –
I have been fain to heel my tutor's stockings
At least seven years. Conspiring with a beard   335
Made me a graduate; then to this Duke's service;
I visited the court, whence I returned,
More courteous, more lecherous by far,
But not a suit the richer; and shall I,
Having a path so open and so free
To my preferment, still retain your milk   340
In my pale forehead? No, this face of mine
I'll arm and fortify with lusty wine
'Gainst shame and blushing.
CORNELIA   O that I ne'er had borne thee.
FLAMINEO   So would I.   345
I would the common'st courtezan in Rome
Had been my mother rather than thyself.
Nature is very pitiful to whores
To give them but few children, yet those children
Plurality of fathers; they are sure   350
They shall not want. Go, go,
Complain unto my great lord Cardinal;

Yet maybe he will justify the act.
Lycurgus wondered much men would provide
Good stallions for their mares, and yet would suffer   355
Their fair wives to be barren.
CORNELIA   Misery of miseries.
          Exit Cornelia
FLAMINEO   The Duchess come to court! I like not that.
We are engaged to mischief and must on:
As rivers to find out the ocean   360
Flow with crook bendings beneath forcèd banks,
Or as we see, to aspire some mountain's top,
The way ascends not straight, but imitates
The subtle foldings of a winter's snake,
So who knows policy and her true aspect,   365
Shall find her ways winding and indirect.
          Exit

Act II Scene I

Enter Francisco de Medici, Cardinal Monticelso,
Marcello, Isabella, young Giovanni, with little
Jaques the Moor

FRANCISCO   Have you not seen your husband since you
   arrived?

ISABELLA   Not yet, sir.

FRANCISCO   Surely he is wondrous kind.
   If I had such a dove-house as Camillo's,
   I would set fire on't, were't but to destroy
   The polecats that haunt to't. [*To Giovanni*] My sweet
     cousin.   5

GIOVANNI   Lord uncle, you did promise me a horse
   And armour.

FRANCISCO   That I did, my pretty cousin;
   Marcello, see it fitted.

MARCELLO [*looking off-stage*] My lord, the Duke is here.

FRANCISCO   Sister, away,
   You must not yet be seen.

ISABELLA   I do beseech you
   Entreat him mildly; let not your rough tongue   10
   Set us at louder variance; all my wrongs
   Are freely pardoned, and I do not doubt,
   As men to try the precious unicorn's horn
   Make of the powder a preservative circle
   And in it put a spider, so these arms   15
   Shall charm his poison, force it to obeying
   And keep him chaste from an infected straying.

FRANCISCO   I wish it may. Be gone.

     Exit [Isabella]. Enter Bracciano and Flamineo
                 Void the chamber.

[*Exeunt Flamineo, Marcello, Giovanni, and little Jaques*]

You are welcome; will you sit? I pray, my lord,
Be you my orator, my heart's too full;   20
I'll second you anon.

MONTICELSO   Ere I begin
Let me entreat your grace forgo all passion
Which may be raised by my free discourse.

BRACCIANO   As silent as i'th' church; you may proceed.

MONTICELSO   It is a wonder to your noble friends,   25
That you that have as 'twere entered the world
With a free sceptre in your able hand,
And have to th' use of nature well applied
High gifts of learning, should in your prime age
Neglect your awful throne for the soft down   30
Of an insatiate bed. O my lord,
The drunkard after all his lavish cups
Is dry, and then is sober; so at length,
When you awake from this lascivious dream,
Repentance then will follow, like the sting   35
Placed in the adder's tail. Wretched are princes
When fortune blasteth but a petty flower
Of their unwieldy crowns, or ravisheth
But one pearl from their sceptre. But alas!
When they to wilful shipwreck loose good fame,   40
All princely titles perish with their name.

BRACCIANO   You have said, my lord.

MONTICELSO   Enough to give you taste
How far I am from flattering your greatness?

BRACCIANO   Now you that are his second, what say you?
Do not like young hawks fetch a course about;   45
Your game flies fair and for you.

FRANCISCO   Do not fear it.
I'll answer you in your own hawking phrase:

Some eagles that should gaze upon the sun
Seldom soar high, but take their lustful ease,
Since they from dunghill birds their prey can seize.   50
You know Vittoria.
BRACCIANO   Yes.
FRANCISCO   You shift your shirt there
When you retire from tennis.
BRACCIANO   Happily.
FRANCISCO   Her husband is lord of a poor fortune,
Yet she wears cloth of tissue.
BRACCIANO   What of this?
Will you urge that, my good lord Cardinal,   55
As part of her confession at next shrift,
And know from where it sails.
FRANCISCO   She is your strumpet.
BRACCIANO   Uncivil sir, there's hemlock in thy breath
And that black slander; were she a whore of mine
All thy loud cannons, and thy borrowed Switzers,   60
Thy galleys, nor thy sworn confederates,
Durst not supplant her.
FRANCISCO   Let's not talk on thunder.
Thou hast a wife, our sister; would I had given
Both her white hands to death, bound and locked fast
In her last winding-sheet, when I gave thee   65
But one.
BRACCIANO   Thou hadst given a soul to God then.
FRANCISCO   True.
Thy ghostly father with all's absolution,
Shall ne'er do so by thee.
BRACCIANO   Spit thy poison.
FRANCISCO   I shall not need, lust carries her sharp
    whip
At her own girdle; look to't, for our anger   70
Is making thunder-bolts.

BRACCIANO   Thunder? in faith,
  They are but crackers.
FRANCISCO   We'll end this with the cannon.
BRACCIANO   Thou'lt get nought by it but iron in
    thy wounds,
  And gunpowder in thy nostrils.
FRANCISCO   Better that
  Than change perfumes for plasters.
BRACCIANO   Pity on thee;   75
  'Twere good you'd show your slaves or men
    condemned
  Your new-ploughed forehead. Defiance! and I'll meet
    thee,
  Even in a thicket of thy ablest men.
MONTICELSO   My lords, you shall not word it any
    further
  Without a milder limit.
FRANCISCO   Willingly.   80
BRACCIANO   Have you proclaimed a triumph that
    you bait
  A lion thus?
MONTICELSO   My lord.
BRACCIANO   I am tame, I am tame, sir.
FRANCISCO   We send unto the Duke for conference
  'Bout levies 'gainst the pirates; my lord Duke
  Is not at home. We come ourself in person,   85
  Still my lord Duke is busied; but we fear
  When Tiber to each prowling passenger
  Discovers flocks of wild ducks, then, my lord –
  'Bout moulting time I mean – we shall be certain
  To find you sure enough and speak with you.
BRACCIANO   Ha?   90
FRANCISCO   A mere tale of a tub, my words are idle;
  But to express the sonnet by natural reason,

When stags grow melancholic you'll find the season.
    Enter Giovanni, [wearing armour, and little Jaques
    with a weapon]
MONTICELSO No more, my lord, here comes a
    champion
  Shall end the difference between you both,   95
  Your son, the prince Giovanni. See, my lords,
  What hopes you store in him; this is a casket
  For both your crowns, and should be held like dear.
  Now is he apt for knowledge; therefore know
  It is a more direct and even way   100
  To train to virtue those of princely blood
  By examples than by precepts. If by examples,
  Whom should he rather strive to imitate
  Than his own father? Be his pattern then,
  Leave him a stock of virtue that may last   105
  Should fortune rend his sails and split his mast.
BRACCIANO Your hand, boy: growing to a soldier?
GIOVANNI Give me a pike.
    [Little Jaques passes Giovanni his weapon]
FRANCISCO What, practising your pike so young,
  fair coz?
GIOVANNI Suppose me one of Homer's frogs, my lord,   110
  Tossing my bulrush thus; pray, sir, tell me,
  Might not a child of good discretion
  Be leader to an army?
FRANCISCO   Yes, cousin, a young prince
  Of good discretion might.
GIOVANNI   Say you so?
  Indeed I have heard 'tis fit a general   115
  Should not endanger his own person oft,
  So that he make a noise, when he's o'horseback,
  Like a Dansk drummer. O 'tis excellent!
  He need not fight; methinks his horse as well

    Might lead an army for him. If I live   120
    I'll charge the French foe, in the very front
    Of all my troops, the foremost man.
FRANCISCO   What, what –
GIOVANNI   And will not bid my soldiers up and follow
    But bid them follow me.
BRACCIANO   Forward lapwing!
    He flies with the shell on's head.
FRANCISCO   Pretty cousin.   125
GIOVANNI   The first year, uncle, that I go to war,
    All prisoners that I take I will set free
    Without their ransom.
FRANCISCO   Ha, without their ransom?
    How then will you reward your soldiers
    That took those prisoners for you?
GIOVANNI   Thus, my lord: 130
    I'll marry them to all the wealthy widows
    That falls that year.
FRANCISCO   Why then, the next year following
    You'll have no men to go with you to war.
GIOVANNI Why then, I'll press the women to the war,
    And then the men will follow.
MONTICELSO   Witty prince.   135
FRANCISCO   See: a good habit makes a child a man,
    Whereas a bad one makes a man a beast;
    Come, you and I are friends.
BRACCIANO   Most wishedly;
    Like bones which broke in sunder and well set
    Knit the more strongly.
FRANCISCO [*to Attendant off-stage*]   Call Camillo hither.   140
    You have received the rumour, how Count Lodovic
    Is turned a pirate?
BRACCIANO   Yes.
FRANCISCO   We are now preparing

Some ships to fetch him in.
   [*Enter Isabella*]
                               Behold your Duchess;
We now will leave you and expect from you
Nothing but kind entreaty.
BRACCIANO   You have charmed me.   145
   Exeunt Francisco, Monticelso, Giovanni
You are in health we see.
ISABELLA   And above health
To see my lord well.
BRACCIANO   So; I wonder much
What amorous whirlwind hurried you to Rome.
ISABELLA   Devotion, my lord.
BRACCIANO   Devotion?
Is your soul charged with any grievous sin?   150
ISABELLA   'Tis burdened with too many, and I think
The oftener that we cast our reckonings up,
Our sleeps will be the sounder.
BRACCIANO   Take your chamber!
ISABELLA   Nay, my dear lord, I will not have you angry;
Doth not my absence from you two months   155
Merit one kiss?
BRACCIANO   I do not use to kiss;
If that will dispossess your jealousy,
I'll swear it to you.
ISABELLA   O my lovèd lord,
I do not come to chide. My jealousy?
I am to learn what that Italian means;   160
You are as welcome to these longing arms
As I to you a virgin.
   [*She tries to embrace him; he turns away.*]
BRACCIANO   O your breath!
Out upon sweet meats and continued physic!
The plague is in them.

ISABELLA   You have oft for these two lips
   Neglected cassia or the natural sweets   165
   Of the spring violet; they are not yet much withered.
   My lord, I should be merry; these your frowns
   Show in a helmet lovely, but on me,
   In such a peaceful interview methinks
   They are too too roughly knit.

BRACCIANO   O dissemblance!   170
   Do you bandy factions 'gainst me? Have you learnt
   The trick of impudent baseness to complain
   Unto your kindred?

ISABELLA   Never, my dear lord.

BRACCIANO   Must I be haunted out, or was't your trick
   To meet some amorous gallant here in Rome   175
   That must supply our discontinuance?

ISABELLA   I pray, sir, burst my heart, and in my death
   Turn to your ancient pity, though not love.

BRACCIANO   Because your brother is the corpulent
       Duke,
   That is the Great Duke, —'s death, I shall not shortly   180
   Racket away five hundred crowns at tennis,
   But it shall rest upon recòrd! I scorn him
   Like a shaved Polack; all his reverend wit
   Lies in his wardrobe; he's a discreet fellow
   When he's made up in his robes of state,   185
   Your brother the Great Duke, because he's galleys,
   And now and then ransacks a Turkish fly-boat –
   Now all the hellish Furies take his soul! –
   First made this match. Accursèd be the priest
   That sang the wedding mass, and even my issue!   190

ISABELLA   O too too far you have cursed.

BRACCIANO   Your hand I'll kiss,
   This is the latest ceremony of my love;
   Henceforth I'll never lie with thee, by this,

This wedding-ring; I'll ne'er more lie with thee.
And this divorce shall be as truly kept,   195
As if the judge had doomed it; fare you well,
Our sleeps are severed.
ISABELLA   Forbid it, the sweet union
Of all things blessèd; why, the saints in heaven
Will knit their brows at that.
BRACCIANO   Let not thy love
Make thee an unbeliever; this my vow   200
Shall never, on my soul, be satisfied
With my repentance; let thy brother rage
Beyond a horrid tempest or sea-fight,
My vow is fixèd.
ISABELLA   O my winding-sheet,
Now shall I need thee shortly! Dear my lord,   205
Let me hear once more what I would not hear:
Never?
BRACCIANO   Never.
ISABELLA   O my unkind lord, may your sins find mercy,
As I upon a woeful widowed bed
Shall pray for you, if not to turn your eyes   210
Upon your wretched wife, and hopeful son,
Yet that in time you'll fix them upon heaven.
BRACCIANO   No more! Go, go, complain to the Great
Duke.
ISABELLA [*weeping*]   No, my dear lord, you shall have
present witness
How I'll work peace between you: I will make   215
Myself the author of your cursèd vow;
I have some cause to do it, you have none.
Conceal it, I beseech you, for the weal
Of both your dukedoms, that you wrought the means
Of such a separation; let the fault   220
Remain with my supposèd jealousy,

And think with what a piteous and rent heart
I shall perform this sad ensuing part.
    Enter Francisco, Flamineo, Monticelso, Marcello
BRACCIANO   Well, take your course. My honourable
    brother!
FRANCISCO   Sister – this is not well, my lord – why,
    sister! –   225
  She merits not this welcome.
BRACCIANO   Welcome, say?
  She hath given a sharp welcome.
FRANCISCO [*to Isabella*]   Are you foolish?
  Come, dry your tears; is this a modest course
  To better what is naught, to rail and weep?
  Grow to a reconcilement, or by heaven,   230
  I'll ne'er more deal between you.
ISABELLA   Sir, you shall not;
  No, though Vittoria upon that condition
  Would become honest.
FRANCISCO   Was your husband loud
  Since we departed?
ISABELLA   By my life, sir, no;
  I swear by that I do not care to lose.   235
  Are all these ruins of my former beauty
  Laid out for a whore's triumph?
FRANCISCO   Do you hear?
  Look upon other women, with what patience
  They suffer these slight wrongs, with what justice
  They study to requite them; take that course.   240
ISABELLA   O that I were a man, or that I had power
  To execute my apprehended wishes,
  I would whip some with scorpions.
FRANCISCO   What? Turned Fury?
ISABELLA   To dig the strumpet's eyes out, let her lie
  Some twenty months a-dying, to cut off   245

Her nose and lips, pull out her rotten teeth,
Preserve her flesh like mummia, for trophies
Of my just anger; hell to my affliction
Is mere snow-water. [*To Bracciano*] By your favour,
   sir –
Brother, draw near, and my lord Cardinal –   250
[*To Bracciano*] Sir, let me borrow of you but one kiss;
Henceforth I'll never lie with you, by this,
This wedding-ring.
FRANCISCO   How? Ne'er more lie with him?
ISABELLA   And this divorce shall be as truly kept,
As if in throngèd court a thousand ears   255
Had heard it, and a thousand lawyers' hands
Sealed to the separation.
BRACCIANO   Ne'er lie with me?
ISABELLA   Let not my former dotage
Make thee an unbeliever; this my vow
Shall never, on my soul, be satisfied   260
With my repentance: *manet alta mente repostum.*
FRANCISCO   Now by my birth you are a foolish, mad,
And jealous woman.
BRACCIANO   You see 'tis not my seeking.
FRANCISCO   Was this your circle of pure unicorn's
   horn
You said should charm your lord? Now horns upon
   thee,   265
For jealousy deserves them; keep your vow,
And take your chamber.
ISABELLA   No, sir, I'll presently to Padua;
I will not stay a minute.
MONTICELSO   O good madam.
BRACCIANO   'Twere best to let her have her humour;   270
Some half day's journey will bring down her stomach,
And then she'll turn in post.

FRANCISCO   To see her come
  To my lord Cardinal for a dispensation
  Of her rash vow will beget excellent laughter.
ISABELLA [*aside*] Unkindness do thy office, poor heart
      break;   275
  Those are the killing griefs which dare not speak.
      Exit [Isabella]. Enter Camillo
MARCELLO   Camillo's come, my lord.
FRANCISCO   Where's the commission?
MARCELLO   'Tis here.
FRANCISCO   Give me the signet.
      [*Monticelso, Francisco, Camillo, and Marcello walk
      apart, and confer in low voices*]
FLAMINEO [*to Bracciano*] My lord, do you mark their
  whispering? I will compound a medicine out of their   280
  two heads, stronger than garlic, deadlier than stibium;
  the cantharides which are scarce seen to stick upon the
  flesh when they work to the heart, shall not do it with
  more silence or invisible cunning.
      Enter Doctor [Julio]
BRACCIANO   About the murder.   285
FLAMINEO   They are sending him to Naples, but I'll
  send him to Candy; here's another property too.
BRACCIANO   O the doctor.
FLAMINEO   A poor quack-salving knave, my lord, one
  that should have been lashed for's lechery, but that he   290
  confessed a judgement, had an execution laid upon
  him, and so put the whip to a *non plus*.
JULIO   And was cozened, my lord, by an arranter knave
  than myself, and made pay all the colourable
  execution.   295
FLAMINEO   He will shoot pills into a man's guts, shall
  make them have more ventages than a cornet or a
  lamprey; he will poison a kiss, and was once minded,

for his masterpiece, because Ireland breeds no poison, to have prepared a deadly vapour in a Spaniard's fart 300 that should have poisoned all Dublin.

BRACCIANO   O Saint Anthony's fire!

JULIO   Your secretary is merry, my lord.

FLAMINEO   O thou cursed antipathy to nature! Look his eye's bloodshed like a needle a chirurgeon stitcheth a 305 wound with. Let me embrace thee, toad, and love thee. O thou abominable loathsome gargarism, that will fetch up lungs, lights, heart, and liver by scruples.

BRACCIANO   No more. I must employ thee, honest doctor;
You must to Padua and by the way 310
Use some of your skill for us.

JULIO   Sir, I shall.

BRACCIANO   But for Camillo?

FLAMINEO   He dies this night by such a politic strain,
Men shall suppose him by's own engine slain.
But for your Duchess' death?

JULIO   I'll make her sure. 315

BRACCIANO   Small mischiefs are by greater made secure.

FLAMINEO   Remember this, you slave: when knaves come to preferment they rise [*aside*] as gallowses are raised i'th' Low Countries, [*aloud*] one upon another's shoulders. 320

    Exeunt [Bracciano, Flamineo, and Doctor Julio]

MONTICELSO   Here is an emblem, nephew, pray peruse it.
'Twas thrown in at your window.

CAMILLO   At my window?
Here is a stag, my lord, hath shed his horns,
And for the loss of them the poor beast weeps –
The word '*Inopem me copia fecit*'.

MONTICELSO   That is, 325
Plenty of horns hath made him poor of horns.

CAMILLO   What should this mean?
MONTICELSO   I'll tell you: 'tis given out
　You are a cuckold.
CAMILLO   Is it given out so?
　I had rather such report as that, my lord,
　Should keep within doors.
FRANCISCO   Have you any children?   330
CAMILLO   None, my lord.
FRANCISCO   You are the happier.
　I'll tell you a tale.
CAMILLO   Pray, my lord.
FRANCISCO   An old tale.
　Upon a time Phoebus, the god of light,
　Or him we call the sun, would need be married.
　The gods gave their consent, and Mercury   335
　Was sent to voice it to the general world.
　But what a piteous cry there straight arose
　Amongst smiths, and felt-makers, brewers and
　　　cooks,
　Reapers and butter-women, amongst fishmongers
　And thousand other trades, which are annoyed   340
　By his excessive heat; 'twas lamentable.
　They came to Jupiter all in a sweat
　And do forbid the bans. A great fat cook
　Was made their speaker, who entreats of Jove
　That Phoebus might be gelded, for if now   345
　When there was but one sun, so many men
　Were like to perish by his violent heat,
　What should they do if he were married
　And should beget more, and those children
　Make fireworks like their father? So say I,   350
　Only I will apply it to your wife:
　Her issue, should not providence prevent it,
　Would make both nature, time, and man repent it.

MONTICELSO   Look you, cousin,
  Go change the air for shame, see if your absence   355
  Will blast your cornucopia: Marcello
  Is chosen with you joint commissioner
  For the relieving our Italian coast
  From pirates.
MARCELLO   I am much honoured in't.
CAMILLO   But, sir,
  Ere I return the stag's horns may be sprouted   360
  Greater than these are shed.
MONTICELSO   Do not fear it,
  I'll be your ranger.
CAMILLO   You must watch i'th' nights,
  Then's the most danger.
FRANCISCO   Farewell, good Marcello.
  All the best fortunes of a soldier's wish
  Bring you o'ship-board.   365
CAMILLO   Were I not best, now I am turned soldier,
  Ere that I leave my wife, sell all she hath
  And then take leave of her?
MONTICELSO   I expect good from you,
  Your parting is so merry.
CAMILLO   Merry, my lord, o'th' captain's humour right;   370
  I am resolvèd to be drunk this night.
    Exit [*Camillo with Marcello*]
FRANCISCO   So, 'twas well fitted; now shall we discern,
  How his wished absence will give violent way
  To Duke Bracciano's lust.
MONTICELSO   Why, that was it;
  To what scorned purpose else should we make choice   375
  Of him for a sea-captain? and besides,
  Count Lodovic which was rumoured for a pirate
  Is now in Padua.
FRANCISCO   Is't true?

MONTICELSO   Most certain.
  I have letters from him, which are suppliant
  To work his quick repeal from banishment;   380
  He means to address himself for pension
  Unto our sister Duchess.
FRANCISCO   O 'twas well.
  We shall not want his absence past six days;
  I fain would have the Duke Bracciano run
  Into notorious scandal, for there's nought   385
  In such cursed dotage to repair his name,
  Only the deep sense of some deathless shame.
MONTICELSO   It may be objected I am dishonourable,
  To play thus with my kinsman; but I answer,
  For my revenge I'd stake a brother's life,   390
  That being wronged durst not avenge himself.
FRANCISCO   Come to observe this strumpet.
MONTICELSO   Curse of greatness!
  Sure he'll not leave her.
FRANCISCO   There's small pity in't;
  Like mistletoe on sere elms spent by weather,
  Let him cleave to her and both rot together.   395
    Exeunt

Act II Scene II

    Enter Bracciano with one in the habit of a Conjurer
BRACCIANO   Now, sir, I claim your promise. 'Tis dead
    midnight,
  The time prefixed to show me by your art
  How the intended murder of Camillo
  And our loathèd Duchess grow to action.
CONJURER   You have won me by your bounty to a deed   5

I do not often practise; some there are,
Which by sophistic tricks aspire that name
Which I would gladly lose, of nigromancer;
As some that use to juggle upon cards,
Seeming to conjure, when indeed they cheat;   10
Others that raise up their confederate spirits
'Bout windmills, and endanger their own necks
For making of a squib; and some there are
Will keep a curtal to show juggling tricks
And give out 'tis a spirit; besides these   15
Such a whole ream of almanac-makers, figure-flingers,
Fellows indeed that only live by stealth,
Since they do merely lie about stol'n goods,
They'd make men think the devil were fast and loose,
With speaking fustian Latin. Pray sit down,   20
Put on this night cap, sir, 'tis charmed;

    [*Bracciano puts on a night cap*]

                        and now

I'll show you by my strong-commanding art
The circumstance that breaks your Duchess' heart.
            A dumb show
    [*Music sounds softly.*] *Enter suspiciously Julio and*
    [*Christopher*]. *They draw a curtain where Bracciano's*
    picture is. They put on spectacles of glass, which
    cover their eyes and noses, and then burn perfumes
    afore the picture, and wash the lips of the picture.
    That done, quenching the fire and putting off their
    spectacles, they depart laughing.
    Enter Isabella in her nightgown as to bedward, with
    lights; after her, Count Lodovico, Giovanni, Guid-
    Antonio, and others waiting on her. She kneels down
    as to prayers, then draws the curtain of the picture,
    does three reverences to it, and kisses it thrice. She
    faints and will not suffer them to come near it; dies.

> Sorrow expressed in Giovanni and in Count
> Lodovico. She's conveyed out solemnly.

BRACCIANO Excellent, then she's dead.

CONJURER   She's poisonèd
By the fumèd picture. 'Twas her custom nightly,   25
Before she went to bed, to go and visit
Your picture and to feed her eyes and lips
On the dead shadow. Doctor Julio
Observing this, infects it with an oil
And other poisoned stuff, which presently   30
Did suffocate her spirits.

BRACCIANO   Methought I saw
Count Lodovic there.

CONJURER   He was, and by my art
I find he did most passionately dote
Upon your Duchess. Now turn another way,
And view Camillo's far more politic fate;   35
Strike louder music from this charmèd ground
To yield, as fits the act, a tragic sound.

> *The second dumb show.*

[*Music sounds, with tragic jarring notes.*] *Enter
Flamineo, Marcello, Camillo, with four more as
Captains. They drink healths and dance. A vaulting-
horse is brought into the room. Marcello and two
more whispered out of the room, while Flamineo and
Camillo strip themselves into their shirts, as to vault;
compliment who shall begin. As Camillo is about to
vault, Flamineo pitcheth him upon his neck, and with
the help of the rest writhes his neck about; seems to
see if it be broke, and lays him folded double as 'twere
under the horse; makes shows to call for help.
Marcello comes in, laments, sends for the Cardinal
[Monticelso] and Duke [Francisco], who comes forth
with armed men; wonder at the act. [Francisco]*

commands the body to be carried home, apprehends
Flamineo, Marcello, and the rest, and go as 'twere to
apprehend Vittoria.

BRACCIANO   'Twas quaintly done, but yet each circumstance
  I taste not fully.

CONJURER   O 'twas most apparent,
  You saw them enter charged with their deep healths   40
  To their boon voyage, and to second that,
  Flamineo calls to have a vaulting-horse
  Maintain their sport. The virtuous Marcello
  Is innocently plotted forth the room,
  Whilst your eye saw the rest and can inform you   45
  The engine of all.

BRACCIANO   It seems Marcello and Flamineo
  Are both committed.

CONJURER   Yes, you saw them guarded,
  And now they are come with purpose to apprehend
  Your mistress, fair Vittoria; we are now   50
  Beneath her roof; 'twere fit we instantly
  Make out by some back postern.

BRACCIANO   Noble friend,
  You bind me ever to you. This shall stand
  As the firm seal annexèd to my hand.
  It shall enforce a payment.

CONJURER   Sir, I thank you.   55

Exit Bracciano

Both flowers and weeds spring when the sun is warm,
And great men do great good, or else great harm.

Exit

Act III Scene I

*Enter Francisco, and Monticelso, their Chancellor
and Register.*

FRANCISCO You have dealt discreetly to obtain the
    presence
Of all the grave lieger ambassadors
To hear Vittoria's trial.

MONTICELSO   'Twas not ill,
For, sir, you know we have nought but circumstances
To charge her with, about her husband's death.   5
Their approbation therefore to the proofs
Of her black lust shall make her infamous
To all our neighbouring kingdoms; I wonder
If Bracciano will be here.

FRANCISCO   O fie,
'Twere impudence too palpable.   10
    *[Exeunt Francisco and Monticelso, and their
    Chancellor and Register. Enter Flamineo and
    Marcello guarded, and a Lawyer]*

LAWYER What, are you in by the week? So, I will try
now whether thy wit be close prisoner. Methinks
none should sit upon thy sister but old whoremasters.

FLAMINEO Or cuckolds, for your cuckold is your most
terrible tickler of lechery. Whoremasters would serve,   15
for none are judges at tilting, but those that have been
old tilters.

LAWYER My lord Duke and she have been very private.

FLAMINEO You are a dull ass; 'tis threatened they have
been very public.   20

LAWYER If it can be proved they have but kissed one
another –

FLAMINEO What then?

LAWYER   My lord Cardinal will ferret them.

FLAMINEO   A cardinal, I hope, will not catch conies.   25

LAWYER   For to sow kisses – mark what I say – to sow
kisses is to reap lechery, and I am sure a woman that
will endure kissing is half won.

FLAMINEO   True, her upper part by that rule; if you
will win her nether part too, you know what follows.   30

LAWYER   Hark, the ambassadors are lighted.

FLAMINEO [*aside*]   I do put on this feignèd garb of
mirth
To gull suspicion.

MARCELLO   O my unfortunate sister!
I would my dagger's point had cleft her heart
When she first saw Bracciano. You, 'tis said,   35
Were made his engine and his stalking-horse
To undo my sister.

FLAMINEO   I made a kind of path
To her and mine own preferment.

MARCELLO   Your ruin.

FLAMINEO   Hum! Thou art a soldier,
Followest the Great Duke, feedest his victories,   40
As witches do their serviceable spirits,
Even with thy prodigal blood. What hast got?
But like the wealth of captains, a poor handful,
Which in thy palm thou bear'st, as men hold water:
Seeking to grip it fast, the frail reward   45
Steals through thy fingers.

MARCELLO   Sir –

FLAMINEO   Thou hast scarce maintenance
To keep thee in fresh chamois.

MARCELLO   Brother.

FLAMINEO   Hear me:
And thus when we have even poured ourselves
Into great fights, for their ambition

Or idle spleen, how shall we find reward?   50
But as we seldom find the mistletoe
Sacred to physic on the builder oak
Without a mandrake by it, so in our quest of gain.
Alas the poorest of their forced dislikes
At a limb proffers, but at heart it strikes: 55
This is lamented doctrine.
MARCELLO   Come, come.
FLAMINEO   When age shall turn thee
White as a blooming hawthorn –
MARCELLO   I'll interrupt you.
For love of virtue bear an honest heart,
And stride over every politic respect,   60
Which where they most advance they most infect.
Were I your father, as I am your brother,
I should not be ambitious to leave you
A better patrimony.
        Enter Savoy [Ambassador]. Here there is a passage of
        the lieger Ambassadors over the stage severally. Enter
        French Ambassador.
FLAMINEO   I'll think on't.
The lord ambassadors.   65
LAWYER   O my sprightly Frenchman: do you know
him? He's an admirable tilter.
FLAMINEO   I saw him at last tilting; he showed like a
pewter candlestick fashioned like a man in armour,
holding a tilting-staff in his hand little bigger than a   70
candle of twelve i'th' pound.
LAWYER   O but he's an excellent horseman.
FLAMINEO   A lame one in his lofty tricks; he sleeps
o'horseback like a poulter.
        Enter English and Spanish [Ambassadors]
LAWYER   Lo you, my Spaniard.   75
FLAMINEO   He carries his face in's ruff, as I have seen a

serving-man carry glasses in a cypress hat-band,
monstrous steady for fear of breaking; he looks like
the claw of a blackbird, first salted and then broiled in
a candle.   80
    Exeunt.

Act III Scene II

Enter Francisco, Monticelso, the six lieger
Ambassadors, Bracciano, Vittoria, [Flamineo,
Marcello], Lawyer, and a guard [and Servant]
MONTICELSO [*to Bracciano*]   Forbear, my lord, here is no
    place assigned you.
This business by his holiness is left
To our examination.
BRACCIANO   May it thrive with you.
   Lays a rich gown under him
FRANCISCO   A chair there for his lordship.
BRACCIANO   Forbear your kindness; an unbidden guest   5
    Should travel as Dutchwomen go to church:
    Bear their stools with them.
MONTICELSO   At your pleasure, sir.
    Stand to the table, gentlewoman. Now, signor,
    Fall to your plea.
LAWYER   *Domine judex converte oculos in hanc pestem*   10
    mulierum corruptissimam.
VITTORIA   What's he?
FRANCISCO   A lawyer that pleads against you.
VITTORIA   Pray, my lord, let him speak his usual
    tongue;
I'll make no answer else.
FRANCISCO   Why, you understand Latin.   15

53

VITTORIA   I do, sir, but amongst this auditory
Which come to hear my cause, the half or more
May be ignorant in't.

MONTICELSO   Go on, sir.

VITTORIA   By your favour,
I will not have my accusation clouded |
In a strange tongue. | All this assembly   20
Shall hear what you can charge me with.

FRANCISCO   Signor,
You need not stand on't much; pray change your
    language.

MONTICELSO   O for God sake! Gentlewoman, your credit
Shall be more famous by it.

LAWYER   Well then, have at you.

VITTORIA   I am at the mark, sir, I'll give aim to you,   25
And tell you how near you shoot.

LAWYER   Most literated judges, please your lordships
So to connive your judgements to the view
Of this debauched and diversivolent woman,
Who such a black concatenation   30
Of mischief hath effected, that to extirp
The memory of't must be the consummation
Of her and her projections.

VITTORIA   What's all this?

LAWYER   Hold your peace.
Exorbitant sins must have exulceration.   35

VITTORIA   Surely, my lords, this lawyer here hath
    swallowed
Some pothecary's bills, or proclamations.
And now the hard and undigestible words
Come up like stones we use give hawks for physic.
Why, this is Welsh to Latin.

LAWYER   My lords, the woman   40
Knows not her tropes nor figures, nor is perfect

54

done in / double / exposure

/ broken from iambic / pentameter

w/o ? ?

In the academic derivation
Of grammatical elocution.

FRANCISCO   Sir, your pains
Shall be well spared, and your deep eloquence
Be worthily applauded amongst those   45
Which understand you.

LAWYER   My good lord.

FRANCISCO (*speaks this as in scorn*)   Sir,
Put up your papers in your fustian bag –
Cry mercy, sir, 'tis buckram – and accept,
My notion of your learn'd verbosity.

the base of the state & useless in the face of the corruption and power at the ?

LAWYER I most graduatically thank your lordship.   50
I shall have use for them elsewhere.
      [*Exit Lawyer*]

MONTICELSO I shall be plainer with you, and paint out
Your follies in more natural red and white
Than that upon your cheek.

VITTORIA   O you mistake.
You raise a blood as noble in this cheek   55
As ever was your mother's.

MONTICELSO I must spare you till proof cry whore
      to that.
Observe this creature here, my honoured lords,
A woman of a most prodigious spirit
In her effected.

VITTORIA   Honourable my lord,   60
It doth not suit a reverend Cardinal   *– separation of / Church and State .*
To play the lawyer thus. *More.*

MONTICELSO O your trade instructs your language!
You see, my lords, what goodly fruit she seems;
Yet like those apples travellers report   65
To grow where Sodom and Gomorrah stood,
I will but touch her and you straight shall see
She'll fall to soot and ashes.

mercy to rarely found in
religion or justice
judge would see ×

VITTORIA   Your envenomed
  Pothecary should do't.
MONTICELSO   I am resolved
  Were there a second paradise to lose   70
  This devil would betray it.
VITTORIA   O poor charity,
  Thou art seldom found in scarlet.
MONTICELSO   Who knows not how, when several night
      by night
  Her gates were choked with coaches, and her rooms
  Outbraved the stars with several kind of lights,   75
  When she did counterfeit a prince's court?
  In music, banquets and most riotous surfeits
  This whore, forsooth, was holy.
VITTORIA   Ha? Whore? What's that?
MONTICELSO   Shall I expound whore to you? Sure
      I shall,
  I'll give their perfect character. They are first,   80
  Sweet-meats which rot the eater; in man's nostril
  Poisoned perfumes. They are cozening alchemy,
whore Shipwrecks in calmest weather! What are whores?
  Cold Russian winters, that appear so barren,
  As if that nature had forgot the spring.   85
  They are the true material fire of hell,
  Worse than those tributes i'th' Low Countries paid,
  Exactions upon meat, drink, garments, sleep;
  Ay, even on man's perdition, his sin.
  They are those brittle evidences of law   90
  Which forfeit all a wretched man's estate
  For leaving out one syllable. What are whores?
  They are those flattering bells have all one tune,
  At weddings, and at funerals; your rich whores
  Are only treasuries by extortion filled,   95
  And emptied by cursed riot. They are worse,

Worse than dead bodies, which are begged at gallows
And wrought upon by surgeons to teach man
Wherein he is imperfect. What's a whore?
She's like the guilty counterfeited coin   100
Which, whosoe'er first stamps it, brings in trouble
All that receive it.
VITTORIA   This character scapes me.
MONTICELSO   You, gentlewoman?
Take from all beasts, and from all minerals,
Their deadly poison.
VITTORIA   Well, what then?
MONTICELSO   I'll tell thee;   105
I'll find in thee a pothecary's shop
To sample them all.
FRENCH AMBASSADOR [*aside*]   She hath lived ill.
ENGLISH AMBASSADOR [*aside*]   True, but the Cardinal's
    too bitter.
MONTICELSO   You know what whore is: next the devil,
    Adult'ry,
Enters the devil, Murder.
FRANCISCO   Your unhappy
Husband is dead.
VITTORIA   O he's a happy husband
Now he owes nature nothing.
FRANCISCO   And by a vaulting engine.
MONTICELSO   An active plot?
He jumped into his grave.
FRANCISCO   What a prodigy was't
That from some two yards' height a slender man   115
Should break his neck!
MONTICELSO   I'th 'rushes.
FRANCISCO   And what's more,
Upon the instant lose all use of speech,
All vital motion, like a man had lain

Wound up three days. Now mark each circumstance.
MONTICELSO   And look upon this creature was his wife.   120
  She comes not like a widow; she comes arm'd
  With scorn and impudence: is this a mourning habit?
VITTORIA   Had I foreknown his death as you suggest,
  I would have bespoke my mourning.
MONTICELSO   O you are cunning.   125
    VITTORIA   You shame your wit and judgement
  To call it so. What, is my just defence
  By him that is my judge called impudence?
  Let me appeal then from this Christian court
  To the uncivil Tartar.
MONTICELSO   See, my lords,   130
  She scandals our proceedings.
    VITTORIA [*bowing*]   Humbly thus,
  Thus low, to the most worthy and respected
  Lieger ambassadors, my modesty
  And womanhood I tender; but withal
  So entangled in a cursèd accusation   135
  That my defence of force, like Perseus,
  Must personate masculine virtue. To the point!
  Find me but guilty, sever head from body –
  We'll part good friends. I scorn to hold my life
  At yours or any man's entreaty, sir.   140
ENGLISH AMBASSADOR   She hath a brave spirit.
MONTICELSO   Well, well, such counterfeit jewels
  Make true ones oft suspected.
    VITTORIA   You are deceived;
  For know that all your strict-combinèd heads,
  Which strike against this mine of diamonds,   145
  Shall prove but glassen hammers: they shall break.
  These are but feignèd shadows of my evils.
  Terrify babes, my lord, with painted devils;
  I am past such needless palsy. For your names

    Of whore and murd'ress, they proceed from you,   150
    As if a man should spit against the wind,
    The filth returns in's face.
MONTICELSO   Pray you, mistress, satisfy me one
      question:
    Who lodged beneath your roof that fatal night
    Your husband brake his neck?
BRACCIANO   That question   155
    Enforceth me break silence: I was there.
MONTICELSO   Your business?
BRACCIANO   Why, I came to comfort her,
    And take some course for settling her estate,
    Because I heard her husband was in debt
    To you, my lord.
MONTICELSO   He was.
BRACCIANO   And 'twas strangely feared   160
    That you would cozen her.
MONTICELSO   Who made you overseer?
BRACCIANO   Why, my charity, my charity, which
      should flow
    From every generous and noble spirit
    To orphans and to widows.
MONTICELSO   Your lust.
BRACCIANO   Cowardly dogs bark loudest. Sirrah priest,   165
    I'll talk with you hereafter. Do you hear?
    The sword you frame of such an excellent temper,
    I'll sheathe in your own bowels.
    There are a number of thy coat resemble
    Your common post-boys.
MONTICELSO   Ha?
BRACCIANO [*preparing to leave*]   Your mercenary
      post-boys.   170
    Your letters carry truth, but 'tis your guise
    To fill your mouths with gross and impudent lies.

SERVANT   My lord, your gown.
BRACCIANO   Thou liest, 'twas my stool.
  Bestow't upon thy master that will challenge
  The rest o'th' household stuff, for Bracciano   175
  Was ne'er so beggarly to take a stool
  Out of another's lodging. Let him make
  Valance for his bed on't, or a demi-footcloth
  For his most reverend mule. Monticelso,
  Nemo me impune lacessit.   180
    Exit Bracciano
MONTICELSO   Your champion's gone.
VITTORIA   The wolf may prey the better.
FRANCISCO   My lord, there's great suspicion of the
      murder,
  But no sound proof who did it. For my part
  I do not think she hath a soul so black
  To act a deed so bloody. If she have,   185
  As in cold countries husbandmen plant vines,
  And with warm blood manure them, even so
  One summer she will bear unsavoury fruit,
  And ere next spring wither both branch and root.
  The act of blood let pass, only descend   190
  To matter of incontinence.
VITTORIA   I discern poison
  Under your gilded pills.
MONTICELSO   Now the Duke's gone, I will produce
      a letter,
  Wherein 'twas plotted he and you should meet,
  At an apothecary's summer-house,   195
  Down by the river Tiber (view't, my lords),
  Where after wanton bathing and the heat
  Of a lascivious banquet – I pray read it,
  I shame to speak the rest.
VITTORIA [*passes the letter round*]   Grant I was tempted,

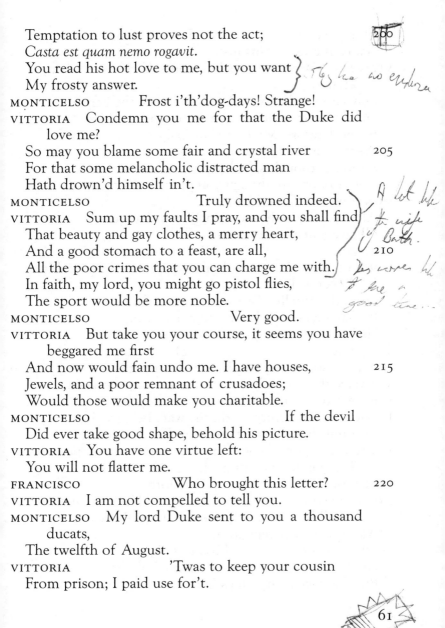

Temptation to lust proves not the act;
Casta est quam nemo rogavit.
You read his hot love to me, but you want
My frosty answer.
MONTICELSO   Frost i'th'dog-days! Strange!
VITTORIA   Condemn you me for that the Duke did
     love me?
So may you blame some fair and crystal river   205
For that some melancholic distracted man
Hath drown'd himself in't.
MONTICELSO   Truly drowned indeed.
VITTORIA   Sum up my faults I pray, and you shall find
That beauty and gay clothes, a merry heart,
And a good stomach to a feast, are all,   210
All the poor crimes that you can charge me with.
In faith, my lord, you might go pistol flies,
The sport would be more noble.
MONTICELSO   Very good.
VITTORIA   But take you your course, it seems you have
     beggared me first
And now would fain undo me. I have houses,   215
Jewels, and a poor remnant of crusadoes;
Would those would make you charitable.
MONTICELSO   If the devil
Did ever take good shape, behold his picture.
VITTORIA   You have one virtue left:
You will not flatter me.
FRANCISCO   Who brought this letter?   220
VITTORIA   I am not compelled to tell you.
MONTICELSO   My lord Duke sent to you a thousand
     ducats,
The twelfth of August.
VITTORIA   'Twas to keep your cousin
From prison; I paid use for't.

MONTICELSO   I rather think
   'Twas interest for his lust.   225
VITTORIA   Who says so but yourself? If you be my
     accuser
   Pray cease to be my judge; come from the bench,
   Give in your evidence 'gainst me, and let these
   Be moderators. My lord Cardinal,
   Were your intelligencing ears as long   230
   As to my thoughts, had you an honest tongue
   I would not care though you proclaimed them all.
MONTICELSO   Go to, go to.
   After your goodly and vainglorious banquet,
   I'll give you a choke-pear.
VITTORIA   O' your own grafting?   235
MONTICELSO   You were born in Venice, honourably
     descended
   From the Vitelli. 'Twas my cousin's fate –
   Ill may I name the hour – to marry you;
   He bought you of your father.
VITTORIA   Ha?
MONTICELSO   He spent there in six months   240
   Twelve thousand ducats, and to my acquaintance
   Received in dowry with you not one julio.
   'Twas a hard pennyworth, the ware being so light.
   I yet but draw the curtain. Now to your picture:
   You came from thence a most notorious strumpet,   245
   And so you have continued.
VITTORIA   My lord.
MONTICELSO   Nay, hear me,
   You shall have time to prate. My Lord Bracciano –
   Alas I make but repetition
   Of what is ordinary and Rialto talk,
   And balladed, and would be played o'th'stage,   250
   But that vice many times finds such loud friends

That preachers are charmed silent.
You gentlemen, Flamineo and Marcello,
The court hath nothing now to charge you with;
Only you must remain upon your sureties   255
For your appearance.

FRANCISCO   I stand for Marcello.
FLAMINEO   And my lord Duke for me.
MONTICELSO   For you, Vittoria, your public fault,
Joined to th'condition of the present time,
Takes from you all the fruits of noble pity.   260
Such a corrupted trial have you made
Both of your life and beauty, and been styled
No less in ominous fate than blazing stars
To princes. Here's your sentence: you are confin'd
Unto a house of convertites, and your bawd –   265

FLAMINEO [aside]   Who, I?
MONTICELSO   The Moor.
FLAMINEO [aside]   O, I am a sound man again.
VITTORIA   A house of convertites, what's that?
MONTICELSO   A house
Of penitent whores.
VITTORIA   Do the noblemen in Rome
Erect it for their wives, that I am sent
To lodge there?
FRANCISCO   You must have patience.
VITTORIA   I must first have vengeance.
I fain would know if you have your salvation
By patent, that you proceed thus.
MONTICELSO   Away with her.
Take her hence.
VITTORIA   A rape, a rape!
MONTICELSO   How?
VITTORIA   Yes, you have ravished justice,   275
Forced her to do your pleasure.

woman who speaks out?
she's mad.

MONTICELSO   Fie, she's mad.

VITTORIA   Die with those pills in your most cursèd maw,
   Should bring you health, or while you sit o'th' bench,
   Let your own spittle choke you.

MONTICELSO   She's turned fury.

VITTORIA   That the last day of judgement may so find
      you,   280
   And leave you the same devil you were before.
   Instruct me some good horse-leech to speak treason,
   For since you cannot take my life for deeds,
   Take it for words. O woman's poor revenge
   Which dwells but in the tongue. I will not weep.   285
   No, I do scorn to call up one poor tear
   To fawn on your injustice. Bear me hence,
   Unto this house of – what's your mitigating title?

MONTICELSO   Of convertites.

VITTORIA   It shall not be a house of convertites.   290
   My mind shall make it honester to me
   Than the Pope's palace, and more peaceable
   Than thy soul, though thou art a cardinal.
   Know this, and let it somewhat raise your spite:
   Through darkness diamonds spread their richest light.   295
      Exit Vittoria [*guarded*]. *Enter Bracciano*

BRACCIANO   Now you and I are friends, sir, we'll shake
      hands,
   In a friend's grave together, a fit place,
   Being the emblem of soft peace t'atone our hatred.

FRANCISCO   Sir, what's the matter?

BRACCIANO   I will not chase more blood from that
      loved cheek;   300
   You have lost too much already. Fare you well.
      [*Exit Bracciano.*]

FRANCISCO   How strange these words sound. What's
      the interpretation?

FLAMINEO [*aside*] Good, this is a preface to the discovery of the Duchess' death; he carries it well. Because now I cannot counterfeit a whining passion for the 305
death of my lady, I will feign a mad humour for the disgrace of my sister, and that will keep off idle questions. Treason's tongue hath a villainous palsy in't; I will talk to any man, hear no man, and for a time appear a politic madman. 310

[*Exit Flamineo*]. *Enter Giovanni, Count Lodovico*

FRANCISCO How now, my noble cousin? What, in black?

GIOVANNI Yes, uncle, I was taught to imitate you
In virtue, and you must imitate me
In colours for your garments. My sweet mother
Is – 315

FRANCISCO How? Where?

GIOVANNI Is there, no yonder; indeed, sir, I'll not tell you,
For I shall make you weep.

FRANCISCO Is dead.

GIOVANNI Do not blame me now,
I did not tell you so.

LODOVICO She's dead, my lord. 320

FRANCISCO Dead?

MONTICELSO Blessèd lady, thou art now above thy woes.
Wilt please your lordships to withdraw a little?

[*Exeunt Ambassadors*]

GIOVANNI What do the dead do, uncle? Do they eat,
Hear music, go a-hunting, and be merry, 325
As we that live?

FRANCISCO No, coz, they sleep.

GIOVANNI Lord, Lord, that I were dead;
I have not slept these six nights. When do they wake?

65

FRANCISCO   When God shall please.
GIOVANNI   Good God let her sleep ever,
For I have known her wake an hundred nights,   330
When all the pillow, where she laid her head,
Was brine-wet with her tears.
I am to complain to you, sir.
I'll tell you how they have used her now she's dead:
They wrapped her in a cruel fold of lead,   335
And would not let me kiss her.
FRANCISCO   Thou didst love her.
GIOVANNI   I have often heard her say she gave me suck,
And it should seem by that she dearly loved me,
Since princes seldom do it.
FRANCISCO   O, all of my poor sister that remains!   340
Take him away for God's sake.
    [Exit Giovanni with Lodovico]
MONTICELSO   How now, my lord?
FRANCISCO   Believe me, I am nothing but her grave,
And I shall keep her blessèd memory
Longer than thousand epitaphs.   345
    [Exeunt]

Act III Scene III

*Enter Flamineo as distracted, [Marcello, and
Lodovico, unobserved by either]*

FLAMINEO   We endure the strokes like anvils or
    hard steel,
Till pain itself make us no pain to feel.
Who shall do me right now? Is this the end of service?
I'd rather go weed garlic; travel through France, and be
mine own ostler; wear sheepskin linings, or shoes that   5

66

stink of blacking; be entered into the list of the forty
thousand pedlars in Poland.
   Enter Savoy [Ambassador]
Would I had rotted in some surgeon's house at
Venice, built upon the pox as well as on piles, ere I had
served Bracciano.

SAVOY AMBASSADOR   You must have comfort.

FLAMINEO   Your comfortable words are like honey.
They relish well in your mouth that's whole; but in
mine that's wounded they go down as if the sting of
the bee were in them. O they have wrought their
purpose cunningly, as if they would not seem to do it
of malice. In this a politician imitates the devil, as the
devil imitates a cannon. Wheresoever he comes to do
mischief, he comes with his backside towards you.
   Enter the French [Ambassador]

FRENCH AMBASSADOR   The proofs are evident.

FLAMINEO   Proof! 'Twas corruption. O gold, what a
god art thou! And O man, what a devil art thou to be
tempted by that cursed mineral! Yon diversivolent
lawyer, mark him; knaves turn informers, as maggots
turn to flies: you may catch gudgeons with either. A
Cardinal! I would he would hear me: there's nothing
so holy but money will corrupt and putrify it, like
victual under the line.
   Enter English Ambassador
You are happy in England, my lord; here they sell
justice with those weights they press men to death
with. O horrible salary!

ENGLISH AMBASSADOR   Fie, fie, Flamineo.

FLAMINEO   Bells ne'er ring well, till they are at their full
pitch, and I hope yon Cardinal shall never have the
grace to pray well, till he come to the scaffold.
   [Exeunt Ambassadors]

If they were racked now to know the confederacy! But
your noblemen are privileged from the rack; and well
may. For a little thing would pull some of them
i'pieces afore they came to their arraignment.
Religion! O how it is commeddled with policy. The 40
first bloodshed in the world happened about religion.
Would I were a Jew.

MARCELLO   O, there are too many.

FLAMINEO   You are deceived. There are not Jews
enough, priests enough, nor gentlemen enough. 45

MARCELLO   How?

FLAMINEO   I'll prove it. For if there were Jews enough,
so many Christians would not turn usurers; if priests
enough, one should not have six benefices; and if
gentlemen enough, so many early mushrooms, whose 50
best growth sprang from a dunghill, should not aspire
to gentility. Farewell. Let others live by begging. Be
thou one of them. Practise the art of Wolner in
England to swallow all's given thee; and yet let one
purgation make thee as hungry again as fellows that 55
work in a sawpit. I'll go hear the screech-owl.
  Exit [Flamineo]

LODOVICO   [*aside*] This was Bracciano's pander, and 'tis
  strange
That in such open and apparent guilt
Of his adulterous sister, he dare utter
So scandalous a passion. I must wind him. 60
  Enter Flamineo

FLAMINEO   [*aside*] How dares this banished count
  return to Rome,
His pardon not yet purchased? I have heard
The deceasèd Duchess gave him pension,
And that he came along from Padua
I'th'train of the young prince. There's somewhat in't. 65

Physicians that cure poisons still do work
With counterpoisons.

MARCELLO [*aside*]   Mark this strange encounter.

FLAMINEO   The god of melancholy turn thy gall to
poison,
And let the stigmatic wrinkles in thy face,
Like to the boisterous waves in a rough tide,   70
One still overtake another.

LODOVICO   I do thank thee,
And I do wish ingeniously for thy sake
The dog-days all year long.

FLAMINEO   How croaks the raven?
Is our good Duchess dead?

LODOVICO   Dead.

FLAMINEO   O fate!
Misfortune comes like the coroner's business,   75
Huddle upon huddle.

LODOVICO   Shalt thou and I join housekeeping?

FLAMINEO   *malcontent*   Yes, content.
Let's be unsociably sociable.

LODOVICO   Sit some three days together, and
discourse.

FLAMINEO   Only with making faces;   80
Lie in our clothes.

LODOVICO   With faggots for our pillows.

FLAMINEO   And be lousy.

LODOVICO   In taffeta linings: that's gentle melancholy;
Sleep all day.

FLAMINEO   Yes, and like your melancholic hare
Feed after midnight.   85

*Enter Antonelli [with Lodovico's pardon, and
Gasparo, both laughing]*

We are observed: see how yon couple grieve.

LODOVICO   What a strange creature is a laughing fool,

As if man were created to no use
But only to show his teeth.

FLAMINEO   I'll tell thee what:
It would do well instead of looking-glasses,   90
To set one's face each morning by a saucer
Of a witch's congealèd blood.

LODOVICO   Precious girn, rogue.
We'll never part.

FLAMINEO   Never: till the beggary of courtiers,
The discontent of churchmen, want of soldiers,   95
And all the creatures that hang manacled,
Worse than strappadoed, on the lowest felly
Of fortune's wheel be taught in our two lives
To scorn that world which life of means deprives.

ANTONELLI   My lord, I bring good news. The Pope on's
death-bed,   100
At the earnest suit of the Great Duke of Florence,
Hath signed your pardon, and restored unto you –

LODOVICO I thank you for your news. Look up again,
Flamineo, see my pardon.

FLAMINEO   Why do you laugh?
There was no such condition in our covenant.

LODOVICO   Why?   105

FLAMINEO   You shall not seem a happier man than I.
You know our vow, sir: if you will be merry,
Do it i'th' like posture, as if some great man
Sat while his enemy were executed:
Though it be very lechery unto thee,   110
Do't with a crabbèd politician's face.

LODOVICO   Your sister is a damnable whore.

FLAMINEO   Ha?

LODOVICO   Look you, I spake that laughing.

FLAMINEO   Dost ever think to speak again?

LODOVICO   Do you hear?

Wilt sell me forty ounces of her blood   115
  To water a mandrake?
FLAMINEO   Poor lord, you did vow
  To live a lousy creature.
LODOVICO   Yes.
FLAMINEO   Like one
  That had for ever forfeited the daylight,
  By being in debt.
LODOVICO   Ha, ha!
FLAMINEO   I do not greatly wonder you do break: 120
  Your lordship learnt long since. But I'll tell you –
LODOVICO   What?
FLAMINEO   And't shall stick by you.
LODOVICO   I long for it.
FLAMINEO   This laughter scurvily becomes your face.
  If you will not be melancholy, be angry.
    Strikes him
  See, now I laugh too.   125
MARCELLO [*to Flamineo*]   You are to blame; I'll force you
      hence.
    [*Marcello hustles Flamineo out, while Antonelli and
    Gasparo restrain Lodovico*]
LODOVICO   Unhand me!
    Exeunt Marcello and Flamineo
  That e'er I should be forced to right myself
  Upon a pander.
ANTONELLI   My lord.
LODOVICO   He'd been as good met with his fist a
    thunderbolt.
GASPARO   How this shows!
LODOVICO   Ud's death, how did my sword miss him?   130
  These rogues that are most weary of their lives
  Still scape the greatest dangers.
  A pox upon him. All his reputation,

71

Nay all the goodness of his family,
Is not worth half his earthquake.   135
I learnt it of no fencer to shake thus.
Come, I'll forget him, and go drink some wine.
    [*Exeunt*]

Act IV Scene I

Enter Francisco and Monticelso

MONTICELSO   Come, come, my lord, untie your folded
    thoughts,
  And let them dangle loose as a bride's hair.
  Your sister's poisoned.

FRANCISCO   Far be it from my thoughts
  To seek revenge.

MONTICELSO   What, are you turned all marble?

FRANCISCO   Shall I defy him, and impose a war
  Most burdensome on my poor subjects' necks,
  Which at my will I have not power to end?
  You know, for all the murders, rapes, and thefts,
  Committed in the horrid lust of war,
  He that unjustly caused it first proceed   10
  Shall find it in his grave and in his seed.

MONTICELSO   That's not the course I'd wish you. Pray,
    observe me.
  We see that undermining more prevails
  Than doth the cannon. Bear your wrongs concealed,
  And, patient as the tortoise, let this camel   15
  Stalk o'er your back unbruised; sleep with the lion,
  And let this brood of secure foolish mice
  Play with your nostrils, till the time be ripe
  For th'bloody audit, and the fatal gripe.
  Aim like a cunning fowler, close one eye,   20
  That you the better may your game espy.

FRANCISCO   Free me, my innocence, from treacherous
    acts.
  I know there's thunder yonder; and I'll stand
  Like a safe valley, which low bends the knee
  To some aspiring mountain, since I know   25

Treason, like spiders weaving nets for flies,
By her foul work is found, and in it dies.
To pass away these thoughts, my honoured lord,
It is reported you possess a book
Wherein you have quoted, by intelligence,   30
The names of all notorious offenders
Lurking about the city.
MONTICELSO   Sir, I do;
And some there are which call it my black book.
Well may the title hold, for though it teach not
The art of conjuring, yet in it lurk   35
The names of many devils.
FRANCISCO   Pray let's see it.
MONTICELSO   I'll fetch it to your lordship.
          Exit Monticelso
FRANCISCO   Monticelso,
I will not trust thee, but in all my plots
I'll rest as jealous as a town besieged.
Thou canst not reach what I intend to act.   40
Your flax soon kindles, soon is out again,
But gold slow heats, and long will hot remain.
          *Enter Monticelso, [who] presents Francisco with a
          book*
MONTICELSO   'Tis here, my lord.
FRANCISCO   First, your intelligencers; pray let's see.
MONTICELSO   Their number rises strangely, and some
          of them   45
You'd take for honest men.
                    [*Turning the pages*] Next are panders.
These are your pirates; and these following leaves
For base rogues that undo young gentlemen
By taking up commodities; for politic bankrupts;
For fellows that are bawds to their own wives,   50
Only to put off horses and slight jewels,

74

Clocks, defaced plate, and such commodities,
At birth of their first children.
FRANCISCO   Are there such?
MONTICELSO   These are for impudent bawds
   That go in men's apparel; for usurers   55
   That share with scriveners for their good reportage;
   For lawyers that will antedate their writs;
   And some divines you might find folded there
   But that I slip them o'er for conscience' sake.
   Here is a general catalogue of knaves.   60
   A man might study all the prisons o'er,
   Yet never attain this knowledge.
FRANCISCO   Murderers.
   Fold down the leaf, I pray.
   Good my lord, let me borrow this strange doctrine.
MONTICELSO   Pray use't, my lord.
FRANCISCO   I do assure your lordship,   65
   You are a worthy member of the state,
   And have done infinite good in your discovery
   Of these offenders.
MONTICELSO   Somewhat, sir.
FRANCISCO   O God!
   Better than tribute of wolves paid in England;
   'Twill hang their skins o'th' hedge.
MONTICELSO   I must make bold   70
   To leave your lordship.
FRANCISCO   Dearly, sir, I thank you.
   If any ask for me at court, report
   You have left me in the company of knaves.
      Exit Monticelso
   I gather now by this, some cunning fellow
   That's my lord's officer, one that lately skipped   75
   From a clerk's desk up to a justice' chair,
   Hath made this knavish summons, and intends,

As the Irish rebels wont were to sell heads,
So to make prize of these. And thus it happens
Your poor rogues pay for't, which have not the means   80
To present bribe in fist; the rest o'th' band
Are razed out of the knaves' record, or else
My lord he winks at them with easy will,
His man grows rich, the knaves are the knaves still.
But to the use I'll make of it: it shall serve   85
To point me out a list of murderers,
Agents for any villainy. Did I want
Ten leash of courtezans, it would furnish me,
Nay, laundress three armies. That in so little paper,
Should lie the undoing of so many men!   90
'Tis not so big as twenty declarations.
See the corrupted use some make of books:
Divinity, wrested by some factious blood,
Draws swords, swells battles, and o'erthrows all good.
To fashion my revenge more seriously,   95
Let me remember my dead sister's face.
Call for her picture? No, I'll close mine eyes,
And in a melancholic thought I'll frame
Her figure 'fore me.
        Enter Isabella's Ghost
                Now I ha't. How strong
Imagination works! How she can frame   100
Things which are not! Methinks she stands afore me,
And by the quick idea of my mind,
Were my skill pregnant, I could draw her picture.
Thought, as a subtle juggler, makes us deem
Things supernatural which have cause   105
Common as sickness. 'Tis my melancholy.
How cam'st thou by thy death? How idle am I
To question mine own idleness. Did ever
Man dream awake till now? Remove this object,

Out of my brain with't. What have I to do   110
With tombs, or death-beds, funerals, or tears,
That have to meditate upon revenge?
   [Exit Ghost]
So now 'tis ended, like an old wives' story.
Statesmen think often they see stranger sights
Than madmen. Come, to this weighty business.   115
My tragedy must have some idle mirth in't,
Else it will never pass. I am in love,
In love with Corombona; and my suit
Thus halts to her in verse.
   He writes
I have done it rarely. O the fate of princes!   120
I am so used to frequent flattery
That, being alone, I now flatter myself;
But it will serve, 'tis sealed.
   Enter Servant
                    Bear this
To the house of convertites; and watch your leisure
To give it to the hands of Corombona,   125
Or to the matron, when some followers
Of Bracciano may be by. Away.
   Exit Servant
He that deals all by strength, his wit is shallow:
When a man's head goes through, each limb will
   follow.
The engine for my business, bold Count Lodovic.   130
'Tis gold must such an instrument procure,
With empty fist no man doth falcons lure.
Bracciano, I am now fit for thy encounter.
Like the wild Irish I'll ne'er think thee dead,
Till I can play at football with thy head.   135
Flectere si nequeo superos, Acheronta movebo.
   Exit

reluctant to allow Bracciano access to Vittoria

Act IV Scene II

Enter the Matron, and Flamineo

MATRON   Should it be known the Duke hath such recourse
To your imprisoned sister, I were like
T'incur much damage by it.

FLAMINEO   Not a scruple.

refers to this a couple of times, taken his age of the God —

The Pope lies on his death-bed, and their heads
Are troubled now with other business   5
Than guarding of a lady.

Enter [Francisco's] Servant

SERVANT [*aside*]   Yonder's Flamineo in conference
With the matrona. [*To the Matron*] Let me speak with you.
I would entreat you to deliver for me
This letter to the fair Vittoria.   10

MATRON   I shall, sir.

Enter Bracciano

SERVANT   With all care and secrecy.
Hereafter you shall know me, and receive
Thanks for this courtesy.

[*Exit Servant*]

FLAMINEO   How now? What's that?

MATRON   A letter.

FLAMINEO   To my sister. I'll see't delivered.

[*Exit Matron*]

BRACCIANO   What's that you read, Flamineo?

FLAMINEO   Look.   15

BRACCIANO   Ha? [*Reads*] 'To the most unfortunate his best respected Vittoria'
Who was the messenger?

FLAMINEO   I know not.

BRACCIANO   No! Who sent it?

FLAMINEO   Ud's foot, you speak as if a man
Should know what fowl is coffined in a baked meat   20
Afore you cut it up.

BRACCIANO   I'll open't, were't her heart. What's here
subscribed?
'Florence'? This juggling is gross and palpable.
I have found out the conveyance. Read it, read it.

FLAMINEO   'Your tears I'll turn to triumphs, be but
mine.   25
Your prop is fall'n. I pity that a vine
Which princes heretofore have longed to gather,
Wanting supporters, now should fade and wither.'
Wine i'faith, my lord, with lees would serve his turn.
'Your sad imprisonment I'll soon uncharm,   30
And with a princely uncontrollèd arm
Lead you to Florence, where my love and care
Shall hang your wishes in my silver hair.'
A halter on his strange equivocation!
'Nor for my years return me the sad willow,   35
Who prefer blossoms before fruit that's mellow?'
Rotten, on my knowledge, with lying too long i'th'
bed-straw.
'And all the lines of age this line convinces:
The gods never wax old, no more do princes.'
A pox on't! Tear it, let's have no more atheists for
God's sake.   40

BRACCIANO   Ud's death, I'll cut her into atomies
And let th'irregular north-wind sweep her up
And blow her int' his nostrils. Where's this whore?

FLAMINEO   That—! what do you call her?

BRACCIANO   O, I could be mad,
Prevent the cursed disease she'll bring me to,   45
And tear my hair off. Where's this changeable stuff?

should be less powerful but lets Bracciano have it

FLAMINEO   O'er head and ears in water, I assure you.
   She is not for your wearing.
BRACCIANO   In, you pander!
FLAMINEO   What, me, my lord, am I your dog?
BRACCIANO   A bloodhound. Do you brave? Do you
   stand me?   50
FLAMINEO   Stand you? Let those that have diseases run;
   I need no plasters.
BRACCIANO   Would you be kicked?
FLAMINEO   Would you have your neck broke?
   I tell you, Duke, I am not in Russia;   *do you know who I am?*
   My shins must be kept whole.
BRACCIANO   Do you know me?   55
FLAMINEO   O, my lord, methodically.   *comment on*
   As in this world there are degrees of evils,   *the class*
   So in this world there are degrees of devils.   *system again*
   You're a great duke, I your poor secretary.
   I do look now for a Spanish fig, or an Italian salad
   daily.   *hasn't been paid*   60
BRACCIANO   Pander, ply your convoy, and leave your
   prating.
FLAMINEO   All your kindness to me is like that
   miserable courtesy of Polyphemus to Ulysses: you
   reserve me to be devoured last. You would dig turves
   out of my grave to feed your larks: that would be   65
   music to you. Come, I'll lead you to her.
BRACCIANO   Do you face me?
FLAMINEO   O, sir, I would not go before a politic enemy
   with my back towards him, though there were behind
   me a whirlpool.   70
   Enter Vittoria to Bracciano and Flamineo
   [*Bracciano hands her the letter*]
BRACCIANO   Can you read, mistress? Look upon that
   letter;

Bold directly to the dukes face.

There are no characters nor hieroglyphics.
You need no comment; I am grown your receiver.
God's precious, you shall be a brave great lady,
A stately and advancèd whore.

VITTORIA   Say, sir?   75

BRACCIANO   Come, come, let's see your cabinet, discover
Your treasury of love-letters. Death and furies,
I'll see them all.

VITTORIA   Sir, upon my soul,
I have not any. Whence was this directed?

BRACCIANO   Confusion on your politic ignorance!   80
    [*Gives her the letter*]
You are reclaimèd, are you? I'll give you the bells
And let you fly to the devil.

FLAMINEO   Ware hawk, my lord.

VITTORIA [*reads*] 'Florence'! This is some treacherous
    plot, my lord.   *← her too innocent*
To me he ne'er was lovely, I protest,   *to see the*
So much as in my sleep.

BRACCIANO   Right: they are plots.   85
    Your beauty! O, ten thousand curses on't.   *dazzled by outward*
    How long have I beheld the devil in crystal?   *appearances*
Thou hast led me, like an heathen sacrifice,
With music, and with fatal yokes of flowers
To my eternal ruin. Woman to man   90
Is either a god or a wolf.   *Perfect or less than human*

VITTORIA   My lord —   *silences her*

BRACCIANO   Away.
We'll be as differing as two adamants:
The one shall shun the other. What? dost weep?
Procure but ten of thy dissembling trade,
Ye'ld furnish all the Irish funerals   95
With howling, past wild Irish.

FLAMINEO   Fie, my lord.

BRACCIANO   That hand, that cursèd hand, which I have
          wearied
     With doting kisses! O my sweetest Duchess,
     How lovely art thou now! [*To Vittoria*] Thy loose
          thoughts
     Scatter like quicksilver. I was bewitched,   100
     For all the world speaks ill of thee.
VITTORIA   No matter.
     I'll live so now I'll make that world recant
     And change her speeches. You did name your
          Duchess.
BRACCIANO   Whose death God pardon.
VITTORIA   Whose death God revenge
     On thee, most godless Duke.   105
FLAMINEO [*aside*]   Now for two whirlwinds.
VITTORIA   What have I gained by thee but infamy?
     Thou hast stained the spotless honour of my house,
     And frighted thence noble society;
     Like those which, sick o'th' palsy and retain   110
     Ill-scenting foxes 'bout them, are still shunned
     By those of choicer nostrils. What do you call this
          house?
     Is this your palace? Did not the judge style it
     A house of penitent whores? Who sent me to it?
     Who hath the honour to advance Vittoria   115
     To this incontinent college? Is't not you?
     Is't not your high preferment? Go, go brag
     How many ladies you have undone, like me.
     Fare you well, sir; let me hear no more of you.
     I had a limb corrupted to an ulcer,   120
     But I have cut it off; and now I'll go
     Weeping to heaven on crutches. For your gifts,
     I will return them all; and I do wish
     That I could make you full executor

To all my sins. O that I could toss myself   125
Into a grave as quickly. For all thou art worth,
I'll not shed one tear more; I'll burst first.
   She throws herself upon a bed
BRACCIANO   I have drunk Lethe. Vittoria?
  My dearest happiness? Vittoria?
  What do you ail, my love? Why do you weep?   130
VITTORIA   Yes, I now weep poniards, do you see?
BRACCIANO   Are not those matchless eyes mine?
VITTORIA   I had rather
  They were not matches.
BRACCIANO   Is not this lip mine?
VITTORIA   Yes: thus to bite it off, rather than give it
    thee.
FLAMINEO   Turn to my lord, good sister.
VITTORIA   Hence, you pander.   135
FLAMINEO   Pander! Am I the author of your sin?
VITTORIA   Yes: he's a base thief that a thief lets in.
FLAMINEO   We're blown up, my lord.
BRACCIANO   Wilt thou hear me?
  Once to be jealous of thee is t'express
  That I will love thee everlastingly,   140
  And never more be jealous.
VITTORIA   O thou fool,
  Whose greatness hath by much o'ergrown thy wit!
  What dar'st thou do that I not dare to suffer,
  Excepting to be still thy whore? For that,
  In the sea's bottom sooner thou shalt make   145
  A bonfire.
FLAMINEO   O, no oaths for God's sake.
BRACCIANO   Will you hear me?
VITTORIA   Never.
FLAMINEO   What a damned imposthume is a woman's
    will.

Can nothing break it? Fie, fie, my lord.
[*Whispers to Bracciano*] Women are caught as you take
    tortoises,   150
She must be turned on her back. [*Aloud*] Sister, by this
    hand
I am on your side. Come, come, you have wronged
    her.
What a strange credulous man were you, my lord,
To think the Duke of Florence would love her?
[*Aside*] Will any mercer take another's ware   155
When once 'tis toused and sullied? [*Aloud*] And yet,
    sister,
How scurvily this frowardness becomes you!
[*To Bracciano*] Young leverets stand not long; and
    women's anger
Should, like their flight, procure a little sport:
A full cry for a quarter of an hour,   160
And then be put to th'dead quat.
BRACCIANO   Shall these eyes,
Which have so long time dwelt upon your face,
Be now put out?
FLAMINEO   No cruel landlady i'th' world,
Which lends forth groats to broom-men, and takes
    use for them,
Would do't.   165
[*Whispers to Bracciano*] Hand her, my lord, and kiss
    her. Be not like
A ferret to let go your hold with blowing.
BRACCIANO   Let us renew right hands.
VITTORIA   Hence.
BRACCIANO   Never shall rage, or the forgetful wine,
Make me commit like fault.   170
FLAMINEO   [*whispers to Bracciano*] Now you are i'th'
    way on't, follow't hard.

84

BRACCIANO   Be thou at peace with me, let all the world
  Threaten the cannon.
FLAMINEO   Mark his penitence.
  Best natures do commit the grossest faults,
  When they're given o'er to jealousy, as best wine   175
  Dying makes strongest vinegar. I'll tell you:
  The sea's more rough and raging than calm rivers,
  But nor so sweet nor wholesome. A quiet woman
  Is a still water under a great bridge.
  A man may shoot her safely.   180
VITTORIA   O ye dissembling men!
FLAMINEO   We sucked that, sister,
  From women's breasts, in our first infancy.
VITTORIA   To add misery to misery.
BRACCIANO   Sweetest.
VITTORIA   Am I not low enough?
  Ay, ay, your good heart gathers like a snowball   185
  Now your affection's cold.
FLAMINEO   Ud's foot, it shall melt
  To a heart again, or all the wine in Rome
  Shall run o'th' lees for't.
VITTORIA   Your dog or hawk should be rewarded better
  Than I have been. I'll speak not one word more.   190
FLAMINEO   Stop her mouth with a sweet kiss, my lord.
  [Bracciano and Vittoria kiss]
  [aside] So now the tide's turned, the vessel's come
    about.
  He's a sweet armful. O we curled-haired men
  Are still most kind to women. This is well.
BRACCIANO   That you should chide thus!
FLAMINEO   O, sir, your little chimneys   195
  Do ever cast most smoke. I sweat for you.
  Couple together with as deep a silence
  As did the Grecians in their wooden horse.

85

They are now planning to
escape whilst she remains
quiet.

My lord, supply your promises with deeds;
You know that painted meat no hunger feeds.   200
BRACCIANO   Stay – ingrateful Rome!
FLAMINEO   Rome! It deserves to be called Barbary, for
   our villainous usage.
BRACCIANO   Soft; the same project which the Duke of
     Florence
   (Whether in love or gullery I know not)   205
   Laid down for her escape, will I pursue.
FLAMINEO   And no time fitter than this night, my lord:
   The Pope being dead, and all the cardinals entered
   The conclave for th'electing a new Pope;
   The city in a great confusion,   *One of*   210
                                            the black
   We may attire her in a page's suit,   *Look.*
   Lay her post-horse, take shipping, and amain
   For Padua.
BRACCIANO   I'll   instantly   steal   forth   the   Prince
     Giovanni,
   And make for Padua. You two with your old mother   215
   And young Marcello that attends on Florence,
   If you can work him to it, follow me.
   I will advance you all. For you, Vittoria,
   Think of a duchess' title.
FLAMINEO   Lo you, sister.
   Stay, my lord, I'll tell you a tale. The crocodile, which   220
   lives in the river Nilus, hath a worm breeds i'th' teeth
   of't, which puts it to extreme anguish. A little bird, no
   bigger than a wren, is barber-surgeon to this crocodile,
   flies into the jaws of't, picks out the worm, and brings
   present remedy. The fish, glad of ease but ingrateful to   225
   her that did it, that the bird may not talk largely of her
   abroad for non-payment, closeth her chaps intending
   to swallow her, and so put her to perpetual silence.
   But nature, loathing such ingratitude, hath armed this

bird with a quill or prick on the head, top o'th' which   230
wounds the crocodile i'th' mouth; forceth her open
her bloody prison; and away flies the pretty tooth-
picker from her cruel patient.

BRACCIANO   Your application is, I have not rewarded
The service you have done me.

FLAMINEO   No, my lord.   235
You, sister, are the crocodile: you are blemished in
your fame, my lord cures it. And though the
comparison hold not in every particle, yet observe,
remember, what good the bird with the prick i'th'
head hath done you, and scorn ingratitude.   240
[*Aside*] It may appear to some ridiculous
Thus to talk knave and madman, and sometimes
Come in with a dried sentence, stuffed with sage.
But this allows my varying of shapes.
Knaves do grow great by being great men's apes.   245
    Exeunt

Act IV Scene III

Enter Lodovico, Gasparo, and six Ambassadors. At
another door [Francisco] the Duke of Florence

FRANCISCO   So, my lord, I commend your diligence.
Guard well the conclave, and, as the order is,
Let none have conference with the cardinals.

LODOVICO   I shall, my lord. Room for the ambassadors.

GASPARO   They're wondrous brave today. Why do they
    wear   5
These several habits?

LODOVICO   O sir, they're knights
Of several orders.
That lord i'th' black cloak with the silver cross

Is Knight of Rhodes; the next Knight of St Michael;
That of the Golden Fleece; the Frenchman there   10
Knight of the Holy Ghost; my lord of Savoy
Knight of th'Annunciation; the Englishman
Is Knight of th'honoured Garter, dedicated
Unto their saint, St George. I could describe to you
Their several institutions, with the laws   15
Annexèd to their orders, but that time
Permits not such discovery.
FRANCISCO   Where's Count Lodovic?
LODOVICO   Here, my lord.
FRANCISCO   'Tis o'th' point of dinner time,
   Marshall the cardinals' service.
LODOVICO   Sir, I shall.
     Enter Servants with several dishes covered
   Stand, let me search your dish. Who's this for?   20
[FIRST] SERVANT   For my Lord Cardinal Monticelso.
LODOVICO   Who's this?
[SECOND] SERVANT   For my Lord Cardinal of Bourbon.
FRENCH AMBASSADOR   Why doth he search the dishes?
     To observe
   What meat is dressed?
ENGLISH AMBASSADOR   No, sir, but to prevent,
   Lest any letters should be conveyed in   25
   To bribe or to solicit the advancement
   Of any cardinal. When first they enter
   'Tis lawful for the ambassadors of princes
   To enter with them, and to make their suit
   For any man their prince affecteth best;   30
   But after, till a general election,
   No man may speak with them.
LODOVICO   You that attend on the lord cardinals
   Open the window, and receive their viands.
     [*A Conclavist appears at the window*]

CONCLAVIST   You must return the service. The lord cardinals   35
  Are busied 'bout electing of the Pope.
  They have given o'er scrutiny, and are fallen
  To admiration.
    [*Conclavist exits*]
LODOVICO   Away, away.
    [*Exeunt Servants*]
FRANCISCO   I'll lay a thousand ducats you hear news
  Of a Pope presently. Hark, sure he's elected.   40
    [*The*] *Cardinal* [*of Aragon appears*] *on the terrace.*
  Behold! my lord of Aragon appears
  On the church battlements.
ARAGON   *Denuntio*   *vobis*   *gaudium*   *magnum.*
  Reverendissimus Cardinalis Lorenzo de Monticelso electus
  est in sedem apostolicam, et elegit sibi nomen Paulum   45
  Quartum.
ALL   *Vivat Sanctus Pater Paulus Quartus.*
    [*Enter Servant*]
SERVANT   Vittoria, my lord –
FRANCISCO   Well, what of her?
SERVANT   Is fled the city.
FRANCISCO   Ha!
SERVANT   With Duke Bracciano.
FRANCISCO   Fled? Where's the prince Giovanni?
SERVANT   Gone with his father.   50
FRANCISCO   Let the matrona of the convertites
  Be apprehended. Fled? O damnable!
    [*Exit Servant*]
  [*Aside*] How fortunate are my wishes. Why, 'twas this
  I only laboured. I did send the letter
  T'instruct him what to do. Thy fame, fond duke,   55
  I first have poison'd; directed thee the way
  To marry a whore. What can be worse? This follows:

The hand must act to drown the passionate tongue,
I scorn to wear a sword and prate of wrong.
    Enter Monticelso in state [as Pope Paul IV]
MONTICELSO *Concedimus vobis apostolicam benedictionem*   60
et remissionem peccatorum.
    [Francisco whispers to him]
    My lord reports Vittoria Corombona
Is stol'n from forth the house of convertites
By Bracciano, and they're fled the city.
Now, though this be the first day of our seat,   65
We cannot better please the divine power
Than to sequester from the holy church
These cursèd persons. Make it therefore known
We do denounce excommunication
Against them both. All that are theirs in Rome   70
We likewise banish. Set on.
    Exeunt [all except Francisco and Lodovico]
FRANCISCO   Come, dear Lodovico,
You have ta'en the sacrament to prosecute
Th'intended murder.
LODOVICO   With all constancy.
But, sir, I wonder you'll engage yourself,   75
In person, being a great prince.
FRANCISCO   Divert me not.
Most of his court are of my faction,
And some are of my counsel. Noble friend,
Our danger shall be 'like in this design;
Give leave, part of the glory may be mine.   80
    Exit Francisco. Enter Monticelso
MONTICELSO   Why did the Duke of Florence with such care
Labour your pardon? Say.
LODOVICO   Italian beggars will resolve you that,
Who, begging of an alms, bid those they beg of

Do good for their own sakes. Or't may be   85
He spreads his bounty with a sowing hand,
Like kings, who many times give out of measure;
Not for desert so much as for their pleasure.

MONTICELSO   I know you're cunning. Come, what devil
    was that
  That you were raising?

LODOVICO   Devil, my lord?

MONTICELSO   I ask you   90
How doth the Duke employ you, that his bonnet
Fell with such compliment unto his knee,
When he departed from you?

LODOVICO   Why, my lord,
He told me of a resty Barbary horse
Which he would fain have brought to the career,   95
The sault, and the ring-galliard. Now, my lord,
I have a rare French rider.

MONTICELSO   Take you heed,
Lest the jade break your neck. Do you put me off
With your wild horse-tricks? Sirrah, you do lie.
O, thou'rt a foul black cloud, and thou dost threat   100
A violent storm.

LODOVICO   Storms are i'th' air, my lord;
I am too low to storm.

MONTICELSO   Wretched creature!
I know that thou art fashioned for all ill,
Like dogs, that once get blood, they'll ever kill.
About some murder? Was't not?

LODOVICO   I'll not tell you;   105
And yet I care not greatly if I do.
Marry, with this preparation. Holy father,
I come not to you as an intelligencer,
But as a penitent sinner. What I utter
Is in confession merely, which you know   110

Must never be revealed.

MONTICELSO You have o'erta'en me.

LODOVICO Sir, I did love Bracciano's duchess dearly;
Or rather I pursued her with hot lust,
Though she ne'er knew on't. She was poison'd,
Upon my soul she was, for which I have sworn   115
T'avenge her murder.

MONTICELSO   To the Duke of Florence?

LODOVICO To him I have.

MONTICELSO   Miserable creature!
If thou persist in this, 'tis damnable.
Dost thou imagine thou canst slide on blood
And not be tainted with a shameful fall?   120
Or like the black and melancholic yew tree,
Dost think to root thyself in dead men's graves,
And yet to prosper? Instruction to thee
Comes like sweet showers to over-hardened ground:
They wet, but pierce not deep. And so I leave thee   125
With all the Furies hanging 'bout thy neck,
Till by thy penitence thou remove this evil,
In conjuring from thy breast that cruel devil.
          Exit Monticelso

LODOVICO I'll give it o'er. He says 'tis damnable.
Besides, I did expect his suffrage,   130
By reason of Camillo's death.
          Enter Servant and Francisco [apart]

FRANCISCO Do you know that count?

SERVANT   Yes, my lord.

FRANCISCO Bear him these thousand ducats to his
          lodging;
Tell him the Pope hath sent them. Happily
That will confirm more than all the rest.
          [*Exit Francisco*]

SERVANT   Sir.   135

92

LODOVICO   To me, sir?

  [*Servant hands over money*]

SERVANT   His Holiness hath sent you a thousand
    crowns,
  And wills you, if you travel, to make him
  Your patron for intelligence.

LODOVICO   His creature

  Ever to be commanded.   140

    [*Exit Servant*]

  Why, now 'tis come about. He railed upon me,
  And yet these crowns were told out and laid ready,
  Before he knew my voyage. O the art,
  The modest form of greatness! that do sit
  Like brides at wedding dinners, with their looks
    turned   145
  From the least wanton jests, their puling stomach
  Sick of the modesty, when their thoughts are loose,
  Even acting of those hot and lustful sports
  Are to ensue about midnight: such his cunning!
  He sounds my depth thus with a golden plummet.   150
  I am doubly armed now. Now to th'act of blood.
  There's but three Furies found in spacious hell,
  But in a great man's breast three thousand dwell.

    [*Exit*]

Act V Scene I

A passage over the stage of Bracciano, Flamineo,
Marcello, Hortensio, [Vittoria] Corombona, Cornelia,
Zanche and others. [Enter Flamineo and Hortensio]

FLAMINEO   In all the weary minutes of my life,
Day ne'er broke up till now. This marriage
Confirms me happy.

HORTENSIO   'Tis a good assurance.
Saw you not yet the Moor that's come to court?

FLAMINEO   Yes, and conferred with him i'th' Duke's
        closet.   5
I have not seen a goodlier personage,
Nor ever talked with man better experienced
In state affairs or rudiments of war.
He hath, by report, served the Venetian
In Candy these twice seven years, and been chief   10
In many a bold design.

HORTENSIO   What are those two
That bear him company?

FLAMINEO   Two noblemen of Hungary, that living in
the emperor's service as commanders, eight years
since, contrary to the expectation of all the court   15
entered into religion, into the strict order of
Capuchins; but being not well settled in their
undertaking, they left their order and returned to
court: for which, being after troubled in conscience,
they vowed their service against the enemies of   20
Christ; went to Malta; were there knighted; and in
their return back, at this great solemnity, they are
resolved for ever to forsake the world, and settle
themselves here in a house of Capuchins in Padua.

HORTENSIO   'Tis strange.   25

94

FLAMINEO   One thing makes it so. They have vowed for
    ever to wear next their bare bodies those coats of mail
    they served in.
HORTENSIO   Hard penance. Is the Moor a Christian?
FLAMINEO   He is.   30
HORTENSIO   Why proffers he his service to our duke?
FLAMINEO   Because he understands there's like to grow
    Some wars between us and the Duke of Florence,
    In which he hopes employment.
    I never saw one in a stern bold look   35
    Wear more command, nor in a lofty phrase
    Express more knowing, or more deep contempt
    Of our slight airy courtiers. He talks
    As if he had travelled all the princes' courts
    Of Christendom; in all things strives t'express   40
    That all that should dispute with him may know
    Glories, like glow-worms, afar off shine bright
    But, looked to near, have neither heat nor light.
    The Duke!
        Enter Bracciano, [Francisco Duke of] Florence
        disguised like Mulinassar; Lodovico, Antonelli,
        Gasparo [disguised], Farnese bearing their swords
        and helmets, [Carlo and Pedro]
BRACCIANO   You're nobly welcome. We have heard at
    full   45
    Your honourable service 'gainst the Turk.
    To you, brave Mulinassar, we assign
    A competent pension, and are inly sorrow
    The vows of these two worthy gentlemen
    Make them incapable of our proffered bounty.   50
    Your wish is you may leave your warlike swords
    For monuments in our chapel. I accept it
    As a great honour done me, and must crave
    Your leave to furnish out our Duchess' revels.

Only one thing, as the last vanity   55
You e'er shall view, deny me not to stay
To see a Barriers prepared tonight.
You shall have private standings. It hath pleased
The great ambassadors of several princes,
In their return from Rome to their own countries,   60
To grace our marriage, and to honour me
With such a kind of sport.
FRANCISCO   I shall persuade them.
To stay, my lord.
BRACCIANO   Set on there to the presence.
      Exeunt Bracciano, Flamineo, and [Hortensio]
CARLO   Noble my lord, most fortunately welcome.
      The conspirators here embrace
You have our vows sealed with the sacrament   65
To second your attempts.
PEDRO   And all things ready.
He could not have invented his own ruin,
Had he despaired, with more propriety.
LODOVICO   You would not take my way.
FRANCISCO   'Tis better ordered.
LODOVICO   T'have poisoned his prayer book, or a pair
      of beads,   70
The pommel of his saddle, his looking-glass,
Or th'handle of his racket. O that, that!
That while he had been bandying at tennis,
He might have sworn himself to hell, and struck
His soul into the hazard! O my lord!   75
I would have our plot be ingenious,
And have it hereafter recorded for example
Rather than borrow example.
FRANCISCO   There's no way
More speeding than this thought on.
LODOVICO   On then.

FRANCISCO   And yet methinks that this revenge is poor,   80
  Because it steals upon him like a thief.
  To have ta'en him by the casque in a pitched field,
  Led him to Florence!
LODOVICO   It had been rare. And there
  Have crowned him with a wreath of stinking garlic,
  T'have shown the sharpness of his government   85
  And rankness of his lust. Flamineo comes.
    Exeunt [all except Francisco]. Enter Flamineo,
    Marcello, and Zanche
MARCELLO   Why doth this devil haunt you? say.
FLAMINEO   I know not.
  For by this light I do not conjure for her.
  'Tis not so great a cunning as men think
  To raise the devil, for here's one up already;   90
  The greatest cunning were to lay him down.
MARCELLO   She is your shame.
FLAMINEO   I prithee pardon her.
  In faith, you see women are like to burs;
  Where their affection throws them, there they'll stick.
ZANCHE   That is my countryman, a goodly person,   95
  When he's at leisure I'll discourse with him
  In our own language.
FLAMINEO   I beseech you do.
    Exit Zanche
  [*To Francisco*] How is't, brave soldier? O that I had seen
  Some of your iron days! I pray relate
  Some of your service to us.   100
FRANCISCO   'Tis a ridiculous thing for a man to be his
  own chronicle; I did never wash my mouth with mine
  own praise for fear of getting a stinking breath.
MARCELLO   You're too stoical. The Duke will expect
  other discourse from you.   105
FRANCISCO   I shall never flatter him. I have studied

man too much to do that. What difference is between the Duke and I? No more than between two bricks, all made of one clay. Only't may be one is placed on the top of a turret, the other in the bottom of a well by mere chance. If I were placed as high as the Duke, I should stick as fast, make as fair a show, and bear out weather equally.

FLAMINEO [*aside*] If this soldier had a patent to beg in churches, then he would tell them stories.

MARCELLO I have been a soldier too.

FRANCISCO How have you thrived?

MARCELLO Faith, poorly.

FRANCISCO That's the misery of peace. Only outsides are then respected. As ships seem very great upon the river, which show very little upon the seas, so some men i'th' court seem Colossuses in a chamber who, if they came into the field, would appear pitiful pigmies.

FLAMINEO Give me a fair room yet hung with arras, and some great cardinal to lug me by th'ears as his endeared minion.

FRANCISCO And thou may'st do the devil knows what villainy.

FLAMINEO And safely.

FRANCISCO Right: you shall see in the country in harvest time, pigeons, though they destroy never so much corn, the farmer dare not present the fowling-piece to them! Why? Because they belong to the lord of the manor; whilst your poor sparrows that belong to the Lord of heaven, they go to the pot for't.

FLAMINEO I will now give you some politic instruction. The Duke says he will give you pension: that's but bare promise; get it under his hand. For I have known men that have come from serving against the Turk; for three or four months they have had

pension to buy them new wooden legs and fresh plasters; but after 'twas not to be had. And this miserable courtesy shows, as if a tormenter should give hot cordial drinks to one three-quarters dead o'th' rack, only to fetch the miserable soul again to   145
endure more dog-days.

Enter Hortensio, a young Lord, Zanche, and two more
How now, gallants; what, are they ready for the Barriers?

[Exit Francisco]

YOUNG LORD   Yes: the lords are putting on their armour.

HORTENSIO   *[aside to Flamineo]* What's he?   150

FLAMINEO   A new upstart: one that swears like a falconer, and will lie in the Duke's ear day by day like a maker of almanacs; and yet I knew him since he came to th'court smell worse of sweat than an under-tennis-court-keeper.

HORTENSIO   Look you, yonder's your sweet mistress.   155

FLAMINEO   Thou art my sworn brother; I'll tell thee, I do love that Moor, that witch, very constrainedly; she knows some of my villainy. I do love her, just as a man holds a wolf by the ears. But for fear of turning upon me, and pulling out my throat, I would let her go   160
to the devil.

HORTENSIO   I hear she claims marriage of thee.

FLAMINEO   'Faith, I made to her some such dark promise, and in seeking to fly from't I run on, like a frighted dog with a bottle at's tail, that fain would bite   165
it off and yet dares not look behind him. *[To Zanche]*
Now, my precious gipsy!

ZANCHE   Ay, your love to me rather cools than heats.

FLAMINEO   Marry, I am the sounder lover. We have many wenches about the town heat too fast.   170

HORTENSIO   What do you think of these perfumed gallants then?

99

FLAMINEO   Their satin cannot save them. I am confident
   They have a certain spice of the disease,
   For they that sleep with dogs shall rise with fleas.   175
ZANCHE   Believe it! A little painting and gay clothes
   make you loathe me.
FLAMINEO   How? Love a lady for painting or gay
   apparel? I'll unkennel one example more for thee.
   Aesop had a foolish dog that let go the flesh to catch   180
   the shadow. I would have courtiers be better diners.
ZANCHE   You remember your oaths.
FLAMINEO   Lovers' oaths are like mariners' prayers,
   uttered in extremity; but when the tempest is o'er, and
   that the vessel leaves tumbling, they fall from   185
   protesting to drinking. And yet amongst gentlemen
   protesting and drinking go together, and agree as well
   as shoemakers and Westphalia bacon. They are both
   drawers-on, for drink draws on protestation, and
   pretestation draws on more drink. Is not this   190
   discourse better now than the morality of your
   sunburnt gentleman?
       Enter Cornelia
CORNELIA   Is this your perch, you haggard? Fly to
   th'stews.
       [*Strikes Zanche*]
FLAMINEO   You should be clapped by th'heels now:
   strike i'th' court!   195
       [*Exit Cornelia*]
ZANCHE   She's good for nothing but to make her maids
   Catch cold o' nights. They dare not use a bedstaff,
   For fear of her light fingers.
MARCELLO   You're a strumpet.
   An impudent one.
       [*Kicks Zanche*]
FLAMINEO   Why do you kick her? Say,

Do you think that she's like a walnut tree?   200
Must she be cudgelled ere she bear good fruit?
MARCELLO   She brags that you shall marry her.
FLAMINEO   What then?
MARCELLO   I had rather she were pitched upon a stake
In some new-seeded garden, to affright
Her fellow crows thence.
FLAMINEO   You're a boy, a fool.   205
Be guardian to your hound, I am of age.
MARCELLO   If I take her near you, I'll cut her throat.
FLAMINEO   With a fan of feathers?
MARCELLO   And for you, I'll whip
This folly from you.
FLAMINEO   Are you choleric?
I'll purge't with rhubarb.
HORTENSIO   O your brother!
FLAMINEO   Hang him.   210
He wrongs me most that ought t'offend me least.
I do suspect my mother played foul play
When she conceived thee.
MARCELLO   Now by all my hopes,
Like the two slaughtered sons of Oedipus,
The very flames of our affection   215
Shall turn two ways. Those words I'll make thee answer
With thy heart blood.
FLAMINEO   Do; like the gests in the progress,
You know where you shall find me.
MARCELLO   Very good.
    [*Exit Flamineo*]
And thou beest a noble friend, bear him my sword,
And bid him fit the length on't.
YOUNG LORD   Sir, I shall.   220
    [*Exeunt all but Zanche.*] *Enter Francisco the Duke of*
    Florence [*disguised as Mulinassar*]

ZANCHE [*aside*]   He comes. Hence petty thought of my
    disgrace.
  [*To him*] I ne'er loved my complexion till now,
  'Cause I may boldly say without a blush,
  I love you.
FRANCISCO   Your love is untimely sown:
  There's a spring at Michaelmas, but 'tis but a faint one;   225
  I am sunk in years, and I have vowed never to marry.
ZANCHE   Alas, poor maids get more lovers than
  husbands; yet you may mistake my wealth. For, as
  when ambassadors are sent to congratulate princes,
  there's commonly sent along with them a rich present,   230
  so that, though the prince like not the ambassador's
  person nor words, yet he likes well of the presentment;
  so I may come to you in the same manner, and be
  better loved for my dowry than my virtue.
FRANCISCO   I'll think on the motion.   235
ZANCHE   Do; I'll now detain you no longer. At your
  better leisure I'll tell you things shall startle your
  blood.
  Nor blame me that this passion I reveal:
  Lovers die inward that their flames conceal.   240
FRANCISCO [*aside*]   Of all intelligence this may prove
  the best.
  Sure I shall draw strange fowl, from this foul nest.
    [*Exeunt*]

Act V Scene II

Enter Marcello and Cornelia
CORNELIA   I hear a whispering all about the court,
  You are to fight. Who is your opposite?
  What is the quarrel?

MARCELLO   'Tis an idle rumour.

CORNELIA   Will you dissemble? Sure you do not well
  To fright me thus. You never look thus pale   5
  But when you are most angry. I do charge you
  Upon my blessing. Nay, I'll call the Duke,
  And he shall school you.

MARCELLO   Publish not a fear
  Which would convert to laughter. 'Tis not so.
  Was not this crucifix my father's?

CORNELIA   Yes.   10

MARCELLO   I have heard you say, giving my brother suck,
  He took the crucifix between his hands,
     Enter Flamineo
  And broke a limb off.

CORNELIA   Yes: but 'tis mended.

FLAMINEO   I have brought your weapon back.
     Flamineo runs Marcello through

CORNELIA   Ha, O my horror!

MARCELLO   You have brought it home indeed.

CORNELIA   Help, O he's murdered.   15

FLAMINEO   Do you turn your gall up? I'll to sanctuary,
  And send a surgeon to you.
     [*Exit Flamineo*]. *Enter* [*Lodovico disguised*] *Carlo,*
     Hortensio, [*Gasparo disguised*], *Pedro*

HORTENSIO   How? O'th'ground?

MARCELLO   O mother, now remember what I told
  Of breaking off the crucifix. Farewell,
  There are some sins which heaven doth duly punish   20
  In a whole family. This it is to rise
  By all dishonest means. Let all men know
  That tree shall long time keep a steady foot
  Whose branches spread no wider than the root.
     [*Marcello dies*]

CORNELIA   O my perpetual sorrow!

HORTENSIO   Virtuous Marcello.   25
   He's dead. Pray leave him, lady; come, you shall.
CORNELIA   Alas, he is not dead: he's in a trance.
   Why, here's nobody shall get any thing by his death.
   Let me call him again for God's sake.
CARLO   I would you were deceived.   30
CORNELIA   O you abuse me, you abuse me, you abuse
   me. How many have gone away thus for lack of
   tendance. Rear up's head, rear up's head; his bleeding
   inward will kill him.
HORTENSIO   You see he is departed.   35
CORNELIA   Let me come to him. Give me him as he is,
   if he be turned to earth. Let me but give him one
   hearty kiss, and you shall put us both into one coffin.
   Fetch a looking-glass, see if his breath will not stain it;
   or pull out some feathers from my pillow, and lay   40
   them to his lips. Will you lose him for a little pains-
   taking?
HORTENSIO   Your kindest office is to pray for him.
CORNELIA   Alas! I would not pray for him yet. He may
   live to lay me i'th' ground, and pray for me, if you'll   45
   let me come to him.
      Enter Bracciano all armed, save the beaver, with
      Flamineo, [Francisco disguised as Mulinassar, a Page,
      and Lodovico disguised]
BRACCIANO   Was this your handiwork?
FLAMINEO   It was my misfortune.
CORNELIA   He lies, he lies, he did not kill him: these
   have killed him, that would not let him be better   50
   looked to.
BRACCIANO   Have comfort my grieved mother.
CORNELIA   O you screech-owl!
HORTENSIO   Forbear, good madam.
CORNELIA   Let me go, let me go.   55

She runs to Flamineo with her knife drawn and,
coming to him, lets it fall

The God of heaven forgive thee. Dost not wonder
I pray for thee? I'll tell thee what's the reason:
I have scarce breath to number twenty minutes,
I'd not spend that in cursing. Fare thee well.
Half of thyself lies there; and may'st thou live   60
To fill an hour-glass with his mouldered ashes,
To tell how thou shouldst spend the time to come
In blessed repentance.

BRACCIANO   Mother, pray tell me,
How came he by his death? What was the quarrel?

CORNELIA   Indeed my younger boy presumed too much   65
Upon his manhood; gave him bitter words;
Drew his sword first; and so I know not how,
For I was out of my wits, he fell with's head
Just in my bosom.

PAGE   This is not true, madam.

CORNELIA   I pray thee peace.   70
One arrow's grazed already; it were vain
T'lose this, for that will ne'er be found again.

BRACCIANO   Go, bear the body to Cornelia's lodging;
    [*Carlo, Pedro, and Hortensio carry off the body*]
And we command that none acquaint our Duchess
With this sad accident. For you, Flamineo,   75
Hark you, I will not grant your pardon.

FLAMINEO   No?

BRACCIANO   Only a lease of your life. And that shall
    last
But for one day. Thou shalt be forced each evening
To renew it, or be hanged.

FLAMINEO   At your pleasure.
    Lodovico sprinkles Bracciano's beaver with a poison
Your will is law now, I'll not meddle with it.   80

BRACCIANO   You once did brave me in your sister's
     lodging;
  I'll now keep you in awe for't. Where's our beaver?
FRANCISCO [*aside*]   He calls for his destruction. Noble
     youth,
  I pity thy sad fate. Now to the Barriers.
  This shall his passage to the black lake further: 85
  The last good deed he did, he pardon'd murder.
     Exeunt

Act V Scene III

*Charges and shouts. They fight at Barriers; first single
pairs, then three to three. Enter Bracciano [in full
armour] and Flamineo with others [following,
including Vittoria, Giovanni, and Francisco disguised
as Mulinassar]*

BRACCIANO   An armourer! Ud's death, an armourer!
FLAMINEO   Armourer! Where's the armourer?
BRACCIANO   Tear off my beaver.
FLAMINEO   Are you hurt, my lord?
BRACCIANO   O my brain's on fire,
     Enter Armourer
                              the helmet is poisoned.
ARMOURER   My lord, upon my soul.
BRACCIANO   Away with him to torture.   5
     [*Exit Armourer, guarded*]
  There are some great ones that have hand in this,
  And near about me.
VITTORIA   O my loved lord: poisoned?
FLAMINEO   Remove the bar. Here's unfortunate revels.
  Call the physicians.
     Enter two Physicians

A plague upon you!
We have too much of your cunning here already.   10
I fear the ambassadors are likewise poisoned.

BRACCIANO   O I am gone already: the infection
Flies to the brain and heart. O thou strong heart!
There's such a covenant 'tween the world and it,
They're loth to break.

GIOVANNI   O my most loved father!   15

BRACCIANO   Remove the boy away.
      [*Exit Giovanni, attended*]
Where's this good woman? Had I infinite worlds,
They were too little for thee. Must I leave thee?
What say yon screech-owls, is the venom mortal?

PHYSICIAN   Most deadly.

BRACCIANO   Most corrupted politic hangman!   20
You kill without book, but your art to save
Fails you as oft as great men's needy friends.
I that have given life to offending slaves
And wretched murderers, have I not power
To lengthen mine own a twelvemonth?   25
[*To Vittoria*] Do not kiss me, for I shall poison thee.
This unction is sent from the Great Duke of Florence.

FRANCISCO   Sir, be of comfort.

BRACCIANO   O thou soft natural death, that art joint-twin
To sweetest slumber, no rough-bearded comet   30
Stares on thy mild departure; the dull owl
Beats not against thy casement; the hoarse wolf
Scents not thy carrion. Pity winds thy corpse
Whilst horror waits on princes.

VITTORIA   I am lost for ever.

BRACCIANO   How miserable a thing it is to die   35
'Mongst women howling!
      [*Enter Lodovico and Gasparo, disguised as Capuchins*]
                 What are those?

FLAMINEO   Franciscans.
  They have brought the extreme unction.
BRACCIANO   On pain of death, let no man name death
    to me.
  It is a word infinitely terrible.
  Withdraw into our cabinet.   40
    Exeunt but Francisco and Flamineo
FLAMINEO   To see what solitariness is about dying
  princes. As heretofore they have unpeopled towns,
  divorced friends, and made great houses unhospitable,
  so now, O justice! where are their flatterers now?
  Flatterers are but the shadows of princes' bodies; the   45
  least thick cloud makes them invisible.
FRANCISCO   There's great moan made for him.
FLAMINEO   'Faith, for some few hours salt water will
  run most plentifully in every office o'th' court. But
  believe it: most of them do but weep over their   50
  stepmothers' graves.
FRANCISCO   How mean you?
FLAMINEO   Why! they dissemble, as some men do that
  live within compass o'th' verge.
FRANCISCO   Come, you have thrived well under him.   55
FLAMINEO   'Faith, like a wolf in a woman's breast, I
  have been fed with poultry. But for money,
  understand me, I had as good a will to cozen him, as
  e'er an officer of them all. But I had not cunning
  enough to do it.   60
FRANCISCO   What didst thou think of him? Faith,
  speak freely.
FLAMINEO   He was a kind of statesman, that would
  sooner have reckoned how many cannon-bullets he
  had discharged against a town, to count his expense   65
  that way, than how many of his valiant and deserving
  subjects he lost before it.

FRANCISCO   O, speak well of the Duke.
FLAMINEO   I have done. Wilt hear some of my court
    wisdom?   70
        Enter Lodovico [disguised]
    To reprehend princes is dangerous, and to over-
    commend some of them is palpable lying.
FRANCISCO   How is it with the Duke?
LODOVICO   Most deadly ill.
    He's fallen into a strange distraction.
    He talks of battles and monopolies,   75
    Levying of taxes, and from that descends
    To the most brainsick language. His mind fastens
    On twenty several, objects, which confound
    Deep sense with folly. Such a fearful end
    May teach some men that bear too lofty crest,   80
    Though they live happiest, yet they die not best.
    He hath conferred the whole state of the dukedom
    Upon your sister, till the Prince arrive
    At mature age.
FLAMINEO   There's some good luck in that yet.
FRANCISCO   See here he comes.
        Enter Bracciano, presented in a bed, Vittoria and
        others, [including Gasparo, disguised]
                          There's death in's face already.   85
VITTORIA   O my good lord!
BRACCIANO *[speaks distractedly]*   Away, you have abused
    me.
    You have conveyed coin forth our territories,
    Bought and sold offices, oppressed the poor,
    And I ne'er dreamt on't. Make up your accounts;
    I'll now be mine own steward.
FLAMINEO   Sir, have patience.   90
BRACCIANO   Indeed I am to blame.
    For did you ever hear the dusky raven

    Chide blackness? Or was't ever known the devil
    Railed against cloven creatures?
VITTORIA   O my lord!
BRACCIANO   Let me have some quails to supper.
FLAMINEO   Sir, you shall.   95
BRACCIANO   No: some fried dog-fish. Your quails feed
    on poison.
    That old dog-fox, that politician Florence –
    I'll forswear hunting and turn dog-killer.
    Rare! I'll be friends with him; for mark you, sir, one
    dog
    Still sets another a-barking. Peace, peace,   100
    Yonder's a fine slave come in now.
FLAMINEO   Where?
BRACCIANO   Why, there.
    In a blue bonnet, and a pair of breeches
    With a great cod-piece. Ha, ha, ha,
    Look you, his cod-piece is stuck full of pins
    With pearls o'th' head of them. Do not you know
    him?   105
FLAMINEO   No, my lord.
BRACCIANO   Why, 'tis the devil.
    I know him by a great rose he wears on's shoe
    To hide his cloven foot. I'll dispute with him.
    He's a rare linguist.
VITTORIA   My lord, here's nothing.
BRACCIANO   Nothing? Rare! Nothing! When I want
    money,   110
    Our treasury is empty. There is nothing.
    I'll not be used thus.
VITTORIA   O! lie still, my lord.
BRACCIANO   See, see, Flamineo that killed his brother
    Is dancing on the ropes there; and he carries
    A money-bag in each hand, to keep him even,   115

For fear of breaking's neck. And there's a lawyer
In a gown whipped with velvet, stares and gapes
When the money will fall. How the rogue cuts capers!
It should have been in a halter.
'Tis there. What's she?
FLAMINEO   Vittoria, my lord.   120
BRACCIANO   Ha, ha, ha. Her hair is sprinkled with orris
    powder, that makes her look as if she had sinned in
    the pastry.

> *Bracciano seems here near his end. Lodovico and*
> *Gasparo in the habit of Capuchins present him in his*
> *bed with a crucifix and hallowed candle*

What's he?
FLAMINEO   A divine, my lord.   125
BRACCIANO   He will be drunk; avoid him. Th'argument
    is fearful when churchmen stagger in't.
    Look you, six grey rats that have lost their tails
    Crawl up the pillow; send for a rat-catcher.
    I'll do a miracle: I'll free the court   130
    From all foul vermin. Where's Flamineo?
FLAMINEO [*aside*]   I do not like that he names me so
        often,
    Especially on's death-bed. 'Tis a sign
    I shall not live long. See, he's near his end.
LODOVICO   Pray give us leave. *Attende Domine Brachiane.*   135
FLAMINEO   See, see, how firmly he doth fix his eye
    Upon the crucifix.
VITTORIA   O hold it constant.
    It settles his wild spirits; and so his eyes
    Melt into tears.
LODOVICO (*by the crucifix*)   *Domine Brachiane, solebas in* 140
    bello tutus esse tuo clipeo, nunc hunc clipeum hosti tuo
    opponas infernali.

GASPARO (*by the hallowed taper*) *Olim hasta valuisti in bello; nunc hanc sacram hastam vibrabis contra hostem animarum.* 145

LODOVICO *Attende Domine Brachiane si nunc quoque probas ea quae acta sunt inter nos, flecte caput in dextrum.*

GASPARO *Esto securus Domine Brachiane: cogita quantum habeas meritorum – denique memineris meam animam pro tua oppignoratam si quid esset periculi.* 150

LODOVICO *Si nunc quoque probas ea quae acta sunt inter nos, flecte caput in laevum.*
He is departing. Pray stand all apart,
And let us only whisper in his ears
Some private meditations, which our order 155
Permits you not to hear.

> *Here the rest being departed, Lodovico and Gasparo discover themselves.*

GASPARO   Bracciano.
LODOVICO Devil Bracciano. Thou art damned.
GASPARO   Perpetually.
LODOVICO A slave condemned, and given up to the gallows
Is thy great lord and master.
GASPARO   True: for thou
Art given up to the devil.
LODOVICO   O you slave! 160
You that were held the famous politician,
Whose art was poison.
GASPARO   And whose conscience murder.
LODOVICO That would have broke your wife's neck down the stairs
Ere she was poisoned.
GASPARO   That had your villainous salads –
LODOVICO And fine embroidered bottles, and perfumes 165
Equally mortal with a winter plague –

GASPARO   Now there's mercury –

LODOVICO   And copperas –

GASPARO   And quicksilver –

LODOVICO   With other devilish pothecary stuff
  A-melting in your politic brains. Dost hear?

GASPARO   This is Count Lodovico.

LODOVICO   This Gasparo.   170
  And thou shalt die like a poor rogue.

GASPARO   And stink
  Like a dead fly-blown dog.

LODOVICO   And be forgotten
  Before thy funeral sermon.

BRACCIANO   Vittoria?
  Vittoria!

LODOVICO   O the cursèd devil,
  Come to himself again! We are undone.   175
    Enter Vittoria and the Attendants.

GASPARO   [*aside to Lodovico*] Strangle him in private.
  [*Aloud*] What? Will you call him again
  To live in treble torments? For charity,
  For Christian charity, avoid the chamber.
    [*Exeunt Vittoria and Attendants*]

LODOVICO   You would prate, sir. This is a true-love knot 180
  Sent from the Duke of Florence.
    Bracciano is strangled.

GASPARO   What, is it done?

LODOVICO   The snuff is out. No woman-keeper i'th'
  world,
  Though she had practised seven year at the pesthouse,
  Could have done't quaintlier. My lords, he's dead. 185
    [*Enter Vittoria, Francisco, and Flamineo, with
    Attendants*]

ALL   Rest to his soul.

VITTORIA   O me! this place is hell.

    Exit Vittoria [followed by all except Lodovico,
    Francisco, and Flamineo]

FRANCISCO   How heavily she takes it.

FLAMINEO   O yes, yes;
  Had women navigable rivers in their eyes
  They would dispend them all. Surely I wonder
  Why we should wish more rivers to the city,   190
  When they sell water so good cheap. I'll tell thee,
  These are but moonish shades of griefs or fears;
  There's nothing sooner dry than women's tears.
  Why, here's an end of all my harvest; he has given me
    nothing.
  Court promises! Let wise men count them cursed,   195
  For while you live he that scores best pays worst.

FRANCISCO   Sure this was Florence' doing.

FLAMINEO   Very likely.
  Those are found weighty strokes which come from
    th'hand,
  But those are killing strokes which come from
    th'head.
  O the rare tricks of a Machiavellian!   200
  He doth not come like a gross plodding slave
  And buffet you to death: no, my quaint knave,
  He tickles you to death, makes you die laughing,
  As if you had swallowed down a pound of saffron.
  You see the feat: 'tis practised in a trice,   205
  To teach court-honesty it jumps on ice.

FRANCISCO   Now have the people liberty to talk
  And descant on his vices.

FLAMINEO   Misery of princes,
  That must of force be censured by their slaves!
  Not only blamed for doing things are ill,   210
  But for not doing all that all men will.
  One were better be a thresher.

Ud's death, I would fain speak with this Duke yet.

FRANCISCO   Now he's dead?

FLAMINEO   I cannot conjure, but if prayers or oaths   215
Will get to th'speech of him, though forty devils
Wait on him in his livery of flames,
I'll speak to him, and shake him by the hand,
Though I be blasted.
    Exit Flamineo.

FRANCISCO   Excellent Lodovico!
What? Did you terrify him at the last gasp?   220

LODOVICO   Yes; and so idly that the Duke had like
T'have terrified us.

FRANCISCO   How?
    Enter [Zanche] the Moor

LODOVICO   You shall hear that hereafter.
See, yon's the infernal that would make up sport.
Now to the revelation of that secret
She promised when she fell in love with you.   225

FRANCISCO [*to Zanche*]   You're passionately met in this
    sad world.

ZANCHE   I would have you look up, sir. These court
    tears
Claim not your tribute to them. Let those weep
That guiltily partake in the sad cause.
I knew last night by a sad dream I had   230
Some mischief would ensue; yet to say truth,
My dream most concerned you.

LODOVICO   Shall's fall a-dreaming?

FRANCISCO   Yes, and for fashion sake I'll dream with her.

ZANCHE   Methought, sir, you came stealing to my bed.

FRANCISCO   Wilt thou believe me, sweeting? By this
    light   235
I was a-dreamt on thee too, for methought
I saw thee naked.

ZANCHE   Fie, sir! As I told you,
  Methought you lay down by me.
FRANCISCO   So dreamt I;
  And lest thou shouldst take cold, I covered thee
  With this Irish mantle.
ZANCHE   Verily, I did dream   240
  You were somewhat bold with me; but to come to't.
LODOVICO   How? How? I hope you will not go to't
    here –
FRANCISCO   Nay, you must hear my dream out.
ZANCHE   Well, sir, forth.
FRANCISCO   When I threw the mantle o'er thee, thou
    didst laugh
  Exceedingly methought.
ZANCHE   Laugh?
FRANCISCO   And cried'st out.   245
  The hair did tickle thee.
ZANCHE   There was a dream indeed.
LODOVICO   Mark her, I prithee: she simpers like the suds
  A collier hath been washed in.
ZANCHE   Come, sir, good fortune tends you. I did tell
    you
  I would reveal a secret: Isabella,   250
  The Duke of Florence' sister, was empoisoned,
  By a fumed picture, and Camillo's neck
  Was broke by damned Flamineo, the mischance
  Laid on a vaulting-horse.
FRANCISCO   Most strange!
ZANCHE   Most true.
LODOVICO [*aside*]   The bed of snakes is broke.   255
ZANCHE   I sadly do confess I had a hand
  In the black deed.
FRANCISCO   Thou kept'st their counsel.
ZANCHE   Right,

For which, urged with contrition, I intend
This night to rob Vittoria.
LODOVICO   Excellent penitence!
Usurers dream on't while they sleep out sermons.   260
ZANCHE   To further our escape, I have entreated
Leave to retire me, till the funeral,
Unto a friend i'th' country. That excuse
Will further our escape. In coin and jewels
I shall, at least, make good unto your use   265
An hundred thousand crowns.
FRANCISCO   O noble wench!
LODOVICO   Those crowns we'll share.
ZANCHE   It is a dowry,
Methinks, should make that sunburnt proverb false,
And wash the Ethiop white.
FRANCISCO   It shall. Away!
ZANCHE   Be ready for our flight.
FRANCISCO   An hour 'fore day.   270
        Exit [Zanche]
O strange discovery! Why, till now we knew not
The circumstance of either of their deaths.
        [Enter Zanche]
ZANCHE   You'll wait about midnight in the chapel.
FRANCISCO   There.
        [Exit Zanche]
LODOVICO   Why, now our action's justified.
FRANCISCO   Tush for justice.
What harms it justice? We now like the partridge   275
Purge the disease with laurel: for the fame
Shall crown the enterprise and quit the shame.
        Exeunt.

At this stage in the play it would be reasonable to see Flamineo to become the main character

Act V Scene IV

Enter Flamineo and Gasparo [disguised as a Knight of St John] at one door, another way Giovanni attended

GASPARO   [*to Flamineo*] The young Duke. Did you e'er see a sweeter prince?

FLAMINEO   I have ~~known a poor~~ woman's bastard better favoured. This is behind him. Now, to his face all comparisons were hateful. Wise was the courtly 5 peacock, that being a great minion, and being compared for beauty, by some dottrels that stood by, to the kingly eagle, said the eagle was a far fairer bird than herself, not in respect of her feathers, but in respect of her long talons. His will grow out in time. 10 [*To Giovanni*] My gracious lord. *fake flattery*

GIOVANNI   I pray leave me, sir.

FLAMINEO   Your grace must be merry. 'Tis I have cause to mourn, for wot you what said the, little boy that rode behind his father on horseback? 15

GIOVANNI   Why, what said he?

FLAMINEO   'When you are dead, father', said he, 'I hope then I shall ride in the saddle'. O, 'tis a brave thing for a man to sit by himself: he may stretch himself in the stirrups, look about, and see the whole 20 compass of the hemisphere; you're now, my lord, i'th' saddle.

GIOVANNI   Study your prayers, sir, and be penitent.
'Twere fit you'd think on what hath former been;
I have heard grief named the eldest child of sin. 25

[*Exeunt Giovanni and Attendants, with Gasparo*]

FLAMINEO   Study my prayers? He threatens me divinely. I am falling to pieces already. I care not,

though like Anacharsis I were pounded to death in a
mortar. And yet that death were fitter for usurers'
gold and themselves to be beaten together, to make a   30
most cordial cullis for the devil.
He hath his uncle's villainous look already,
    Enter Courtier
In *decimo-sexto*. Now, sir, what are you?

COURTIER   It is the pleasure, sir, of the young Duke
  That you forbear the presence, and all rooms   35
  That owe him reverence.

FLAMINEO   So, the wolf and the raven
  Are very pretty fools when they are young.
  Is it your office, sir, to keep me out?

COURTIER   So the duke wills.

FLAMINEO   Verily, master courtier, extremity is not to   40
  be used in all offices. Say that a gentlewoman were
  taken out of her bed about midnight, and committed
  to Castle Angelo, to the tower yonder, with nothing
  about her, but her smock: would it not show a cruel
  part in the gentleman porter to lay claim to her upper   45
  garment, pull it o'er her head and ears, and put her in
  naked?

COURTIER   Very good: you are merry.
    [*Exit Courtier*]

FLAMINEO   Doth he make a court ejectment of me? A
  flaming firebrand casts more smoke without a   50
  chimney, than within't. I'll smoor some of them.
    Enter [Francisco Duke of] Florence, [disguised as
    Mulinassar]
How now? Thou art sad.

FRANCISCO   I met even now with the most piteous
  sight.

FLAMINEO   Thou met'st another here: a pitiful
  Degraded courtier.

FRANCISCO   Your reverend mother   55
  Is grown a very old woman in two hours.
  I found them winding of Marcello's corpse,
  And there is such a solemn melody
  'Tween doleful songs, tears, and sad elegies
  (Such as old grandames, watching by the dead,   60
  Were wont t'outwear the nights with), that, believe
      me,
  I had no eyes to guide me forth the room,
  They were so o'ercharged with water.
FLAMINEO   I will see them.
FRANCISCO   'Twere much uncharity in you, for your
      sight
  Will add unto their tears.
FLAMINEO   I will see them.   65
  They are behind the traverse. I'll discover
  Their superstitious howling.
      [*Draws the traverse*]. *Cornelia*, [*Zanche*] *the Moor*
      and three other Ladies [*are*] *discovered, winding*
      Marcello's corpse. A song
CORNELIA   This rosemary is withered, pray get fresh;
  I would have these herbs grow up in his grave
  When I am dead and rotten. Reach the bays,   70
  I'll tie a garland here about his head:
  'Twill keep my boy from lightning. This sheet
  I have kept this twenty year, and every day
  Hallowed it with my prayers; I did not think
  He should have wore it.
ZANCHE   Look you: who are yonder?   75
CORNELIA   O reach me the flowers.
ZANCHE   Her ladyship's foolish.
LADY   Alas, her grief
  Hath turned her child again.
CORNELIA (*to Flamineo*)   You're very welcome.

There's rosemary for you, and rue for you,
Heart's-ease for you. I pray make much of it.   80
I have left more for myself.
FRANCISCO   Lady, who's this?
CORNELIA   You are, I take it, the grave-maker. *← I more since be notes*
FLAMINEO   So. *killed him.*
ZANCHE   'Tis Flamineo.
CORNELIA   Will you make me such a fool? Here's a
      white hand:
Can blood so soon be washed out? Let me see: 85
When screech-owls croak upon the chimney-tops,
And the strange cricket i'th' oven sings and hops,
When yellow spots do on your hands appear,
Be certain then you of a corpse shall hear.
Out upon't, how 'tis speckled! H'as handled a toad
      sure.   90
Cowslip-water is good for the memory:
Pray buy me three ounces of't.
FLAMINEO   I would I were from hence.
CORNELIA   Do you hear, sir?
I'll give you a saying which my grandmother
Was wont, when she heard the bell toll, to sing o'er   95
Unto her lute.
FLAMINEO   Do an you will, do.
Cornelia [sings] this in several forms of distraction
CORNELIA   *Call for the robin red breast and the wren,*
  Since o'er shady groves they hover,
  And with leaves and flowers do cover
  The friendless bodies of unburied men.
  Call unto his funeral dole
  The ant, the field-mouse, and the mole
  To rear him hillocks, that shall keep him warm,
  And, when gay tombs are robb'd, sustain no harm;
  But keep the wolf far thence, that's foe to men,   105

For with his nails he'll dig them up again.
[*Speaks*] They would not bury him 'cause he died in a
    quarrel,
But I have an answer for them.
[*Sings*] *Let holy church receive him duly,*
Since he paid the church tithes truly.   110
[*Speaks*] His wealth is summed, and this is all his store:
This poor men get; and great men get no more.
Now the wares are gone, we may shut up shop.
Bless you all, good people.
        Exeunt Cornelia, [Zanche], and Ladies
FLAMINEO   I have a strange thing in me, to th'which   115
    I cannot give a name, without it be
    Compassion. I pray leave me.
        Exit Francisco
    This night I'll know the utmost of my fate,
    I'll be resolv'd what my rich sister means
    T'assign me for my service. I have lived   120
    Riotously ill, like some that live in court;
    And sometimes, when my face was full of smiles
    Have felt the maze of conscience in my breast.
    Oft gay and honoured robes those tortures try;
    We think caged birds sing, when indeed they cry.   125
        Enter Bracciano's Ghost, in his leather cassock and
        breeches, boots, [and] a cowl, [in his hand] a pot of
        lily-flowers with a skull in't
    Ha! I can stand thee. Nearer, nearer yet.
    What a mockery hath death made of thee?
    Thou look'st sad.
    In what place art thou? In yon starry gallery,
    Or in the cursèd dungeon? No? Not speak?   130
    Pray, sir, resolve me, what religion's best
    For a man to die in? Or is it in your knowledge
    To answer me how long I have to live?

read, put out fragments of his imagination

That's the most necessary question.
Not answer? Are you still like some great men   135
That only walk like shadows up and down,
And to no purpose? say.
> *The Ghost throws earth upon him and shows him the*
> *skull*

What's that? O fatal! He throws earth upon me.
A dead man's skull beneath the roots of flowers.
I pray, speak, sir. Our Italian churchmen   140
Make us believe dead men hold conference
With their familiars, and many times
Will come to bed to them, and eat with them.
> *Exit Ghost*

He's gone; and see, the skull and earth are vanished.
This is beyond melancholy. I do dare my fate   145
To do its worst. Now to my sister's lodging,
And sum up all these horrors: the disgrace
The prince threw on me; next the piteous sight
Of my dead brother, and my mother's dotage;
And last this terrible vision. All these   150
Shall with Vittoria's bounty turn to good,
Or I will drown this weapon in her blood.
> *Exit*

or he will kill her.

Act V Scene V

Enter Francisco, Lodovico, and Hortensio
[overhearing them]

LODOVICO   My lord, upon my soul you shall no
further:
You have most ridiculously engaged yourself
Too far already. For my part, I have paid

All my debts, so if I should chance to fall
My creditors fall not with me; and I vow   5
To quit all in this bold assembly
To the meanest follower. My lord, leave the city,
Or I'll forswear the murder.
FRANCISCO   Farewell, Lodovico.
  If thou dost perish in this glorious act,
  I'll rear unto thy memory that fame   10
  Shall in the ashes keep alive thy name.
      [*Exeunt Francisco and Lodovico severally*]
HORTENSIO   There's some black deed on foot. I'll presently
  Down to the citadel, and raise some force.
  These strong court factions that do brook no checks,
  In the career oft break the riders' necks.   15
      [*Exit*]

Act V Scene VI

Enter Vittoria with a [prayer-] book in her hand,
Zanche; [and] Flamineo, following them
FLAMINEO   What, are you at your prayers? Give o'er.
VITTORIA   How, ruffin?
FLAMINEO   I come to you 'bout worldly business.
  Sit down, sit down [*Zanche begins to leave*] – Nay, stay,
      blowze, you may hear it,
  The doors are fast enough.
VITTORIA   Ha, are you drunk?
FLAMINEO   Yes, yes, with wormwood water; you shall taste   5
  Some of it presently.
VITTORIA   What intends the fury?

FLAMINEO   You are my lord's executrix, and I claim
  Reward for my long service.
VITTORIA   For your service?
FLAMINEO   Come therefore, here is pen and ink, set
    down
  What you will give me.   10
    She writes
VITTORIA   There.
FLAMINEO   Ha, have you done already?
  'Tis a most short conveyance.
VITTORIA   I will read it.
  [*Reads*] 'I give that portion to thee, and no other,
  Which Cain groaned under, having slain his brother.'
FLAMINEO   A most courtly patent to beg by.   15
VITTORIA   You are a villain.
FLAMINEO   Is't come to this? They say affrights cure
    agues.
  Thou hast a devil in thee; I will try
  If I can scare him from thee. Nay, sit still:
  My lord hath left me yet two case of jewels   20
  Shall make me scorn your bounty; you shall see them.
    [*Exit Flamineo*]
VITTORIA   Sure he's distracted.
ZANCHE   O, he's desperate.
  For your own safety give him gentle language.
    Enter [Flamineo] with two case of pistols
FLAMINEO   Look, these are better far at a dead lift
  Than all your jewel house.
VITTORIA   And yet methinks   25
  These stones have no fair lustre, they are ill set.
FLAMINEO   I'll turn the right side towards you; you
    shall see
  How they will sparkle.
VITTORIA   Turn this horror from me.

What do you want? What would you have me do?
Is not all mine, yours? Have I any children? 30
FLAMINEO   Pray thee, good woman, do not trouble me
With this vain worldly business. Say your prayers.
I made a vow to my deceasèd lord,
Neither yourself, nor I should outlive him
The numbering of four hours.
VITTORIA   Did he enjoin it? 35
FLAMINEO   He did, and 'twas a deadly jealousy,
Lest any should enjoy thee after him,
That urged him vow me to it. For my death,
I did propound it voluntarily, knowing
If he could not be safe in his own court 40
Being a great Duke, what hope then for us?
VITTORIA   This is your melancholy and despair.
FLAMINEO   Away,
Fool thou art to think that politicians
Do use to kill the effects of injuries
And let the cause live. Shall we groan in irons, 45
Or be a shameful and a weighty burden
To a public scaffold? This is my resolve:
I would not live at any man's entreaty
Nor die at any's bidding.
VITTORIA   Will you hear me?
FLAMINEO   My life hath done service to other men, 50
My death shall serve mine own turn. Make you ready.
VITTORIA   Do you mean to die indeed?
FLAMINEO   With as much pleasure
As e'er my father gat me.
VITTORIA [*whispers to Zanche*]   Are the doors locked?
ZANCHE [*whispers to Vittoria*]   Yes, madam. 55
VITTORIA   Are you grown an atheist? Will you turn
your body,
Which is the goodly palace of the soul,

To the soul's slaughter house? O the cursed devil
Which doth present us with all other sins
Thrice candied o'er; despair with gall and stibium,   60
Yet we carouse it off; – [*whispers to Zanche*] cry out for
    help –
Makes us forsake that which was made for man,
The world, to sink to that was made for devils,
Eternal darkness.
ZANCHE   Help, help!
FLAMINEO   I'll stop your throat
With winter plums.
VITTORIA   I prithee yet remember   65
Millions are now in graves, which at last day
Like mandrakes shall rise shrieking.
FLAMINEO   Leave your prating,
For these are but grammatical laments,
Feminine arguments, and they move me
As some in pulpits move their auditory   70
More with their exclamation than sense
Of reason, or sound doctrine.
ZANCHE [*whispers to Vittoria*]   Gentle madam,
Seem to consent, only persuade him teach
The way to death: let him die first.
VITTORIA [*whispers to Zanche*] 'Tis good, I apprehend it.   75
[*Aloud*] To kill one's self is meat that we must take
Like pills, not chew't, but quickly swallow it;
The smart o'th' wound, or weakness of the hand
May else bring treble torments.
FLAMINEO   I have held it
A wretched and most miserable life,   80
Which is not able to die.
VITTORIA   O but frailty!
Yet I am now resolved. Farewell, affliction.

Behold Bracciano, I that while you lived
Did make a flaming altar of my heart
To sacrifice unto you, now am ready   85
To sacrifice heart and all. Farewell, Zanche.

ZANCHE   How, madam! Do you think that I'll outlive
    you?
Especially when my best self Flamineo
Goes the same voyage.

FLAMINEO   O most lovèd Moor!

ZANCHE   Only by all my love let me entreat you: 90
Since it is most necessary none of us
Do violence on ourselves, let you or I
Be her sad taster, teach her how to die.

FLAMINEO   Thou dost instruct me nobly. Take these
    pistols:
Because my hand is stained with blood already,   95
Two of these you shall level at my breast,
Th'other 'gainst your own, and so we'll die,
Most equally contented. But first swear
Not to outlive me.

VITTORIA *and* ZANCHE   Most religiously.

FLAMINEO   Then here's an end of me. Farewell,
    daylight,   100
And O contemptible physic! that dost take
So long a study, only to preserve
So short a life: I take my leave of thee.
    Showing the pistols
These are two cupping-glasses, that shall draw
All my infected blood out. Are you ready?   105

VITTORIA *and* ZANCHE   Ready.

FLAMINEO   Whither shall I go now? O Lucian, thy
    ridiculous purgatory! To find Alexander the Great
    cobbling shoes, Pompey tagging points, and Julius
    Caesar making hair buttons, Hannibal selling   110

blacking, and Augustus crying 'garlic', Charlemagne
selling lists by the dozen, and King Pepin crying
'apples' in a cart drawn with one horse.
Whether I resolve to fire, earth, water, air,
Or all the elements by scruples, I know not   115
Nor greatly care. Shoot, shoot,
Of all deaths the violent death is best,
For from ourselves it steals ourselves so fast
The pain once apprehended is quite past.
     They shoot and run to him and tread upon him
VITTORIA   What, are you dropped?   120
FLAMINEO   I am mixed with earth already. As you are
     noble,
Perform your vows, and bravely follow me.
VITTORIA   Whither, to hell?
ZANCHE   To most assurèd damnation.
VITTORIA   O thou most cursed devil.
ZANCHE   Thou art caught.
VITTORIA   In thine own engine. I tread the fire out   125
     That would have been my ruin.
FLAMINEO   Will you be perjured? What a religious oath
     was Styx that the gods never durst swear by and
     violate? O that we had such an oath to minister, and to
     be so well kept in our courts of justice.   130
VITTORIA   Think whither thou art going.
ZANCHE   And remember.
     What villanies thou hast acted.
VITTORIA   This thy death
Shall make me like a blazing ominous star,
Look up and tremble.
FLAMINEO   O I am caught with a springe!
VITTORIA   You see the fox comes many times short
     home;   135
     'Tis here proved true.

FLAMINEO   Killed with a couple of braches.
VITTORIA   No fitter offering for the infernal Furies
  Than one in whom they reigned while he was living.
FLAMINEO   O the way's dark and horrid! I cannot see.
  Shall I have no company?
VITTORIA   O yes, thy sins   140
  Do run before thee to fetch fire from hell,
  To light thee thither.
FLAMINEO   O I smell soot,
  Most stinking soot, the chimney is afire,
  My liver's parboiled like Scotch holy bread;
  There's a plumber, laying pipes in my guts, it scalds.   145
  Wilt thou outlive me?
ZANCHE   Yes, and drive a stake
  Through thy body; for we'll give it out
  Thou didst this violence upon thyself.
FLAMINEO   O cunning devils! now I have tried your
      love,
  And doubled all your reaches.
      Flamineo riseth
                              I am not wounded;   150
  The pistols held no bullets: 'twas a plot
  To prove your kindness to me, and I live
  To punish your ingratitude. I knew
  One time or other you would find a way
  To give me a strong potion. O men   155
  That lie upon your death-beds, and are haunted
  With howling wives, ne'er trust them: they'll re-marry
  Ere the worm pierce your winding-sheet, ere the
      spider
  Make a thin curtain for your epitaphs.
  How cunning you were to discharge! Do you practise   160
  at the Artillery Yard? Trust a woman? Never, never.
  Bracciano be my precedent: we lay our souls to pawn

to the devil for a little pleasure, and a woman makes
the bill of sale. That ever man should marry! For one
Hypermnestra that saved her lord and husband, forty-   165
nine of her sisters cut their husbands' throats all in
one night. There was a shoal of virtuous horse-
leeches.
Here are two other instruments.

Enter Lodovico, Gasparo, [disguised as Capuchins,]
Pedro [and] Carlo

VITTORIA   Help, help!
FLAMINEO   What noise is that? Ha, false keys i'th'
     court!   170
LODOVICO   We have brought you a masque.
FLAMINEO   A matachin, it seems,
     By your drawn swords. Churchmen turned revellers!
CARLO   Isabella, Isabella!
LODOVICO   Do you know us now?
     [*They throw off their disguises*]
FLAMINEO   Lodovico and Gasparo.
LODOVICO   Yes, and that Moor the Duke gave pension to, 175
     Was the Great Duke of Florence.
VITTORIA   O we are lost.
FLAMINEO   You shall not take justice from forth my
     hands;
     O let me kill her. I'll cut my safety
     Through your coats of steel. Fate's a spaniel,
     We cannot beat it from us. What remains now?   180
     Let all that do ill take this precedent:
     Man may his fate foresee, but not prevent.
     And of all axioms this shall win the prize:
     'Tis better to be fortunate than wise.
GASPARO   Bind him to the pillar.
     [*Pedro and Carlo tie up Flamineo*]
VITTORIA   O your gentle pity. 185

I have seen a blackbird that would sooner fly
To a man's bosom, than to stay the grip
Of the fierce sparrow-hawk.
GASPARO   Your hope deceives you.
VITTORIA   If Florence be i'th' court, would he would
      kill me.
GASPARO   Fool! Princes give rewards with their own
      hands,   190
But death or punishment by the hands of others.
LODOVICO   Sirrah, you once did strike me; I'll strike
      you
Into the centre.
FLAMINEO   Thou'lt do it like a hangman; a base
      hangman;
Not like a noble fellow, for thou seest   195
I cannot strike again.
LODOVICO   Dost laugh?
FLAMINEO   Wouldst have me die, as I was born, in
      whining?
GASPARO   Recommend yourself to heaven.
FLAMINEO   No, I will carry mine own commendations
      thither.
LODOVICO   O could I kill you forty times a day,   200
And use't four year together, 'twere too little.
Nought grieves but that you are too few to feed
The famine of our vengeance. What dost think on?
FLAMINEO   Nothing; of nothing. Leave thy idle
      questions,
I am i'th' way to study a long silence,   205
To prate were idle; I remember nothing.
There's nothing of so infinite vexation
As man's own thoughts.
LODOVICO   [*to Vittoria*]   O thou glorious strumpet,
Could I divide thy breath from this pure air

When't leaves thy body, I would suck it up   210
And breathe't upon some dunghill.
VITTORIA   You, my death's-man;
Methinks thou dost not look horrid enough,
Thou hast too good a face to be a hangman;
If thou be, do thy office in right form:
Fall down upon thy knees, and ask forgiveness.   215
LODOVICO   O thou hast been a most prodigious comet,
But I'll cut off your train. Kill the Moor first.
VITTORIA   You shall not kill her first. Behold my
          breast:
I will be waited on in death; my servant
Shall never go before me.   220
GASPARO   Are you so brave?
VITTORIA   Yes, I shall welcome death,
As princes do some great ambassadors;
I'll meet thy weapon half way.
LODOVICO   Thou dost tremble.
Methinks fear should dissolve thee into air.
VITTORIA   O thou art deceived, I am too true a woman;   225
Conceit can never kill me. I'll tell thee what:
I will not in my death shed one base tear,
Or if look pale, for want of blood, not fear.
GASPARO   Thou art my task, black Fury.
ZANCHE   I have blood
As red as either of theirs: wilt drink some?   230
'Tis good for the falling sickness; I am proud
Death cannot alter my complexion,
For I shall ne'er look pale.
LODOVICO   Strike, strike,
With a joint motion.
          [*They strike*]
VITTORIA   'Twas a manly blow.
The next thou giv'st, murder some sucking infant,   235

And then thou wilt be famous.
FLAMINEO   O what blade is't?
A Toledo, or an English fox?
I ever thought a cutler should distinguish
The cause of my death, rather than a doctor.
Search my wound deeper, tent it with the steel   240
That made it.
VITTORIA   O my greatest sin lay in my blood;
Now my blood pays for't.
FLAMINEO   Thou'rt a noble sister:
I love thee now. If woman do breed man,
She ought to teach him manhood. Fare thee well.   245
Know many glorious women that are famed
For masculine virtue, have been vicious:
Only a happier silence did betide them.
She hath no faults, who hath the art to hide them.
VITTORIA   My soul, like to a ship in a black storm,   250
Is driven I know not whither.
FLAMINEO   Then cast anchor.
Prosperity doth bewitch men seeming clear,
But seas do laugh, show white, when rocks are near.
We cease to grieve, cease to be fortune's slaves,
    [*Zanche dies*]
Nay cease to die by dying. [*To Zanche*] Art thou gone, 255
[*to Vittoria*] And thou so near the bottom? False report
Which says that women vie with the nine Muses
For nine tough durable lives. I do not look
Who went before, nor who shall follow me;
No, at myself I will begin and end: 260
While we look up to heaven we confound
Knowledge with knowledge. O I am in a mist.
VITTORIA   O happy they that never saw the court,
Nor ever knew great man but by report.
    Vittoria dies

FLAMINEO   I recover like a spent taper, for a flash,   265
  And instantly go out.
  Let all that belong to great men remember th'old
  wives' tradition, to be like the lions i'th' Tower on
  Candlemas day, to mourn if the sun shine, for fear of
  the pitiful remainder of winter to come.   270
  'Tis well yet there's some goodness in my death,
  My life was a black charnel: I have caught
  An everlasting cold. I have lost my voice
  Most irrecoverably. Farewell, glorious villains.
  This busy trade of life appears most vain,   275
  Since rest breeds rest, where all seek pain by pain.
  Let no harsh flattering bells resound my knell
  Strike, thunder, and strike loud to my farewell.
      [*Flamineo*] *dies*
ENGLISH AMBASSADOR   [*within*] This way, this way,
      break ope the doors, this way.
LODOVICO   Ha, are we betrayed?   280
  Why then, let's constantly die all together,
  And having finished this most noble deed,
  Defy the worst of fate, not fear to bleed.
      Enter [*Ambassador*] *and Giovanni* [*with Guards*]
ENGLISH AMBASSADOR   Keep back the Prince! Shoot,
      shoot!
      [*They shoot, and wound Lodovico*]
LODOVICO   O I am wounded.   285
  I fear I shall be ta'en.
GIOVANNI   You bloody villains,
  By what authority have you committed
  This massacre?
LODOVICO   By thine.
GIOVANNI   Mine?
LODOVICO   Yes, thy uncle,
  Which is a part of thee, enjoined us to't.

Thou know'st me, I am sure: I am Count Lodovic,   290
And thy most noble uncle in disguise
Was last night in thy court.
GIOVANNI   Ha!
CARLO   Yes, that Moor
Thy father chose his pensioner.
GIOVANNI   He turned murderer?
Away with them to prison, and to torture;
All that have hands in this shall taste our justice,   295
As I hope heaven.
LODOVICO   I do glory yet,
That I can call this act mine own. For my part,
The rack, the gallows, and the torturing wheel
Shall be but sound sleeps to me. Here's my rest:
I limned this night-piece, and it was my best.   300
GIOVANNI   Remove the bodies.
     [*The Guards begin to remove the bodies*]
                                   See, my honoured lord,
What use you ought make of their punishment.
Let guilty men remember their black deeds
Do lean on crutches, made of slender reeds.
     [*Exeunt*]

*Sin will be
found
out*

Epilogue

Instead of an epilogue only this of Martial supplies me:
Haec fuerint nobis praemia si placui.

For the action of the play, 'twas generally well, and I dare
affirm, with the joint testimony of some of their own
quality, for the true imitation of life, without striving to   5
make nature a monster, the best that ever became them;
whereof as I make a general acknowledgement, so in
particular I must remember the well approved industry
of my friend Master Perkins, and confess the worth of
his action did crown both the beginning and end.   10

Notes

sd=stage direction

Title page

Webster here refers to the historical characters upon whom he based his play.

The Persons of the Play

Jaques, Christophero, Guid-Antonio and Ferneze are 'ghost' characters who do not speak; they may have had speaking roles in earlier drafts of the play.

To the Reader

1 **challenge to myself** claim for myself.
3 **nos... nihil** 'we know these things are nothing'. This is a quotation from Marcus Valerius Martialis, known in English as Martial, a Latin poet and writer of witty epigrams in the first century CE, whom Webster admired.
5 **so open and black a theatre** The play was probably first performed in February or March 1612, at the outdoor theatre, the Red Bull at Clerkenwell. The audience would be exposed to the 'black' sky.
7 **understanding auditory** intelligent audience.
11 **it** i.e. *this tragedy* (line 1).
13–14 **Nec... molestas** 'You [the play] will not fear the sneers of the malicious, nor be execution garments for mackerels' (a quotation from Martial, see Note to line 3).
15–23 **no true dramatic poem** Webster rejects the classical 'laws' of tragedy as defined by Aristotle. Drama following these rules was said by some to be the only *true* form.

16–17 **non... dixi** 'you cannot say more against my trifles than I have said myself' (another quotation from Martial, see Note to line 3).

17–18 **Willingly... faulted** Webster asserts that he has deliberately broken the classical 'laws' of tragedy. He aligns his drama with the native English tradition.

19 **sententious** Seneca's drama was full of aphorisms and *sententiae* (moral sayings).

22, 23 **Chorus, Nuntius** traditional roles in classical drama. The *Chorus* is a group of characters who comment on the action; the *Nuntius* is a messenger who relates events that occur offstage.

22 **lifen death** make the presentation of death come alive.

23–4 **O dura messorum ilia** 'O strong stomachs of harvesters' (a quotation from Horace, a Roman lyric poet of the first century BCE).

26 **Horace** See Note to lines 23–4.

27 **Haec... relinques** 'What you leave today will be food for pigs' (another quotation from Horace, see Note to lines 23–4).

29–30 **I confess... two feathers** Webster alludes to the fact that he published nothing between 1605 and 1611, probably while working on *The White Devil*.

31–2 **Euripides to Alcestides** Presumably Webster is referring to the traditional story that a writer called Alcestis claimed he could write a hundred verses while Euripides (one of the great tragedians of classical Athens) wrote just three.

41–7 **Chapman, Jonson, Beaumont, Fletcher, Dekker, Heywood** Great Elizabethan and Jacobean playwrights who were writing at the same time as Webster.

51 **Martial** See Note to line 3.

52 **non... mori** 'these monuments know not death', implying that unlike decaying tombs, literature will not die.

Act I Scene I

This scene is set in Rome, as are all the others except Act V, which takes place in Padua (the city to which Bracciano and Vittoria retreat, see Interpretations page 246). All the settings are indoors, reflecting Webster's interest in people's inner lives and the ways they interact, their hidden motives, and the psychology of the evildoer. Webster opens the play with Lodovico expressing his views on society and the powerful; his words introduce the central issues of the play relating to corruption and injustice. It becomes evident that bright young men have no future other than through service (often involving dishonourable deeds) to powerful lords, as reflected in his comments about Bracciano. His feelings of resentment towards Vittoria are also made evident, and Webster introduces the dominant images that will echo throughout the play.

1 sd   **Enter**   It is not clear whether the men enter separately or together. Perhaps his friends enter separately to hand the documents of banishment to Lodovico, and so visually re-enact the court sentence.

   2   **Democritus**   Greek philosopher of the fifth century BCE; he did not hold the views about *Courtly reward,/And punishment* that are suggested in lines 3–4. These were from Antonio de Guevara's *Diall of Princes*, translated by Thomas North, 1557.

   4   **Fortune**   This is a reference to the theory of *de casibus* tragedy (see page 8) about the rise and inevitable fall of great men. See III.iii.98 and Note.

   5   **parcels**   portions.

   6   **swoop**   stroke.

   7   **quite**   take revenge on.

8–9   **Your wolf... she's hungry**   Webster introduces the play's animal imagery by comparing great men to wolves who no longer seem dangerous when their appetites are satisfied. What is the effect of such an image?

  12   **pashed**   dashed.

  16   **mummia**   the flesh of a dead person. It was said to make an excellent, if unpalatable, medicine. Webster introduces the imagery of disease, which characterizes the society of the play.

  18   **kennel**   gutter.

  20   **Is**   who is.

  21   **caviare**   Webster's reference to this rare and expensive delicacy suggests self-indulgence.

23 **phoenix** a legendary bird (which would be the rarest and
most expensive dish of all). At the end of its long life, the
phoenix was said to build a nest and set fire to itself; a young
bird would then arise from the ashes.

25 **idle** worthless.

meteor a falling star that burns itself out; these were
perceived as ill omens. Webster's use of astronomical imagery
suggests the inevitable decline and fall of great men and
women.

29–30 **This well... of either** This proverbial image of two buckets
alternately drawing water from a well mimics the dual attacks
of Gasparo and Antonelli on Lodovico; it also captures the
difficult balancing act of servants and advisers in this society.
Webster may have made this image visual by the positions of
the characters onstage. There could also be echoes of the
medieval morality play, as the friends act as Good Counsel to
Lodovico.

31 **acted** carried out.

36 **This gentle penance** Lodovico's punishment is less harsh
than his actions may have justified. There is an ironic echo at
the end of the play in Giovanni's harsh punishment of him (see
V.vi.294–5).

41 **close** secret.

44 **Have a full man within you** be a purposeful and self-
sufficient man.

50 **painted** presented in false colours. Webster uses imagery of
painting to suggest the differences between appearance and
reality.

51 **Italian cut-works** fashionable openwork embroidery. This
domestic image heightens the bloodiness of Lodovico's acts,
and suggests that he takes pleasure in doing things subtly.

55 **knave** low villain.

59 sd *sennet* a ceremonial trumpet call, which announces the arrival
of Bracciano and Vittoria. The trumpeters may have entered
during the last speeches, creating a seamless movement.

60 **alms** charitable donation. This is a sarcastic reference to the
'charity' given to Lodovico in his punishment. The line could also
suggest that he gives money to his friends to bribe his way out of
banishment, an ironic reversal that corrupts the idea of charity.

61–2 This rhyming couplet forms a *sententia* or moral saying, which sums up the ideas expressed in the scene as Webster moves from the particular incident to the universal. What is the effect of this?

Act I Scene II

This scene is set at Vittoria's house and it is dark (as signalled by the *Attendants carrying torches*), which suggests that there may be mischief afoot. Bracciano despairs of seeing Vittoria alone, but Flamineo steps in to offer his services. Webster's stagecraft is important as the wooing of the lovers is framed by three commentators: Flamineo, Zanche and Cornelia. They each provide their own interpretations for the audience; the first is bawdy, the second conspiratorial and the third speaks of sin.

1 sd **Vittoria Corombona** She is given her full name as Webster reminds his audience of the historical Vittoria. In staging the scene, she may cross the stage in the same way as she does after her trial (III.ii.295) and again at her wedding (V.i), to create ironic parallels.

1 **Your best of rest** good night to you.

3 **lost** Webster uses this word ironically, to suggest that while Bracciano may have lost his heart, he will also lose his life and, in Christian terms, his soul. This echoes Lodovico's sense of being lost in I.i, linking the two characters who may be representatives of the chivalric tradition.

6 sd **Whispers** Webster uses this word throughout the play to suggest secret and corrupt politics.

8 **caroche** luxurious coach used for town visits.

9 This line marks a change to intimate darkness as the crowded stage empties.

10 **Can't** can it.

15 Zanche's eagerness to help Bracciano is reflected ironically in her confession to Francisco, V.iii.250–54.

18 **talk freely** In this informal situation Flamineo relaxes, and Webster changes the dialogue from verse to prose.

25 **buttery-hatch** serving hatch for food and drinks. Webster again links the imagery of food and appetite with corruption.

29–30 Gilders used mercury (*quicksilver*) in their work, and the fumes caused brain damage. Flamineo compares the sick worker to the feeble Camillo; the *liver* was supposedly the seat of passion.

31 **great barriers** medieval tournament in which knights fought each other over low barriers (as at Bracciano's wedding in V.iii), losing their decorative *feathers* as they did so. Webster uses wordplay to link this idea with Camillo's loss of hair and his impotence, symptoms of syphilis. Ironically, at his own barriers Bracciano is to lose his life, not his feathers.

32–4 **An Irish gamester... more venturous** It was said that an Irish gambler would gamble away not only all his clothes but even his own body parts, just as Camillo has gambled away his virility through catching syphilis.

35–6 **like a Dutch doublet... his breeches** The *Dutch doublet* was tight-fitting but the accompanying *breeches* were loose; the suggestion is that Camillo's sexual organs have shrunk. A weak *back* also suggests impotence. Flamineo's fluent wordplay would make him a popular character with Webster's audience.

37 Bracciano perhaps crouches behind a stage prop here, remaining visible to Flamineo. The word *Shroud* carries connotations of death, which in fact results from this wooing.

43 **under-age protestation** immature declaration of love.

50–51 His long robes make Camillo look like a state councillor or an old man. Webster uses the word *politician* repeatedly to suggest corruption.

53 **foot-cloth** the ceremonial, elaborate cloth that covered a noble's horse. Camillo would be fool enough to use it on an *ass*.

54 **travelling** A double meaning is implied: both travelling, and labouring hard. This is more mockery of Camillo's impotence. Again Webster raises the serious issue of the suitability of Vittoria's marriage.

58 **lose your count** A crude pun on female anatomy is made here.

61 **flaw** a sudden squall that separates two ships at anchor; also a passionate outburst; also, in the sense of a 'crack', a reference to female sexual anatomy.

65–6 Camillo comments that the passionate Bracciano is inclined towards Vittoria, just as a bowler leans the way he wants his

bowl to run. There is also the universal sense of women being
fair game for men in this society.

67 **bowl booty**   cheat at bowls. Webster uses gaming imagery to
suggest how two players can conspire to defeat a third, as with
Bracciano and Flamineo against Camillo.

67–9 **his cheek… my mistress**   Camillo uses bowling terms to
suggest that just as in the game of bowls the larger bowl is
aimed at the small white ball, so Bracciano aims to get
extremely close to Vittoria. *Jump with*, as well as being a
bowling term, suggests sexual activity.

70 **your Aristotle**   your study of logic and philosophy such as
Aristotle's.

71 **ephemerides**   tables that showed the predicted course of
astronomical bodies on successive days.

73 **Pew wew**   This is a foolish-sounding exclamation, which an
actor would probably 'ham up'.

76 **God boy you**   God be with you.

78 **horn-shavings**   horns were supposed to grow on the foreheads
of cuckolds (men whose wives were unfaithful).

82–3 **hound/In lyam**   dog on a leash.

89 **wrings me**   pinches me (because of his cuckold's horns).

90 **large ears**   asses' ears.

96 **Jacob's staff**   measuring instrument.

97–8 **These politic… the flesh**   Flamineo uses a series of puns
depending on the word *mutton* meaning a promiscuous woman.
Just as, at this time, nobles suffered peasant rebellions because
they fenced off the land, so restraining a woman leads to
promiscuity.

98–9 **provocative electuaries**   aphrodisiacs.

99 **uttered**   supplied.

Jubilee   a year that the Pope ordained when people could be
granted forgiveness for all their sins in return for pious acts and
a pilgrimage to Rome. The year 1600 was one such, and they
occurred every 25 years.

103 **spectacles fashioned with such perspective art**   specially
faceted glasses that create multiple images. Webster uses this as
an image for his play, as our perspective on events changes with
different viewpoints.

113–15 **like so many bubbles… cuckold-maker**   just as bubbles reflect a face many times, so a jealous man imagines many men making him a cuckold.

119 **Ida** in Greek mythology, a sacred mountain near Troy in whose green groves Paris lived as a boy. There is an ironic effect as Paris was to cause the Trojan wars by taking Helen as his wife.

119–20 **ivory of Corinth** This is another irony since Corinth was famous for luxury and debauchery; 'Corinth' was slang for a brothel. The term 'ivory' could describe sexually provocative flesh.

120–21 **blackbird's bill… blackbird's feather** The blackbird's bill is yellow, while its feathers are black. Fair-haired women were traditionally seen as more beautiful.

122 **friends** lovers.

124 **walk you aloof** Flamineo sends Camillo a short distance away while he takes Vittoria aside to talk privately; the audience attends to all parts of the stage.

125 sd *whispers to Vittoria* While the audience hear all of this conversation, Camillo cannot hear the asides to Vittoria.

131 **carved him** Flamineo puns on the idea of castration.
capon a castrated cock, a eunuch.

135 **blackguard** the lowest and therefore the dirtiest of household staff, who cleaned the kitchens and their huge open fires.

137 **tickle her** rouse her interest; but the meaning 'sexually arouse' is also suggested.

139 **calf's brains without any sage** This is a pun on the herb *sage* and the meaning 'wise'; calf's brains cooked without the herb are compared to the minds of fools without wisdom.

140 **crouching in the hams** bending his legs in a crouching position, as if begging.

142 **glass-house** glass factory where a fire always burned.

146 **foil** setting for a jewel, designed to show its beauty.

147–8 **covered with false stone** Webster introduces the image of jewellery to suggest that Vittoria is a lovely setting paired with a cheap stone (Camillo). There is also a pun on *stone* to mean testicle.

150–51 **thou shalt go to bed to my lord** Flamineo tops his wordplay with this comment, where *my lord* could in fact refer to Bracciano or Camillo.

154–5 **opening your case hard** Flamineo is continuing his sexual innuendos.

157–8 **philosopher's stone**   a mythical substance that alchemists believed could turn base metal into gold, and extend life. Again there is a pun on 'testicle'. What is the cumulative effect of all these sexual puns?

160 **turtles**   turtle doves, an image of faithful love.

167 How can we get rid of him?

168–9 **put breeze... gadding**   send him flying off like a gadfly. Gadflies use the wind for flight.

170 **coming**   responsive; also, sexually aroused.

177 **tumultuary**   confused or irregular.
quae negata grata   whatever is denied is desired.

178 **adamant**   magnet.

180 **philosophical**   wise, logical.

182 **progress**   royal or state procession. The reference is to Bracciano's formal visit, but an actor might play Camillo parading up and down in front of Vittoria at this point.

190–91 **I shall have you**   I suspect you will.

193 **gull**   trick or deceive.

199 **scurvily**   ungraciously.

204 sd *Exit Camillo*   The foolish Camillo leaves Vittoria alone with Flamineo.

208 **cursed**   vicious.

210 sd *Enter Bracciano*   Bracciano reappears from his hiding place to reveal himself to Vittoria.

212 **Give credit**   believe me. Bracciano asks Vittoria to believe him as he switches to the elevated language of courtly love to woo her.

214 sd While Bracciano speaks nobly, the laying out of the carpet and cushions visually reminds the audience that this profession of love is about sex. Cornelia's entrance, presumably wearing her crucifix (see V.ii.10–13) brings a reminder that in the Christian context, these actions are sinful. As in I.i, Webster uses effects from the medieval morality play as Zanche (signifying Vice), and Cornelia (Virtue) may frame the lovers from opposite sides of the stage.

217 **Loose**   reject, or force him to let go of his *vows*.

220–22 **a loathèd... their credit**   cruelly rejecting men loses a woman her reputation, just as a doctor loses his when many patients die.

224 **close**   Zanche approvingly comments on the lovers reaching agreement and moving together.

226–30   Cornelia comments on the effects of the couple's adultery, offering the Christian and moral perspective.

227   **house**   family (especially their honourable reputation).

231–8   **this jewel... jewel lower**   Exchanging jewels is a sign of betrothal, but Bracciano and Flamineo both pun on *jewel* meaning chastity, or sexual organs.

239–40   **I'll tell your grace/A dream**   Perhaps Vittoria wishes to defuse the sexually charged moment and move away from Bracciano. She may walk around the stage as she describes the dream, but Bracciano would pull her close to him again (line 270).

243   **yew-tree**   the tree traditionally grown in graveyards, echoed in Monticelso's warning to Lodovico (IV.iii.121). The *goodly yew-tree* in the dream may represent lawful marriage, as symbolized by Isabella and Camillo; in which case Bracciano is the *whirlwind* in line 262. However, the *yew-tree* may also represent Bracciano himself, whom Vittoria will transform into a *withered* shrub (line 253) if she yields to him. Vittoria puns on *yew* and 'you' (i.e. Bracciano) at the end of her description (line 264).

246   **cross-sticks**   wooden crosses that mark the head of a grave; or perhaps twigs crossing overhead as they hang above the graveyard, creating criss-cross patterns and shadows; or perhaps witches' devices used to summon storms. Whatever the precise meaning, Webster creates the suggestion of death overshadowing everything.

260   **the devil**   Flamineo links the dream to sin and evil; his use of this word is ironic as Bracciano sees the devil coming for his soul on his death (V.iii.106).

262   Vittoria is explicit about the *massy arm* around her; she might indicate this onstage by moving closer to Bracciano. The *whirlwind* suggests the duke's anger and power. The word is ironically repeated by Flamineo during the lovers' quarrel (IV.ii.106).

266–8   Flamineo interprets the dream as an attempt by Vittoria to urge Bracciano to murder Isabella and Camillo. Do you think this is the case?

270–78   Bracciano ironically promises to *protect* Vittoria, and elevate her *above law*, a vow that brings about murders and social disintegration. His words suggest his arrogance as he places himself above the law; he is utterly absorbed in self-interest, and blind to wrongdoing.

275 **government**   ruling the duchy.

279 Cornelia has been listening to all of this, perhaps forgotten by the lovers.

280 **Fury**   one of the avenging goddesses in classical myth, presented with snakes coiling around their heads. This is ironic, as Cornelia here represents Christian belief, believing that the snake in the Garden of Eden was the devil.

280 sd **Exit Zanche**   Why do you think Zanche leaves here?

286 **Thessaly**   an area of northern Greece, traditionally home to poisonous herbs and witches. The imagery of *witchcraft* (288) suggests the evil actions of society.

290 Perhaps Vittoria kneels to her mother for love and forgiveness here so that Cornelia has to *bend* to her. She is much more respectful to her mother than Flamineo is.

299–301 Cornelia touches upon one of the major themes of the play when she accuses Bracciano of neglecting his responsibilities as a *prince*, to set an *example* to society, in corrupting her daughter.

303 sd **kneels**   Vittoria shows deep respect for her mother, but she is not prepared to give up her new lover; Vittoria is thus shown to be a highly ambiguous character.

304 **blood**   Webster introduces one of the key images of the play. Here, *blood* could refer to Vittoria's life-blood, to the bloodshed of the murders of the two spouses, to her anger and also her passion. Ironically she repeats this at her death (V.vi.242–3).

310 **Judas-like**   In the Bible, Judas betrays Christ with a kiss, as Vittoria betrays her mother and Camillo.

320 **honour**   This is another key word, which will be redefined in the course of the play.

325–6 **bear my beard... lord's stirrup**   be in a less subservient position than a lowly foot-attendant to a lord riding a horse.

327–44 Do you think Webster gains some audience sympathy for Flamineo here, as he points out the lack of opportunity for such young men in this society?

329–31 **My father... spent**   This forms a parallel with Lodovico, who spent all of his fortune (I.i.); Flamineo's father also wasted his.

335–6 **Conspiring... a graduate**   The meaning is ambiguous: perhaps Flamineo only graduated because he had grown older and fulfilled the requirements for residence at the university; perhaps he was helped by his tutor or an older man; perhaps he carried out services for one, or even sold himself to men for sex.

338 **courteous**   trained in the manners of a courtier.

354–6 Plutarch, the first-century CE Greek historian, wrote that the Spartan law-giver Lycurgus suggested senators might share their wives with others to ensure that good stock was bred; ironically, unlike Isabella, Vittoria has no children.

359 Flamineo declares that he is a malcontent in league with evil.

361 **forcèd**   artificial. This emphasizes Flamineo's lack of freedom and opportunity.

364 **winter's snake**   a snake that is coiled up while hibernating. This image illuminates the idea of Flamineo's pact with evil, and the methods that malcontents such as he might use.

364–6 **subtle, policy, indirect**   Webster clusters together some important words here: they suggest the skills of a Machiavel (see Interpretations page 191).

Act II Scene I

This busy scene is set in Francisco's palace in Rome. There are many exits and entrances, with changes from a crowded stage to an intimate meeting, and the audience needs to absorb events happening all over the stage. There are many changes of mood, pace and tone. The first part is concerned with Bracciano's and Isabella's divorce agreement, interrupted by her public chastisement of Bracciano; in the second part, Flamineo assures the duke about his murder plan, and the two great men start their revenge action, looking forward to the return of Lodovico.

1 sd **with little Jacques the Moor**   Jaques is mentioned only in this scene, and never speaks. If he does appear, he is a young boy contrasting to the corruption of the older men, as Giovanni does.

3 **dove-house**   This is an ironical reference to Bracciano's situation with Vittoria, since doves were regarded as loving and innocent.

5 **polecats**   predatory animals with a vile smell; also a slang term for prostitutes.

My sweet cousin Francisco immediately expresses affection for his nephew Giovanni, to prepare the audience for his act of revenge.

9–17 **I do beseech... infected straying** What do you make of Isabella's optimism about mending her marriage? What does it reveal of her character?

13–15 **unicorn's horn... spider** It was believed that powder made from a unicorn's horns would have magical powers against poison. Since spiders were believed to be poisonous, the powder could be tested on a spider.

18 **Void the chamber** Webster boldly empties the stage for the confrontation between the three men, which echoes I.i. This pattern is repeated several times throughout the play.

30 **awful** awe-inspiring.

35–6 **the sting/Placed in the adder's tail** It was believed that adders carried a sting in their tail as well as their fangs; so Vittoria carries a double threat to Bracciano, wrecking his dukedom as well as his marriage. Monticelso here seems to be honourable and noble.

37–8 **fortune blasteth... unwieldy crowns** In this reference to *fortune* (see Note to I.i.4) there is a pun on *crowns* as flower heads.

41 **name** reputation.

45 Do not change direction like inexperienced *hawks* hunting their prey.

46–50 **Do not fear... can seize** Francisco drops the pretence of courtesy. How does the mood change here?

50 **dunghill birds** carrion birds that feed on dunghills, in contrast to *eagles* (48), which fly high. In other words, Bracciano is drastically lowering his standards with Vittoria.

51 **shift your shirt** Francisco speaks directly about Bracciano's encounters with Vittoria.

52 **happily** perhaps. There is also a pun on the modern meaning of *happily*.

54 **cloth of tissue** Camillo would not be able to afford this very expensive material for dresses, which noblewomen wear; nor is Vittoria entitled to wear it.

58 **hemlock** poison.

60 **borrowed Switzers** Bracciano sneers at the paid Swiss Guard, who were hired to act as security men at courts across Europe. At this point, he is threatening war on Francisco.

62 **Let's not talk on thunder** Francisco moves quickly to change the subject from the threat of war.

65 **winding-sheet** the sheet in which dead bodies were wrapped; here there is a suggestion that Isabella's wedding gown became hers.

66 **Thou hadst given a soul to God then** Bracciano seems to suggest that Isabella is too saintly to make a good wife.

67 **ghostly** spiritual.

72 **crackers** fire-crackers (fireworks). Notice how the two men share lines here in their angry speeches.

75 **change perfumes for plasters** the sweetness of self-indulgence can lead to the *plasters* necessary for treating venereal disease.

77 **new-ploughed forehead** Francisco is frowning deeply in anger.

80 **milder limit** more control. Monticelso steps in to avert war.

81–2 **Have you proclaimed... lion thus?** In Roman celebrations of victory, lions were baited in the Colosseum. Bracciano refers to himself as a tormented *lion*.

87 **Tiber** the river flowing through Rome.

88 **wild ducks** slang term for prostitutes.

89 **moulting time** Francisco alludes to the loss of hair of a man inflicted with venereal disease.

91 **tale of a tub** a cock-and-bull story. There is also a reference to the sweating-tub treatment for venereal disease.

92 To explain his meaning in plain terms.

93 **stags grow melancholic** Male deer (which have horns on their heads like cuckolds) retreat into isolation after mating.

93 sd Giovanni, wearing the armour his uncle gave him, is a visual emblem of the chivalric ideal which Bracciano represents ironically. Monticelso uses the arrival of the innocent child to try to make peace.

109 **practising your pike** Francisco's use of an innuendo here serves to emphasize the boy's innocence in contrast to his father.

110 **Homer's frogs** *The Battle of Frogs and Mice* is a satire attributed to Homer in which frogs use bulrushes as pikes; this shows Giovanni's education.

112 **discretion** wisdom and prudence.

117 **So that** so long as.

118 **Dansk** Danish.

124 **lapwing** a bird whose chicks are able to run as soon as they hatch, so were seen as precocious or forward for their age.

136 **habit** a pun meaning clothing (Giovanni's armour) as well a customary way of behaving.

149 **Devotion** Isabella means love for her husband, but Bracciano pretends that he thinks she means religious worship.

152 **cast our reckonings up** admit the extent of our sins.

154 **Nay** Isabella refuses to be sent straight to her room, which prepares the audience for her strong-mindedness.

156 **I do not use to kiss** I am not in the habit of kissing.

160 **to learn** as yet ignorant of.
that Italian the 'Italian' emotion of jealousy. Italians were reputed to be passionate in love.

165 **cassia** tree with an aromatic bark used as a substitute for the spice cinnamon.

171 **bandy factions** form a conspiracy.

174 **haunted out** hunted out, visited often.

176 **supply** make up for.

178 **ancient** former.

179 **corpulent** fat. This insult is a pun based on his title as the *Great Duke* (180) rather than his physical size.

180 **–'s death** by God's death (an oath or swearword).

182 **rest upon recòrd** be written down and used as evidence.

183 **a shaved Polack** a barbarian, someone of no account. Poles were reputed to shave their heads.

187 **fly-boat** fast sailing boat.

190 **issue** child or children.

192 **latest** last.

193–7 **Henceforth I'll... are severed** Bracciano reverses the gesture he made to Vittoria with their *jewels* at I.ii.233, as he 'divorces' Isabella. While divorce was legal in Jacobean England, divorced people could not remarry.

204 **winding-sheet** See line 65, and Note.

229 **naught** worthless, wicked.

233 **honest** chaste.

242 **apprehended** fully understood.

243 **whip some with scorpions** This is a reference to biblical threats of punishment. See 1 Kings 12:11 and 2 Chronicles 10:11.
Turned Fury? This echoes Flamineo's words to Cornelia at I.ii.280. See the Note to that line.

247 **mummia** See Note to I.i.16.

248 **to** compared to.

252–3 **Henceforth I'll... wedding-ring** Isabella echoes Bracciano's words at 193–4.

254–7 **And this divorce... the separation** Once again she echoes Bracciano's words (at 195–6), but adds the *throngèd court* and *thousand ears* of an audience who sympathize with her plight (see Interpretations page 210). Her words also anticipate those of Vittoria at IV.ii.119–21.

258–61 **Let not... my repentance** For a third time Isabella echoes Bracciano (see 199–202), sealing their divorce.

261 *manet alta mente repostum* it is stored deeply in my heart. This is an echo of the words the Roman poet Virgil gave to the goddess Juno, expressing her anger that Paris chose Venus, rather than Juno or her daughter Minerva, as the fairest of the goddesses. This incident led to the Trojan war.

265 **horns upon thee** Isabella now has the cuckold's horns.

267–8 Isabella is again told to go to her room (see 153), this time by her brother, but again refuses to obey.

271 **bring down her stomach** calm her anger.

272 **turn in post** return post-haste.

276 This is a proverbial idea, that pent-up grief will break the heart.

278 sd Webster now splits the stage action into two parts, and the audience will attend to both.

281 **stibium** a poisonous metallic element.

282 **cantharides** a dried beetle, known as Spanish fly, which causes blisters when applied to the skin but was also swallowed as an aphrodisiac. It is poisonous when too much is swallowed.

287 **Candy** Crete, where the inhabitants were believed to eat poisonous snakes, so visitors would die there. Flamineo means that he will send Camillo to his death.
    property stage prop for the conspiracy.

289 **quack-salving** pretending to cure.

291 **confessed a judgement** pleaded that he was already under a sentence for debt, which meant he would be taken into custody.
    execution claim for payment of debt.

292 **to a *non-plus*** beyond use.

294–5 **colourable execution** pretended debt.

297–8 **more ventages than a cornet or a lamprey** more holes than a cornet (a trumpet-like musical instrument) or an eel (thought to have several breathing-holes on top of its head).

298 **poison a kiss** This is indeed the way Isabella dies; the *kiss* is an important image in the play.

299 **Ireland breeds no poison** There are no poisonous snakes in Ireland; St Patrick is believed to have banished them.

302 **Saint Anthony's fire** an infection causing a severe skin rash and fever.

305 **bloodshed** bloodshot.

307 **gargarism** fluid gargled up.

308 **lights** lungs.
　　by scruples little by little.

313 **politic strain** cunning strategy.

314 **engine** device, method.

318–20 **as gallowses... another's shoulders** In the *Low Countries* (the Netherlands), Flamineo claims, instead of standing on gallows with the rope around his neck, the condemned convict stands on another man's shoulders.

321 **emblem** a picture accompanied by a moral saying.

325 **'Inopem me copia fecit'** 'Plenty has made me poor' (a quotation from Ovid's *Metamorphoses*).

326 This punning line can be interpreted in several ways: Camillo has become impotent; Bracciano's sexual activity with Vittoria has left Camillo deprived; Bracciano has worn out his sexual drive with Vittoria.

332–53 Francisco deftly suggests several possible meanings with this allegory. *Phoebus* (the sun) could relate to the cuckolded Camillo, or the 'hot' Bracciano, who should both be *gelded* (345) or castrated. Vittoria is the target (see 351–3), for if she were to have children with Bracciano, Giovanni's inheritance would be threatened.

350 **fireworks** the fire, heat and light of the sun.

355 **Go change the air** go away from here.

356 **cornucopia** horn of plenty. Traditionally this symbolizes fertility, but here it is used to symbolize cuckoldry.

360–61 **the stag's... are shed** Camillo fears he will be shown to be an even greater cuckold.

362 **ranger** gamekeeper.

372 **'twas well fitted** the plan is working out nicely.

382 **our sister Duchess** She is Francisco's sister; Monticelso is showing solidarity with him.

385–7 **for there's nought... deathless shame** Francisco hopes that Bracciano, if he causes a scandal by an affair with Vittoria in Camillo's absence, may then realize he has gone too far and lost his reputation through her, so will get rid of her. Francisco appears to be trying to avoid bloodshed at this point.

390–91 Monticelso expresses his determination to avenge, at any cost, a relative who cannot avenge himself.

394–5 Francisco hopes that Bracciano and Vittoria remain together until they *rot*, like *mistletoe* on dried-up, weather-worn *elms*. What is the effect of the image, at the end of this long scene?

Act II Scene II

This short, dramatic scene takes place at midnight when traditionally spirits arise; the device of the dumb-shows distances the audience from the cruelty.

1 sd *Conjurer* magician who may be involved in the black arts.

  8 **nigromancer** one who practises the black arts and claims to communicate with the dead.

  9 **juggle** play tricks, cheat.

11 **confederate** allied, companion.

12 **windmills** fanciful plans.

13 **squib** small explosion; trivial effect.

14 **curtal** horse with a docked tail. This is a reference to 'Marocco', a horse taught to do tricks, to great public acclaim in London in the 1590s; people believed that the owner, Banks, was a magician and that the horse was his attendant demon (*spirit*, 15).

16 **ream** a large amount of paper (and, here, those who publish with it).

    figure-flingers people who pretend to practise astrology.

18 **lie about stol'n goods** cast horoscopes to find stolen property.

20 **fustian** overblown or gibberish.

21 sd *night cap* This is part of the magic spell.

23 sd The two dumb-shows may be played either in the discovery
space or for greater visual impact on either side of the stage. In
the first, soft music and the reference to *perfumes* bring out the
gentle and religious aspects of Isabella's character. The
distancing of Bracciano from the murder, by framing, distances
the audience as well, but the grief of Giovanni and of
Lodovico reminds us that there will be repercussions. The
enactment of the kiss echoes the divorce (II.i.191), and will be
ironically repeated on Bracciano's death (V.iii.26). References
are made here to the 'ghost' characters Christopher and Guid-
Antonio, who partly parallel Antonelli and Gasparo, plotters
against Bracciano, to emphasize the revenge theme. Perhaps the
same actors played both for visual effect. In the second dumb-
show, Flamineo and Marcello play loosely equivalent roles.

24 **Excellent** Bracciano's response to his wife's death is shocking
and shows his total ruthlessness; he is further condemned by
being involved in the black arts.

25 **fumèd** contaminated, poisoned.

28 **dead shadow** Notice the irony of this description. The portrait
is in itself lifeless, but Bracciano himself is now effectively 'a
dead man walking' as this action has sentenced him to death.

35 **politic** cunning.

36 The music comes from below, as if from hell; it is harsher this
time, in accordance with the masculine content of this dumb-
show.

37 sd *vaulting-horse* In Jacobean slang 'to vault' meant to have sex;
but Camillo ends up *under the horse* – where his body is
arranged so that it looks like an accident – showing that he
cannot 'jump'.
to apprehend Vittoria Francisco's revenge against Vittoria
begins.

38 **quaintly** skilfully.

39 **taste** Bracciano seems to relish each moment of the murder.

40 **charged with their deep healths** intoxicated by drinking
extravagant toasts.

41 **boon** successful.

46 **engine** strategy, method.

50–51 **we are now/Beneath her roof** There is an abrupt change of
perspective as the action shifts into the present.

52 **Noble**   Note the irony in the use of this word.
53–5 **This shall... a payment**   Perhaps they shake hands, or
     Bracciano gives the Conjurer a token as a promise of payment.

Act III Scene I

There is continuous action throughout Act III, with no major
scene changes, and probably the stage is never cleared. The scene
divisions have been inserted for the convenience of readers. As a
prelude to the trial, Webster allows the audience to hear the
thoughts of most of the major characters, but not Vittoria.
Differences between Marcello and Flamineo are made plain, and
so is the seriousness of Vittoria's plight. Flamineo's satirical
comments about the ambassadors suggest that they are not
immune from corruption, and the foolishness of the Lawyer
hints at the quality of justice to be meted out to Vittoria. The
actor who plays Camillo may double up as the Lawyer, to
underline the point.

1 sd **Register**   Registrar.
1–3 **You have... Vittoria's trial**   The attendance of the ambassadors
     at Vittoria's trial will help to legitimize the proceedings.
  2 **lieger**   resident.
4–8 **For, sir... neighbouring kingdoms**   The revengers know that
     there is no evidence to link Vittoria to Camillo's murder; they
     intend to proceed by blackening her reputation.
 11 **in by the week**   caught out.
 13 **sit upon**   sit in judgement upon. The phrase also suggests a
     sexual meaning. Webster suggests the crudeness and unfitness
     of the Lawyer.
 15 **tickler**   punisher, but also provoker.
 16 **tilting**   jousting. Also, illicit sex.
 18 **private**   intimate.
 20 **public**   open or indiscreet.
 24 **ferret them**   catch them out. A ferret is used for catching
     rabbits (*conies*, 25).

25 **catch conies**   play tricks on fools (as well as 'catch rabbits', see above).

36 **stalking-horse**   horse trained to approach game quietly, so it may be caught.

37–8 **I made... own preferment**   Flamineo has tied his own advancement to that of his sister.

41 Witches were said to feed their demons with their own milk from an extra teat hidden on their body.

42 **prodigal**   wasteful.

47 **chamois**   soft leather jerkin worn below armour. Flamineo implies that Marcello, for all his virtue, can hardly afford to buy necessities.

51–3 **mistletoe... by it**   Mistletoe, which was believed to have healing qualities (*Sacred to physic*) grew alongside poisonous *mandrake*, which was believed to scream when uprooted and to grow below the gallows.

52 **builder**   used for building.

54–5 The smallest of actions arising from great men's *dislikes* seems only to injure their target superficially, but in fact deals a mortal blow. Flamineo will realize that this is true for himself.

60–61 Rise above all considerations of policy, which though it seems to advance a cause, by doing so also corrupts.

64 sd As the ambassadors enter in a splendid procession, Flamineo and the lawyer make disrespectful remarks upon them; Webster is again offering his audience a dual perspective. The ambassadors include those from Savoy (a powerful duchy between France and Italy, see page 230), France, Spain, and England.

73 **lofty tricks**   acrobatics.

73–4 **sleeps o'horseback like a poulter**   poulterers rode to market very early in the morning and were known to fall asleep while riding along.

77 **cypress hat-band**   hat-band made of very fine material such as crepe. Just as glasses would have to be carried very carefully in such material, this vain ambassador does not move his head inside his fashionable *ruff* (76).

78–80 **he looks like... in a candle**   The wide Spanish ruff is compared to the claw of a blackbird, which is spread wide for grilling.

80 sd They both exit to re-enter as part of a larger group, with Flamineo as a prisoner.

Act III Scene II

This is one of the most important scenes of the play, and Webster gave it its own title, 'The Arraignment of Vittoria'. The stage would be set out as a court with a high throne from which Monticelso would preside. Vittoria would be lower than the cardinal, probably behind a barrier.

- 1 sd The scene begins with another formal procession.
- 1 Monticelso, probably shocked by Bracciano's entrance (see III.i.8–10), tries in vain to get rid of him.
- 3 sd This action recalls the *carpet... and two fair cushions* which Zanche lays on the floor at I.ii.214 to promote adultery.
- 10–11 **Domine... corruptissimam** Lord Judge, turn your eyes upon this plague, the most corrupt of women.
- 15 Most women would not have learned Latin, so would be unable to follow proceedings. Vittoria does know Latin, and will use it later in the scene (201).
- 16 **this auditory** As Isabella does at II.i.254–7, Vittoria refers to the entire audience who may hear her (see Interpretations page 195).
- 22 **stand on't** insist upon it.
- 23–4 **your credit/Shall be more famous** your (bad) reputation will be more widely known (because of the use of easily understood language).
- 25 **give aim** This is an image from archery, where an archer is helped to find direction by being given the results of a previous shot.
- 28 **connive your judgements** The Lawyer is using high-sounding and pretentious language but gets it wrong here, as *connive* means to conspire with. Ironically he is correct, as the trial is a conspiracy against Vittoria.
- 29 **diversivolent** wishing to cause strife.
- 33 **projections** projects.
- 35 **exulceration** lancing of an ulcer.
- 37 **pothecary's bills** medical prescriptions, which use Latin and technical terms.
  proclamations official notices and formal orders, which are often phrased obscurely.

39 **Come up**   are vomited up.
   stones... for physic   This refers to a remedy used for sick hawks.
40 **Welsh to Latin**   a language just as remote as the other.
41 **tropes, figures**   images and flourishes in rhetorical language.
47 **fustian**   fabric made of a mixture of cotton and flax. This is an image for the mixed-up and unintelligible language of the lawyer.
48 **buckram**   coarse, hard fabric used for stiffening.
50 **graduatically**   as a graduate would.
51 sd Monticelso, a cardinal, becomes prosecuting counsel on the departure of the Lawyer. What is the significance of this?
53–4 **more natural... your cheek**   He begins with a personal attack on Vittoria's appearance, by suggesting that she is wearing make-up that makes her look like a whore.
59 **spirit**   courage, perhaps with a pun on spirited or vigorous sexually.
60 **effected**   achieved.
66 **Sodom and Gomorrah**   two cities that according to the Bible were destroyed by God, and were regarded as symbols of vice. For the origin of stories about Sodom and Gomorrah's fruit becoming ash, see Deuteronomy 32:32.
68–9 **Your envenomed/Pothecary should do't**   Vittoria is referring to the Lawyer (see 36–7).
70–1 **Were there... betray it**   Monticelso believes that Vittoria is as dangerous as Eve, whose temptation of Adam caused all humankind to lose Paradise, according to the Bible (Genesis 3:6).
72 **scarlet**   The colour of the robes of a cardinal or a judge, and also the colour of blood and of passion.
80 **character**   character sketch.
82 **Poisoned perfumes**   Webster reminds the audience of Isabella's death, shown in the first dumb-show.
87 **tributes i'th' Low Countries**   taxes in the Netherlands (which were famously high).
97–9 **which are... he is imperfect**   The bodies of executed criminals were used in anatomy lessons and experiments.
100 **guilty**   This is a pun on the gilt that covers a counterfeit coin, concealing the base metal underneath. The suggestion is that although Vittoria looks attractive, she has no inner worth.

107 **She hath lived ill** France is a near neighbour, and its
ambassador supports the accusation.

108 The more distanced English Ambassador is critical of
Monticelso. Is the audience likely to agree with him, or the
French Ambassador, or both?

112 He has repaid his debt to *nature* by giving up his life.

116 **rushes** dried stems of marsh plants, used as a floor covering.

119 **Wound up** i.e. in his shroud.

129 **Christian court** Vittoria reminds the audience that Christian
principles should govern the behaviour of the court. At that
time 'Courts Christian' heard divorce cases.

130 **Tartar** Turk or Mongol; a byword for cruelty.

131 sd Vittoria behaves courteously to the ambassadors.

136 **of force** by necessity.
Perseus a warrior hero of Greek mythology.

137 **personate** imitate.
masculine virtue *Virtue* implies both strength and goodness.
Webster suggests that in order to survive, Vittoria must act like
a man.

144 **strict-combinèd heads** closely allied forces.

148 **painted devils** the frightening images Monticelso has created
(possibly with a side-swipe at the images of devils in Roman
Catholic churches).

149 **palsy** weakness and shaking.

155–6 **That question... I was there** Bracciano speaks for the first
time, but only in self-interest, offering an alibi for himself.

167 **sword** This is the emblem of justice, but also of the strength
of Bracciano's anger, which he will use against Monticelso. He
cannot respond as intelligently as Vittoria.

169 **of thy coat** who wear robes like yours. Bracciano throws out
insults.

178 **Valance** curtains around the canopy of a bed.
demi-footcloth the covering for a horse used by people of
lower status.

180 No one harms me with impunity.

180 sd Bracciano is too angry to stay any longer, so abandons Vittoria
to her fate.

192 **gilded** covered in gold (to make them more attractive and easy
to swallow).

196 **(view't, my lords)** The audience's attention is drawn to the ambassadors, who are also making judgements.

201 'The chaste woman is the one nobody has asked.' This is a quotation from Ovid's *Amores*, 1.viii.43, but Vittoria makes a tactical error in using it here as its context is of a woman being persuaded into bed.

202 **want** lack.

203 **dog-days** sultry, oppressively hot weather.

212 **pistol flies** shoot flies.

216 **crusadoes** Portuguese coins of gold or silver, bearing a cross.

217–18 **If the devil... his picture** This is a reference to the title of the play, and to people whose appearance suggests goodness in contrast to the inner reality.

222 **ducats** gold or silver coins.

224 **use** interest.

228 **these** the ambassadors.

230 **intelligencing** spying.

235 **choke-pear** inedible pear; metaphorically, a severe reprimand.

237 **the Vitelli** a Venetian family. Venice was notorious for prostitutes.

242 **julio** silver coin. Ironically Doctor Julio is implicated in Bracciano's murder plots.

243 **the ware being so light** the goods being less than the weight that was paid for. *Light* also means unchaste.

247 **prate** repeat endlessly, rant and rave.

249 **Rialto talk** gossip exchanged at the Rialto, in the heart of Venice.

250 **balladed** sung about in popular ballads.
    would be... o'th'stage Many scandals were turned into plays and staged; Webster himself echoes some of them.

255 **sureties** people who pay bail to guarantee that the accused will reappear in court.

263 **blazing stars** comets, which were considered ill omens, especially for powerful men.

265 **house of convertites** place of correction run by nuns. The historical Vittoria was imprisoned in Castel Sant'Angelo, Rome.

273 **patent** special licence.

277 **pills** Probably a reference to the *gilded pills* of 192, this implies hypocritical words.

maw   throat.

282 **horse-leech**   blood-sucker.

301 **You have lost too much**   Bracciano may be referring to Francisco looking pale with anger, or to the fact that family blood has been lost with his sister's (yet-to-be-announced) death.

306 **feign a mad humour**   Flamineo will pretend to have become mad because of his sister's *disgrace*, to keep himself clear of blame for the murders.

308 **hath a villainous palsy**   moves uncontrollably.

310 sd   Webster changes the look of the stage dramatically; while Monticelso and the ambassadors talk after the trial, Giovanni and Lodovico enter to change the pace and direction of the scene.

314 **My sweet mother**   Webster reminds the audience of the innocent Isabella's death when Vittoria's trial is barely over.

335 **fold of lead**   lead-lined coffin. The lead will enclose the poisonous fumes.

336 **would not let me kiss her**   This is a reminder of the poisoned kiss that caused Isabella's death.

337–9 **she gave me suck… seldom do it**   Isabella breastfed her child, which was unusual for a noblewoman as wet nurses were usually employed. As the perfect mother, she is contrasted again with Vittoria, who is childless.

341   Giovanni is to be protected from the full horror of the murder and its consequences.

Act III Scene III

As he vowed (III.ii.306), Flamineo pretends he is mad (*distracted*), a typical device in revenge tragedy. Similarities and differences between Flamineo and Lodovico and their situations are brought out. The audience begins to see a decline in Flamineo, originally Bracciano's companion, especially as Lodovico is pardoned while Flamineo is not.

3 The usually sure-footed Flamineo is uncertain about his life and where he now stands. Notice the key word *service*.

5 **ostler** stable-boy or groom.

7 **pedlars in Poland** Poles were regarded as poverty-stricken.

9 **upon the pox as well as on piles** This is a pun; Venice was built upon piles driven into the ground, but also was famous for pox (venereal disease), and men made fortunes treating pox and hemorrhoids (piles).

11 The ambassadors of Savoy, France and England take turns in this scene to try to console Flamineo, fooled by his trick; they accept the court's judgement.

19 **he comes... towards you** A person who faces you can be seen as a threat; the devil is too sly to do this, as is a politician.

23 **diversivolent** Flamineo throws the Lawyer's word back at him (see III.ii.29).

25 **gudgeons** small fish used as bait; people who are readily tricked.

28 **victual under the line** food at the equator.

30–31 **those weights... death with** The English devised the press, an instrument of torture in which people were crushed to death by loading heavy weights on top of them.

31 **salary** reward.

33–4 **full pitch** highest point in the church bell-tower.

37–8 **well may** so should they be.

40 **policy** plotting.

40–41 **The first... about religion** Cain killed his brother Abel out of jealousy as his own sacrifice did not please God as much as his brother's (Genesis 4). Note the irony in Flamineo, who will kill his own brother, making this allusion.

50 **early mushrooms** precocious young men.

53 **Wolner** famous English glutton who died after eating a raw eel.

56 **screech-owl** small owl with a noisy cry, considered a bad omen.

60 **wind** find out about.

62 **purchased** granted.

68 **gall** bitterness.

69 **stigmatic** ugly.

72 **ingeniously** truthfully (also, cleverly).

73 **raven** bird whose croak is said to predict death; a bird of ill omen.

76 Tumbling over each other.

82 **faggots** bundles of sticks.

84 **melancholic hare** The hare was said to be depressive, so eating it would make a person melancholy too.

86 **grieve** Pretending to be mad, Flamineo 'mistakes' laughter for sorrow.

91 **saucer** small dish that would be used in blood-letting to catch the blood.

92 **witch's congealèd blood** Witches were said to be melancholy.
   girn grin that is really a snarl.

97 **strappadoed** hoisted from the ground by the arms tied behind the back.
   felly wheel rim.

98 **fortune's wheel** Flamineo here links the Wheel of Fortune (see Interpretations page 225) with the torture of the rack.

100 **My lord, I bring good news** As soon as Antonelli brings Lodovico the news of his pardon, he changes his attitude towards Flamineo. Is Webster suggesting there can be no real loyalty between men?

118 **for ever forfeited the daylight** been imprisoned for life.

119 **being in debt** going bankrupt.

120 **break** break our agreement.

122 **stick by you** This is a pun, meaning 'stab you' as well as 'remain in your memory'.

130 **Ud's death** by God's death (an oath).

136 **to shake thus** i.e. with rage. Lodovico feels scorn at Flamineo and does not seem to believe in his madness, so Flamineo's powers have failed again.

Act IV Scene I

In this great revenge scene, the time of decision arrives for Monticelso and Francisco. Instead of suggesting that he pray, the cardinal urges Francisco to take revenge through murder, by using an agent listed in his own *black book* (33). Rejecting the supernaturalism of the ghost, Francisco decides to use Lodovico and begins the revenge plot.

2 **loose as a bride's hair** Jacobean women wore their hair loose as a sign of their virginity for their wedding; Francisco is a 'virgin' in plotting revenge. Loose hair was also a sign of madness, and Francisco claims to be maddened by grief for his sister.

13–14 **undermining more... the cannon** In order to knock down walls in a siege, the more subtle method of *undermining* them was often more effective than using the *cannon*.

15–16 **patient as... back unbruised** The tortoise, whose *back* is protected by a shell, and therefore will remain *unbruised*, represents the virtues of patience and persistence.

18–19 **till the time... fatal gripe** Monticelso speaks in the typical register of the revenger, but here it is to persuade another revenger into action, not himself.

20 **fowler** hunter of fowl.

22 **Free me, my innocence** This reinforces the 'virginal' image of the line 2.

23–5 **I'll stand... aspiring mountain** This is an ambiguous comment; Francisco may mean that he will leave the revenge to God, or that he will pretend to be humble in order to ensure his own safety.

33 **black book** a register bound in black. There is a pun on the idea of the black arts, as Monticelso goes on to explain.

39 **jealous** watchful.

40 **reach** grasp.

49 **taking up commodities** lending goods, then claiming payment for more than they are worth.

50–53 **fellows that... first children** husbands who force their wives' lovers to buy goods at inflated prices when the wives give birth to their children.

54–5 **bawds/That go in men's apparel** pimps and prostitutes who cross-dress as men.

55–6 **usurers... good reportage** moneylenders who share their profits with the notaries who recommend them to customers.

57 **antedate their writs** change the date on a document to an earlier one in order to falsify a legal case.

69 **tribute of wolves** King Edgar reputedly imposed a tribute of 300 wolves a year on Wales in the tenth century, to get rid of the animals.

70 **hang their skins o'th' hedge**   Dogs and wolves who bit sheep were hung up to frighten away others.

78 **to sell heads**   Elizabeth I paid a reward for the heads of Irish rebels.

88 **leash**   set of three hunting animals or birds.

91 **declarations**   official proclamations.

93 **wrested by some factious blood**   stirred by some rebellious, violent passion.

99–100 **How strong/Imagination works!**   After closing his eyes to imagine Isabella (97–9), Francisco is certain that the ghost is a figment of his imagination. This is unusual in revenge drama. What does it tell us about Francisco's character?

102 **quick**   life-like.

106 **melancholy**   It was believed that melancholic people suffered from hallucinations.

108 **idleness**   folly.

129 This is a reference to the proverb that once a fox has got his head through a fence his body will follow. Francisco intends to succeed by using his head (his wits).

132 Falcons are trained by holding out meat to entice them to return to their handler.

134 **wild Irish**   The Irish were thought to be very cruel and violent.

136 If I cannot prevail on the will of heaven, I shall appeal to hell (Virgil's *Aeneid*, vii.312).

Act IV Scene II

This scene is set in the House of Convertites, where Bracciano and Vittoria argue bitterly over Francisco's letter. Vittoria may be thought to approach tragic status in this scene. Flamineo, keen to make peace for his own purposes, proposes a plan for Vittoria's escape and flight with Bracciano; effectively he seals his sister's fate.

1 **recourse**   access.

10 The letter allows for plenty of stage business as it is passed from hand to hand.

20 **coffined** sealed inside a pie crust.

24 **conveyance** dishonest activity.

26–8 **a vine... fade and wither** Compare III.ii.186–9.

29 Flamineo scornfully says that bad wine would be good enough for Francisco.

31 **uncontrollèd** free from constraint.

34 He should be hanged for quibbling with words (picking up the word *hang*, 33).

35 **sad willow** Willows 'weep', as do unsuccessful lovers.

37 **bed-straw** Straw was used for mattresses as well as for keeping fruit while it ripened.

38 There is a pun on *convince*: 'this saying takes precedence over earlier ones' and 'this saying is good because of my wisdom (from age)'.

40 **atheists** Flamineo suggests that Francisco has blasphemed by claiming that princes are equal to the gods.

42 **irregular** erratic.

45–6 **Prevent the... hair off** This is another reference to hair loss caused by venereal disease.

46 **changeable stuff** fickle woman.

47–8 **O'er head... your wearing** This refers both to the fact that Vittoria is in deep trouble, and to the *wearing* of a dress of shot ('watered', changeable) silk.

50 **bloodhound** hunting hound. The connotations of 'blood', as we have seen, include sex, passion and death.
    stand me stand up to me, defy me.

53 **neck broke** This is a reminder of Camillo's murder.

54–5 **I am not... kept whole** In Russia, those defaulting on debt were beaten on their shins.

60 **Spanish fig, Italian salad** poisoned food. *Spanish fig* is also an expression of contempt.

61 **ply your convoy** carry on with your trade (of being a pimp).

63 **Polyphemus, Ulysses** According to Homer's *Odyssey*, the one-eyed monster *Polyphemus* imprisoned *Ulysses* and his ship's crew, eating two at each meal, offering 'kindly' to leave the hero till last.

64 **turves** pieces of grass.

67 **face** defy.

68–70 Flamineo puns on *face me* (67) by declaring that he cannot trust Bracciano enough to turn his back on him.

70 sd   Vittoria makes a dramatic entrance and so takes control of the scene. She may enter through the discovery space.

72   **characters**   coded symbols.

73   **receiver**   clerk whose job is to receive payments; probably also suggesting a pimp.

74   **God's precious**   by God's precious blood (an oath).

81   **reclaimèd**   reformed; also, of a hawk, called back.
      bells   A trained hawk would wear these.

82   **Ware hawk**   be on your guard. Flamineo takes up the imagery of falconry that Bracciano has been using.

87   **beheld the devil in crystal**   been deceived. This is another allusion to the title of the play; devils were said to appear in a piece of crystal, but this was a byword for trickery.

92   **adamants**   magnets.

95–6   **furnish all... past wild Irish**   Women were hired to wail loudly at Irish funerals.

98   **doting kisses**   The *kisses* recall his divorce from Isabella, and the method of her death; Bracciano remembers her in the same line.

110–12   **Like those... choicer nostrils**   Foxes were thought to cure palsy, but their smell made the sufferer unsuitable for company.

120   This is a reference to a saying in the Bible. In Matthew 18:8, Jesus compares amputation of an infected limb with giving up sinfulness rather than losing heaven.
      ulcer   The historical Bracciano is said to have died from an ulcerous leg.

131   **weep poniards**   weep tears that sting like daggers.

133   **not matches**   squinting.

148   **imposthume**   abscess.

155   **mercer**   trader in expensive fabrics.

157   **frowardness**   perverse obstinacy.

158   **Young leverets stand not long**   Flamineo advises Bracciano that Vittoria's defiance is like that of young hares being hunted – they cannot resist capture for long.

166   **Hand**   handle, fondle.

166–7   **Be not... blowing**   It was said that when blown at, ferrets would release their prey.

169   **forgetful wine**   wine that makes one forgetful or oblivious.

180   **shoot**   navigate rough water. Flamineo's phrase also suggests sexual activity.

194 **still** always.

198 **wooden horse** In Virgil's *Aeneid*, Greek soldiers hide inside a huge wooden horse presented as a gift to the city of Troy; once inside the walls, they emerge and capture the city.

212 **Lay her post-horse** prepare relays of post-horses for her.

215–16 **You two... young Marcello** Bracciano promises to reward and protect the whole family.

220–33 Flamineo's fable is ambiguous, as Bracciano sees (234–5). Again a fable is used to relate the particular situation to humankind generally. It also demonstrates the interdependent relationship between the three characters. See Interpretations page 221.

243 **sage** This is a pun on the herb *sage* and the meaning 'wise', as at I.ii.139.

Act IV Scene III

The setting is the Vatican, Rome, where the papal election takes place. Lodovico, newly pardoned, now has considerable power in return for his services in the murder plot; he is primed for action.

2 **conclave** the private rooms in which cardinals meet to elect a pope.

4 Probably the characters are in two groupings on the stage after this line: Francisco with the ambassadors, and Gasparo with Lodovico.

5 **brave** impressive, showy. Webster offers another splendid spectacle, which reminds the audience of the inner corruption of the powerful characters.

9–14 **Knights of Rhodes... St George** Knights of Rhodes belonged to the Order of St John, founded during the First Crusade in the eleventh century; the Orders of St Michael and of the Holy Ghost were French; the Order of the Golden Fleece was from Burgundy; the Order of the Annunciation was from Savoy; and Knights of the Garter were English. All wore colourful and costly robes.

34 **viands** food.

37 **given o'er scrutiny** finished taking the vote in the secret ballot.

38 **admiration** acclamation, where the cardinals unanimously proclaim one of the cardinals to be pope. It is less secure than a secret ballot, as the stronger could bully the weaker cardinals.

43–6 'I bring you tidings of great joy. The most Reverend Cardinal Lorenzo de Monticelso has been elected to the Apostolic See, and has chosen for himself the title of Paul the Fourth.' The historical source was Cardinal Montalto, who became Sixtus the Fifth.

47 Long live Holy Father Paul the Fourth.

60–61 We grant you the apostolic blessing and forgiveness of sins.

61 sd Webster uses the word *whispers* to denote conspirators at work. Francisco distracts the new pope from Church matters in order to pursue revenge.

65 **seat** occupancy of the papal throne.

73 **ta'en the sacrament** Lodovico has taken communion before his task, as knights did before going on crusades. Francisco merely wants a guarantee that he will carry out his job.

83 **resolve you** answer you.

87 **out of measure** out of control, excessively.

88 **cunning** crafty; also, possessing magical skills.

94 **resty Barbary horse** hot-tempered Arab horse.

95–6 **the career... ring-galliard** riding at full speed, then making the horse leap and putting it through the motions of dancing.

98 **jade** broken-down or useless horse or, insultingly, woman.

102 **I am too low to storm** Lodovico refers to both his position at court, and to kneeling as a sinner about to say confession.

110–11 Confession is a sacrament, so the content may never be revealed to anyone. Lodovico thus prevents Monticelso from giving evidence against Francisco. To this extent, it makes no difference whether Monticelso is reformed or not.

111 **o'erta'en me** trapped me.

130 **suffrage** support.

132 sd Again Webster uses split staging for ironic effect.

138–9 Politicians often paid travellers to bring foreign news.

142 **told out** counted out.

145 **Like brides at wedding dinners** This simile foreshadows the wedding in the following scene.

146 **puling** protesting feebly.

151 **act of blood**   act of revenge. Although Lodovico acts as
  Francisco's agent, his love for Isabella and resentment against
  Vittoria (I.i.43–4) make him a personal revenger also.

Act V Scene I

This long and complex act is half the length of the four previous
acts put together. The setting is unchanged throughout,
becomingly increasingly dark as the denouement approaches.

  1 sd This third procession is presumably Bracciano's and Vittoria's
    wedding, and would be presented with some splendour. Despite
    their reservations, Cornelia and Marcello have joined
    Bracciano's household. The ambassadors are probably included
    in *others*, as Bracciano expresses concern for their safety when
    he is poisoned (V.iii.11). Their presence indicates political
    acceptance of the wedding of a murderer and a whore, and
    reinforces Vittoria's status as the new duchess.
16–17 **strict order of Capuchins**   an order of monks that separated
    from the Franciscans, vowing a return to their original austerity.
  21 **knighted**   became part of the Order of St John.
  38 **airy**   superficial.
44 sd Bracciano's extended household are included, as are *Carlo* and
    Pedro; although some editors believe that these two characters
    are Lodovico and Gasparo in disguise, in some editions all four
    appear together. It is likely that they are Bracciano's servants in
    the pay of Francisco, which is confirmed by their words to the
    disguised Francisco (64–8). Also, extra hands are needed for the
    three murders later (V.vi.185 sd).
  50 **incapable of**   unable to accept.
51–4 Bracciano is so easily duped that the audience may think he
    does not have the necessary skills to survive in such a ruthless
    political environment. On the other hand, do you think his
    chivalrous generosity, at odds with his selfishness, makes an
    audience warm towards him before his death?
  52 **monuments**   memorials.
  57 **Barriers**   See Note to I.ii.31.

63 **presence** ducal presence chamber.

68 **despaired** been suicidal.

70–72 The victim's hands, having touched any of these objects, would carry the poison to the mouth.

70 **pair** set (which could be more than two).

74–5 **struck... into the hazard** A stroke *into the hazard* was a winning one on the indoor Jacobean tennis court. The pun, of course, also means 'put his soul in danger'.

82 To have taken him by the helmet on the field of battle (i.e. honourably).

93–4 'To stick like a burr' is a proverbial phrase, referring to the sticky, seed-carrying burrs of plants.

107–13 **What difference... weather equally** This speech is ironic, as the disguised Francisco is in fact equal in status to Bracciano.

114–15 Beggars used to claim they were veteran soldiers, to avoid being whipped for begging.

122 **Colossuses** giants (like the statue at Rhodes, one of the seven wonders of the world).

124 **arras** tapestry wall-hanging.

138 **under his hand** in the form of a signed promise.

143 **miserable** a pun, meaning both 'miserly' and 'compassionate'.

150 Hortensio's question gives Flamineo the opportunity to rail against flattery and sycophancy as the young lords curry favour at court; ironically, he tries to do the same thing.

152–3 **maker of almanacs** fortune-teller.

157 **constrainedly** under duress.

159 **holds a wolf by the ears** This is a proverbial expression; it is just as dangerous to let go of the wolf's ears as it is to keep hold of them.

167 **gypsy** person with dark skin.

168–70 Zanche says that Flamineo's love has cooled, but he twists her meaning to claim that he satisfies her lust.

170 **heat** become sexually aroused.

173 **satin** There is a pun on 'Satan'.

176 **painting** cosmetics.

180–1 **Aesop had... the shadow** This story comes from a proverb.

184–6 **uttered in... to drinking** Flamineo links a series of sexual images to images of sailors on a ship in a storm. The verb *tumbling* is often used for sexual activity.

188–9 **shoemakers and… both drawers-on** Bacon, being salty, draws
men to drink just as shoemakers draw shoes onto feet.

192 **sunburnt** dark-skinned.

192 sd Cornelia's entrance and attack, parallel to that in I.ii.279,
interrupts proceedings. She is again opposed to Zanche.

193 **haggard** wild female hawk, a term also used for a prostitute.
stews brothels.

194 **clapped by th'heels** put in prisoners' irons.

195 Violence at court was a serious offence under English law.

197 **bedstaff** a support for a mattress or a stick for turning the
bed, which Cornelia would use as a weapon; also suggesting the
men who might keep the maids warm in bed.

200–1 A proverb stated that women, like asses and the walnut tree,
are better the more they are beaten.

203–4 **pitched upon… new-seeded garden** This image suggests a
combination of a witch being burnt at the stake, and a
scarecrow.

205 **boy** Flamineo mocks Marcello, suggesting he lacks virility.

208 **fan of feathers** Flamineo taunts Marcello by saying he carries
a courtier's fan rather than a weapon of war.

209–10 **choleric… with rhubarb** The bad-tempered humour of choler
was often treated with rhubarb.

214 **two slaughtered sons of Oedipus** Eteocles and Polynices,
who were enemies even after death, when the *flames* (215) of
their funeral pyres vied for height.

217 **gests in the progress** stopping places on a royal progress.

219–20 **bear him… length on't** Marcello issues the challenge of a
duel to his brother, inviting him to match his sword.

225 **Michaelmas** autumn feast day (29 September).
Mulinassar/Francisco is in the autumn of his life, whereas love
belongs to spring.

Act V Scene II

Tension is ratcheted up in this scene where, although Flamineo
kills his brother, Bracciano neither tells Vittoria nor cancels the
celebratory barriers. His typical self-centredness will cost him his

life as the conspirators poison the mouth-protector (*beaver*) of his helmet, a reminder of the poisonous kiss on the lips that has killed Isabella.

10 **this crucifix** It presumably hangs at Cornelia's neck; it is used here to suggest Flamineo's evil nature, but it could be a visual reminder of the corrupt pope, Monticelso, who would also wear a crucifix.

14 sd Flamineo's sudden entrance and violent action parallel those of his mother in the previous scene.

16 **turn your gall up** 'Turning up one's toes' is a phrase used for 'dying', and perhaps Flamineo refers to the blood that Marcello coughs up.

    sanctuary a place such as a church, where fugitives from justice have a temporary refuge.

26 **come, you shall** Cornelia is presumably dragged away from the body of her son.

46 sd *save the beaver* This offers a clue about Bracciano's fate.

71 **grazed** grassed, i.e. lost in the grass; a second arrow would be shot after it in order to find it. But there is also a reference to the wound Flamineo has inflicted on Marcello.

85 **black lake** Acheron, the river or lake in the underworld.

Act V Scene III

The audience is not spared the anguish of the great prince dying helpless in bed, while the conspirators laugh and torment him. Perhaps Francisco seems to have gone too far in his merciless revenge, but he will go even further. Flamineo's heartless treatment of Zanche, a sign of his increasing loss of judgement, leads to the discovery of the details of the earlier murders, which will trigger yet more.

1 sd Webster offers the audience another grand spectacle. This one is linked to the medieval chivalric tradition, as the knights fight singly and then in groups of three. Bracciano is contextualized

as a noble knight, recalling his status as a courtly lover; this perhaps gains audience sympathy prior to his death. Does Webster suggest that he is an anachronism in the new political age, as perhaps is Flamineo?

8 **bar** either the clasp of Bracciano's helmet, or the barrier in front of the joust.

11 Bracciano's concern for the safety of the ambassadors, who are his guests, underlines his courtesy.

16 For the second time, attempts are made to shield Giovanni from the horror of a parent's death (see III.ii.341).

19 **screech-owls** See Note to III.iii.56; here, physicians who can foretell death.

21 **without book** without study or difficulty.

26 Webster makes clear the ironic parallel with Isabella's death.

27–34 **This unction… waits on princes** Bracciano refers to the elements of revenge tragedy in referencing Francisco and the fall of the great.

30 **rough-bearded comet** comet with a very long tail; seen as a particularly bad omen.

36 **Franciscans** Lodovico and Gasparo belong to Francisco's faction, just as the Capuchins belonged to the Franciscans. Webster employs a double visual image; the two servants are marked out as Francisco's men, while the white hood of the Capuchins might suggest that he is a white devil.

37 **extreme unction** in Roman Catholicism, the last sacrament before death, which prepares the soul for salvation.

40 Perhaps the discovery space is used here.

54 **verge** technically, an area within 12 miles of a ruler's court.

57 **fed with poultry** it was believed that ulcers (called 'wolves') could be cured by 'feeding' them with meat or poultry applied to the skin.

85 sd **Bracciano, presented in a bed** There is a visual reminder of the bed that Zanche made on the floor for Bracciano and Vittoria (I.ii.214), and the bed present at their reconciliation (IV.ii.127).

87 **conveyed coin forth our territories** This was a serious offence under English law.

92–3 **the dusky raven/Chide blackness** The raven, black like hell, was seen as evil.

95 **quails** Quails were a delicacy, yet were believed to feed off poison; the term was also slang for promiscuous women.

96 **dog-fish** This is cheap food for the lower classes, and also a term of abuse.

103 **cod-piece** part of a man's clothing: the pouch covering the genitals. Bracciano thus links sex with hell.

107 **rose** Shoes were often decorated with a rosette.

108 **dispute** discuss.

109 **a rare linguist** eloquent.

117 **whipped** trimmed.

118 **rogue** i.e. Flamineo.
cuts capers dances.

121–2 **Her hair... orris powder** Vittoria's hair was probably sprinkled with powder (as was fashionable) for her wedding earlier.

123 sd *a crucifix* Perhaps this crucifix, used in a parody of a religious service, is another visual image of the corrupt Monticelso.

135 ***Attende Domine Brachiane*** Listen, Lord Bracciano.

140–52 Lord Bracciano, you used to be safe in war behind your shield; now you shall oppose this shield to your infernal enemy. / Once you prevailed in battle with your spear; now you shall wield this holy spear against the enemy of souls. / Listen, Lord Bracciano, if you now approve what has been done between us, turn your head to the right. / Rest assured, Lord Bracciano: think of the many good deeds to your credit – finally, remember that my soul is pledged for yours, if there should be any peril. / If you now also approve what has been done between us, turn your head to the left.

153–6 **Pray stand... not to hear** The conspirators send the witnesses away so that they can parody the sacrament by commending Bracciano's soul to the devil.

162 **conscience** inmost thoughts.

163 This is probably a contemporary reference to the Earl of Leicester who, it was asserted, in 1560 employed a real-life Doctor Julio to poison his wife; this failed, so he had her thrown downstairs so that he might be free to marry Elizabeth I.

165 **fine embroidered bottles** possibly glass or silver, decorated with gems.

179 **avoid** empty.

180 **true-love knot** This image ironically links Bracciano's death with his courtship of Vittoria and with Francisco's 'love' letter to her.

183 **woman-keeper** nurse.

184 **pesthouse** plague hospital.

185 **quaintlier** with more skill.

190 **more rivers to the city** This alludes to work on a system for supplying London with fresh water, begun in 1609.

192 **moonish** both changeable and insubstantial (the moon has no light of its own but reflects that of the sun).
shades ghosts.

196 **scores** obtains goods on credit.

200 **Machiavellian** See Interpretations pages 191 and 200.

204 **swallowed down a pound of saffron** Taken as a cordial, *saffron* was believed to create merriness, but to be fatal in large doses.

206 To teach those engaged in courtly intrigue that they are foolish to feel safe.

208 **descant** comment or discuss at length.

219 **Excellent Lodovico** Francisco is respectful of Lodovico.

223 **infernal** evil spirit. Zanche is seen as a spirit from hell as she is black; ironically, so is Francisco, in his disguise.

226 **passionately** with both passion and suffering.

230 **a sad dream** This parallels Vittoria telling Bracciano of her dream in I.ii.239, reminding the audience of the effects of their affair.

240 **Irish mantle** a plaid blanket, such as that worn by the Irish poor.

268-9 **make that... Ethiop white** This recalls the proverb, 'The leopard cannot change his spots'.

275-7 **like the partridge... the shame** Pliny, a Roman writer, recorded that quails and other fowl purged their systems by eating laurel. Francisco picks up this idea, and adds the image of the victor's laurel *crown*; he implies that by their own success they will remove evidence of the foul methods used in their *enterprise*.

Act V Scene IV

Flamineo's judgement fails as he is expelled by Giovanni; then, although frightened by the appearance of Bracciano's ghost, he presses ahead in trying to extort unpaid wages from his sister, as his lord's widow. In addition, his mother descends into madness as she tries to bury his brother, further alienating Flamineo.

   7 **dottrels** dolts, fools.
  10 **talons** Flamineo compares Giovanni to an eagle, a bird of prey; later he calls him *villainous* (32); how much trust does the audience now have in Flamineo's judgement?
  23 This is a more mature Giovanni, who will not tolerate Flamineo's insensitivity; Flamineo seems increasingly isolated after Bracciano's death.
  28 *Anacharsis* a sixth-century BCE Scythian prince famed for his wisdom. He is probably here confused with Anaxarchus, a philosopher from Thrace who remained calm, throwing out insults, as he was tortured by being pounded to death in a mortar.
  31 **cullis** thick broth.
  33 **In *decimo-sexto*** in miniature. *Decimo-sexto* is the page size in a very small book, where each page is one-sixteenth of a full sheet.
  43 **Castle Angelo... the tower yonder** Castel Sant'Angelo, an ancient round fortress in Rome which seems to remind Webster of the Tower of London (where James I imprisoned Arabella Stuart for her crimes related to love, see page 3).
43–4 **nothing about her** with no clothes on.
  50 **flaming firebrand** Flamineo is probably punning on his own name.
  51 **smoor** suffocate.
  60 **watching by the dead** Roman Catholic practice was to keep a candle-lit vigil over the dead, lasting all night.
  66 **traverse** curtain or screen.
67 sd **winding** wrapping in a winding-sheet ready for burial.
  68 **rosemary** herb associated with remembrance, used at funerals.
70–72 **the bays... from lightning** Bay leaves were given to poets and victorious generals; they were also thought to protect a person from lightning.

76 **flowers** Like the herbs, these may be imaginary, showing Cornelia's madness.

79 **rue** herb with bitter, strong-smelling leaves; the word also means 'regret'.

80 **Heart's-ease** wild pansy; also, comfort in affliction.

84–5 **Here's a white... be washed out?** Webster here seems to echo Shakespeare's Lady Macbeth trying to wash blood from her hands (*Macbeth* V.i), which some of the audience will recognize. It intensifies the feelings of guilt and horror here.

87 **strange** eerie.
cricket i'th' oven sings The sound of a cricket chirping in the house was sometimes considered a bad omen.

88–90 The (imaginary) spots she sees on Flamineo's hand indicate death because they suggest he has touched the *toad*, believed to be poisonous, which also has these spots.

91 This was a popular belief of the time.

96 sd *in several forms of distraction* Webster skilfully creates the sense of fragmentation as this society continues to fall apart; Cornelia's madness is at odds with her attempt to sing a melodious dirge.

97–100 The *robin* and the *wren* (his wife) were believed to cover the bodies of the unburied dead.

101 **dole** rites, ceremony.

105–6 Wolves were thought to dig up the bodies of murder victims, perhaps acting as God's revengers.

111 **this** the grave or wrapped body, which is all that is left of Marcello.

116 **without** unless.

123 **the maze of conscience** my conscience in a state of confusion. Does this awareness of sin allow Flamineo to reach heroic status?

125 sd *leather cassock* long, loose leather coat worn by soldiers, and traditionally by ghosts in revenge tragedy.
a pot of lily-flowers Lilies are traditionally linked to death. They are a visual emblem of beauty, combined with the *skull* as a sign of death.

126 Flamineo initially defies the ghost, as he has defied Bracciano at IV.ii.51.

127 **mockery** parody.

129–30 **yon starry gallery... cursèd dungeon**   This is a reference both
to the heaven of God and the 'heavens' of the theatre, and to
the *dungeon* of hell and the space below the stage.

135 **Not answer?**   The ghost's silence and mimed gestures heighten
Flamineo's increasingly frenzied manner.

145 **beyond melancholy**   beyond melancholic imaginings. Unlike
Francisco when he sees a ghost in IV.i, Flamineo believes in the
supernatural, which makes his suffering at his death worse.

152 **weapon**   Flamineo probably rushes off-stage brandishing a
dagger or sword.

Act V Scene V

This short scene allows a pause in the build-up of suspense.
Lodovico persuades Francisco the leave the scene to maintain his
appearance of innocence; Lodovico's concern for his lord's
spiritual as well as his physical well-being sharply contrasts with
Flamineo's attitude to Bracciano. Hortensio goes for help, leaving
the audience to wonder whether it will arrive in time.

1 sd   Perhaps the conspirators enter at one side of the stage, Hortensio
from another. Perhaps the conspirators are swaggering and
over-confident as they do not notice Hortensio – their first
mistake.

7 **To**   including.

12 **presently**   immediately.

Act V Scene VI

Webster skilfully controls the pace and mood of the long final
scene, to maximize the effect on the audience of the climactic
events. The bleak comedy of Flamineo's assumed death, the
dramatic heights where Flamineo and Vittoria reach moments of

heroic status, and then the final massacre culminate in a suspended ending when Giovanni appears. For the third time he has been shielded from horror; but the justice he metes out reverses the gentle justice at the start of the play. Lodovico has chivalrously defended his lord by preventing Monticelso from giving evidence in a future trial. What are the hopes for the future of this society? Has England anything to learn from the society of *The White Devil*?

1 **ruffin** devil. There is evidently little affection left between the siblings.

3 sd Zanche also rejects Flamineo and attempts to leave.

3 **blowze** red-faced woman; an insult.

5 **wormwood** herb with a bitter taste, therefore bitter to the soul.

6 **fury** Vittoria turns Flamineo's insult to Cornelia (I.ii.280) against him as the play begins to come full circle.

13–14 **that portion... his brother** This is a reference to Genesis 4:14: 'Behold, thou hast driven me out this day from the face of the earth; and from thy face shall I be hid; and I shall be a fugitive and a vagabond in the earth.' See Note to III.iii.40–41.

20 **case of jewels** Flamineo ironically reworks the jewel image (I.ii.234) to refer to pistols.

24 **dead lift** emergency, with a double-meaning on 'dead'.

33–7 This is possibly a reference to the story that King Herod ordered that his wife be killed on his death.

47–9 **This is my... any's bidding** There is an echo here of Vittoria's defiant words at her trial (III.ii.139–40).

54–5 The exchange between Vittoria and Zanche here and the aside at 61 heighten the tension of the scene while implying that they are plotting.

56–8 **turn your body... slaughter house?** Killing the body by suicide also murders the soul, because suicide is a sin.

59–61 **other sins... carouse it off** other sins taste sweet as if covered in sugar (*candied o'er*), but despair tastes bitter and is poisonous (like *stibium*), yet we drink it greedily.

65 **winter plums** plums that are cold and unnatural (unseasonal) – like bullets.

68 **grammatical** formal, empty of meaning.

71 **exclamation** rhetorical declaration.

84 The *flaming* or sacred *heart* on an *altar* is an image of God's presence, but there is a suggestion of destructive and sinful passion here, as in 105 below.

93 **taster** one who tastes a ruler's food to test for poison.

104 **cupping-glasses** glass vessels applied to the skin in medical treatments to draw blood to the surface.

107–8 **Lucian, thy ridiculous purgatory** classical Greek writer who presented purgatory as a place where monarchs and rulers do menial chores. These tasks are ironically relevant to what each did in life.

109 **tagging points** drawing together the laces that fastened Elizabethan garments.

111 **crying 'garlic'** offering garlic for sale in the street.

112 **lists** strips of cloth.
King Pepin King of the Franks in the eighth century, and father of Charlemagne. His name suggests 'pippin' (a type of apple).

128 **Styx** a river in the Greek underworld, upon which the gods swore their oaths.

134 **springe** trap for catching small animals and birds.

135 Even the cunning fox often ends up dead without his tail (kept as a trophy by hunters).

136 **braches** bitches.

144 **Scotch holy bread** sheep's liver.

146–7 **drive a stake/Through thy body** This was the usual treatment of suicide victims' bodies.

150 **doubled all your reaches** outwitted all your plots.

150 sd Is Webster here reminding the audience that all stage deaths are artificial?

155–7 **O men... howling wives** There is an echo here of Bracciano's words at his death (V.iii.35–6).

161 **Artillery Yard** an area used for military practice in Bishopsgate, East London.

165 **Hypermnestra** the youngest of the 50 daughters of Danaus. According to Ovid's *Heroides*, she was the only one of the 50 who refused to kill her husband.

167–8 **horse-leeches** blood-suckers.

169 **instruments** weapons. Zanche and Vittoria are regarded as two

instruments of death.

171 **masque** a performance or entertainment that is often a device in revenge tragedy for carrying out the final murders.
matachin dance using swords.

186–8 **I have seen... fierce sparrow-hawk** Vittoria uses the metaphor of the *blackbird* to say that she would rather trust her natural enemies than be left to the mercy of a predator of her own kind – her brother.

193 **centre** heart or soul.

194 **hangman** executioner.

208 **glorious** vainglorious, proud.

215 **ask forgiveness** Executioners conventionally asked forgiveness from the condemned person before carrying out the sentence.

216 **train** comet's tail. He is referring to her servant, Zanche.

226 **Conceit** imagination.

227 This is an echo of Vittoria's refusal to weep at her trial (III.ii.285).

230 **red** Zanche's blood, courage and passion are red, although her skin is black.

231 **falling sickness** epilepsy, with a punning reference to death.

237 **Toledo** a finely made and strong sword.
fox a kind of sword bearing the figure of a wolf (often mistaken for a fox).

238 **cutler** one who makes or sells knives and other cutting tools.

240 **tent** keep (a wound) open for cleaning. There is a pun on 'tend'.

242–3 **O my greatest... pays for't** All the connotations of the word *blood* are gathered here.

248 But fortunately they met with silence (their vices were not discovered).

256 **the bottom** death, extending the image of *a ship in a black storm* (250).

260–62 **No, at myself... with knowledge** Flamineo says that his knowledge is confined to his own experience, and that a greater knowledge – of matters related to heaven or hell – lies outside the scope of human intelligence.

268 **lions i'th' Tower** There was a small zoo at the Tower of London.

269 **Candlemas** feast day held on 2 February. It was said that sunshine on that day meant severe weather later.

275 **trade** business, profession. Perhaps there is the hint of an acknowledgement by Flamineo that he, like many people, has

been obsessed with acquiring money.

276 **where** whereas.

278 **Strike, thunder** Conventionally, the death of a great man was accompanied by thunder; perhaps this is also Webster making a joke about stage effects.

281 **constantly** bravely or determinedly.

284 **Keep back the Prince!** The English Ambassador shields Giovanni from the horrors; he is protected for the final time in the play, suggesting once more his youth and inexperience.

299 **rest** peace of mind, with a pun on 'the rest of my story'.

300 **limned** drew, painted. With this confession Lodovico takes all the blame upon himself rather than involving Francisco. What is the effect of this?

night-piece picture of a scene set at night time (by extension, a scene of evil). So Lodovico brings the play full circle, having introduced many of the issues for the audience in I.i.

Epilogue

2 These things will be our reward, if I have pleased you (a quotation from Martial, see Note to 'To the Reader', 3).

3 **action** acting.

5 **quality** profession.

5–6 **to make nature a monster** to distort natural aspects through exaggeration.

9 **Master Perkins** Richard Perkins, a member of the Queen's Men. It is usually assumed that he played Flamineo in the first production. Calling him *friend*, Webster praises his actions at *both the beginning and end* of the play, which might rather suggest that he played Lodovico; but perhaps Webster's meaning is that his great acting skills illuminated the play from start to finish.

Interpretations

Webster's use of sources

As described on page 9, Webster's drama is based quite extensively on historical events, making it partly a history play. It is a sensational story involving midnight assignations and conspiracies, elopements and flight, imprisonment and ruthless murders. Much of the criticism of Webster as 'sensationalist' can therefore be referred to the facts as he found them. Webster changed the names slightly, suggested that Vittoria may have been involved in the murder of her first husband, developed the role of her brother Flamineo, and greatly elaborated the role of Isabella's brother, Francisco. He added most of the so-called 'Gothic' elements, such as the ghosts and the madness of Bracciano and Cornelia. Of course, he created all of the dialogue and shaped the drama both to offer a critique of contemporary society and to raise those universal issues connected with tragedy as a genre.

When studying a seventeenth-century text it is important to think about how Webster's contemporary audience might have viewed the play, and also to explore what the text might offer to audiences of other periods, including your own. An example of differing responses can be seen in attitudes to Bracciano's marriage to Vittoria. While the Jacobean audience would have felt some sympathy for him, they would have had serious doubts about his wisdom, as a powerful ruler, in infringing the rules of 'degree' or social order by marrying a woman beneath him in class. To a modern audience, this class difference might not matter, if his great passion for her were believed to be genuine.

The concept of revenge, too, offered particular resonances to a Jacobean audience. Religious and state law forbade violent revenge, and James I banned private duelling because too many young courtiers were being killed in this way. Yet social codes of honour supported the idea of a man taking revenge on behalf of a relative or friend who could not defend himself, or herself. It would have been a case of the head versus the heart; as a compromise, in a play it was expected that the revenger himself would die in the name of justice by the end. *The White Devil* raises questions concerning Francisco: should he at least have halted his revenge once Bracciano was dead? Furthermore, he himself does not die.

The interpretation of this play, as with any work of art, does not rely solely on the author; every spectator and reader brings an individual reading that extends the author's original purposes. When new readings arise that are relevant to successive periods of history, a text may be described as universal; such is the case with *The White Devil*.

Webster's worldview in *The White Devil*

The issues that Webster raises about the society presented in *The White Devil* fall generally into two interrelated categories: matters of identity and matters of integrity. The first relates to the social, economic and political pressures that shape the life of every character in the play. The second moves inward; in Webster's tragedy the concept of integrity implies fulfilling one's personal potential while adhering to a principled moral code, such as Christianity. In this play he questions whether a Vittoria or a Flamineo can achieve this integrity, rather than merely submitting to the social roles that are thrust upon them.

As early as the first scene of the play, Webster makes clear that this society rests on a system of patronage governed by corrupt and absolute leaders, both of State and Church. It quickly becomes apparent that there is no justice, no rule of law, no spiritual guidance and no system for rewarding merit. Bracciano and Francisco, the two dukes, act entirely out of self-interest; Isabella and Camillo are quickly murdered to satisfy the former's lust. Francisco, concerned for his nephew Giovanni's inheritance, orders two more murders, and a further three killings occur as a result. The sinful head of the Church, the cardinal Monticelso, also seems to be concerned with wealth and family 'honour' in the corrupt trial to which he submits Vittoria, and his excessive zeal suggests the far-reaching power of the Church. There can be no appeal for justice to these authority figures, who uphold no recognizable moral code. Corruption is evident everywhere.

Webster shows the ways in which this corruption spreads through all of society. Flamineo reveals (I.ii.327–344) that he cannot fulfil his potential and achieve an identity; instead he must be a puppet in the hands of the powerful. Flamineo represents an entire social group, the less privileged, just as Vittoria represents powerless women; the play raises the question of whether it is the system of patronage itself that is corrupt rather than only the rulers. The audience is invited to consider the problems revealed and think about what the alternatives might be. Perhaps James I will be able to create an alternative in his English court? (See page 231 below.)

Activity

Explore the ways in which Webster presents the problem of corruption spreading through society in *The White Devil*.

Discussion

Webster shows how corruption spreads from the rulers to extend throughout society as a whole. The actions of the great men are seen to be corrupting as they force the less privileged to serve them, which inevitably involves committing evil deeds. This is evident in the relationships between Bracciano and Flamineo, and Francisco and Lodovico. Flamineo first prostitutes his sister (I.ii) then murders Camillo (II.ii). Lodovico is involved in four murders (V.iii, V.vi).

Webster develops this concept most clearly through his use of imagery, notably that related to poison, sickness, witchcraft and the black arts. Through these images he externalizes the inner corruption of this society, presenting it for all to see and hear. References to poison and infections are widespread; for example, in the opening scene Gasparo uses the image of dangerous food causing sickness (I.i.15–16). Isabella refers to her husband's illicit love, hoping to *charm his poison* and cure him from his *infected straying* (II.i.16–17).

Webster parallels this imagery with the literal use of poison as a murder weapon in Isabella's fatal kiss, and Bracciano's death; imagery and dramatic action work together. Likewise, allusions to witchcraft are underlined by its presentation onstage in the two dumb-shows.

It might be helpful to make lists of the types of imagery used, and note how they interlink to present a vision of a poisoned, corrupt and evil society.

Characterization

In I.ii, the audience is amused by Flamineo's gulling of Camillo. As part of his strategy he offers a significant image: *I have seen a pair of spectacles fashioned with such perspective art that, lay down but one twelvepence o'th' board, 'twill appear as if there were twenty* (I.ii.102–105).

This is a concise description of Webster's dramatic technique, as characters, situations and issues are all shown from multiple perspectives. Every character is ambiguous, contradictory and elusive; to make any judgement the audience must hold together all of the different aspects that are revealed. Webster achieves such complexity by the use of framing devices, repetition, echoes and stage management, which come together in a cumulative scheme. As in the society of *The White Devil* itself, all judgements are relative, perhaps seemingly incoherent.

A second aspect of Webster's method is that he allows us limited, if any, access to the minds of his characters, unlike the access we have to the thoughts and feeling of a Shakespearean tragic hero. Webster's aim is different. His characters constantly change along with their circumstances, and he explores the effects of certain inescapable and often crushing social forces on nobles and on their less privileged subjects.

Flamineo

Flamineo is probably the leading character in *The White Devil*, and is one of the four Machiavellian characters. ('Machiavellian' means related to the ideas of Niccolò Machiavelli, 1469–1527, an Italian politician who advocated the cynical use of ruthless tactics to gain and hold power.) From Lodovico's comments at the beginning of the play about *Courtly reward, /And punishment!* (I.i.3–4), the audience are aware that Flamineo will be forced into dependency on Bracciano; Webster has thus provided a perspective from which to assess both characters.

Flamineo's character is quickly established as a crafty manipulator in his gulling of Camillo; he is a cunning and able servant of Bracciano, and is ruthless and self-seeking enough to encourage the sexual exploitation of his sister, presumably hitherto an innocent woman. His first soliloquy reveals his links with evil and his dramatic role (I.ii.358–366). He relishes his role as a Machiavel – *We are engaged to mischief and must on* – and is able to imitate *The subtle foldings of a winter's snake*. Webster has placed Flamineo, through this analogy, as the snake in the Garden of Eden, as the stage villain linked to hell, as a malcontent and a commentator who connects with the audience. Like Lodovico, he is a cynical observer, conscience-free, completely absorbed in self-interest.

But Webster has complicated this introduction to Flamineo through the exchanges with his mother, Cornelia, where the writer effectively pleads the malcontent's case, beginning with the arresting question: *Pray what means have you/To keep me from the galleys, or the gallows?* (I.ii.327–328). The rhythm of this speech, the run-on lines, the rhetorical questions, the pauses and the elisions establish Flamineo's self-control and persuasive powers, but the speech also sums up many of the economic, social and political difficulties that young men like Flamineo face. Humiliated by his poverty while at university, but educated and intelligent, he can find no honest place in this corrupt society. He is forced to court the favour of a 'great' man. Despite the shocking contempt Flamineo shows for family and religion, Webster has balanced the weight of our judgement: yes, Flamineo is indeed the stage and court villain, but what else is open to him?

In the first part of *The White Devil* Flamineo is in the ascendant, but his fortunes change when he is *committed* (II.ii.47–48) with Marcello for Camillo's death. Webster uses a parallel to suggest that his fortunes are not secure in the trial scene: both men are bailed by the court, but while Francisco stands as surety for Marcello (III.ii.256), Flamineo has to speak for himself and fears that he is being condemned along with Vittoria as her *bawd* (III.ii.265–266). In a later parallel, when he has killed his brother, Bracciano grants him only a conditional *lease of... life*, refusing him a pardon (V.ii.76–79), whereas Francisco secures the murderer Lodovico a pardon (III.iii.100–102).

In the curious scene between Flamineo and Lodovico (III.iii.68ff), Webster invites his audience to consider Flamineo's status at this point in the play. Mistrustful and isolated, he sounds out Lodovico, and has every reason to do so. His patron, Bracciano, appears to have made peace with Francisco and Monticelso (*You have charmed me*, II.i.145). Perhaps his offer to *join housekeeping* (III.iii.77) with Lodovico indicates his loss of social, political and economic status. More than this, perhaps Webster uses the feigned madness in this scene with irony. A madman has no grasp on his surroundings; similarly, Flamineo is losing both this position and his judgement.

Nevertheless, Flamineo continues to voice his acute and accurate perceptions of society: *As in this world there are degrees of evils,/So in this world there are degrees of devils* (IV.ii.57–58).

Here the *degree* necessary for order, normally indicating unalterable social ranking, is inverted to suggest rankings in hell; or could it be that, at the climax of events, Webster presents the society of the play as hell itself? One reading of the last act supports this idea.

Flamineo becomes increasingly isolated: he admits the truth of his relationship with Zanche (V.i.156ff); he has killed his brother (V.ii) and will drive his mother to madness (V.iv); he is ejected from court by Giovanni (V.iv.34–36). He finally realizes the extent of his own decline (*I am falling to pieces already*, V.iv.27), and his rejection by his sister Vittoria (V.vi.13ff) completes his isolation.

However, Webster does not leave matters here as a warning about the dangers of living an evil life. Instead, he adds a fresh dimension to the audience's perception of Flamineo and allows him to achieve, even if only momentarily, tragic status. In response to Cornelia's madness, Webster introduces a new, Christian register, as the villain admits to feeling *Compassion* and *the maze of conscience* (V.iv.115ff). His soliloquy here is persuasive, and the appearance of Bracciano's ghost triggers thoughts about his own imminent death. He shows courage and resolve: *I do dare my fate/To do its worst* (V.iv.145–146).

Now the audience wait to see this fate. Flamineo meets his death with a courage that appeals to the audience, and reconciling himself to his sister (V.vi.243–244), he finds some peace and self-knowledge: *'Tis well yet there's some goodness in my death,/My life was a black charnel... This busy trade of life appears most vain* (V.vi.271–275).

Webster thus has Flamineo taking his leave with a question hanging in the air: what is the *goodness* in his death? There are several possible interpretations: his death will cure society of one source of evil; his death has allowed him a final 'honest' vision; and as a metatheatrical device (see page 220), the dying revenger comes out of role to remind the audience that the conventions of revenge tragedy have been fulfilled as he dies for transgressing moral laws. Thus Webster unifies all Flamineo's social and dramatic functions; he has indeed demonstrated that this corrupt society has no honourable place for him, as he explained to Cornelia in I.ii.327ff.

Vittoria

In his presentation of Vittoria, as with all the female characters in *The White Devil*, Webster shows that in this society women can only define themselves through men; it is their only route to some limited power. Vittoria is at the height of her power at the beginning of the play, because she has not yet submitted to Bracciano's passion for her; Lodovico claims she *might have got my pardon/For one kiss to the duke* (I.i.43 44). Whether through marriage or more illicit means, women's sexuality is their only means of social mobility. Vittoria is therefore a representative character, but she is also individual in her role in the play.

These considerations make the outcome of Bracciano's pursuit of her seem inevitable, so Webster leaves the audience free to consider the nuances of Vittoria's responses and what they reveal about her character. Vittoria accepts Bracciano's advances, skilfully side-stepping the lewd wordplay about the *jewel* (I.ii.231ff), by speaking about her dream. Her story of meeting Camillo and Isabella in the churchyard is full of ambiguity, so the audience cannot know Vittoria's intentions, but the dream clearly links her to murder, as Flamineo remarks (lines 267–278), and this conflicts with the apparent passiveness of her surrender to Bracciano.

Bracciano's language of courtly love in this scene suggests that his is a whole-hearted and passionate love, no mere exercise in lust, which makes Flamineo's crude commentary and the interruption of Cornelia's conventional rant of condemnation seem almost irrelevant. Nevertheless Cornelia's words terrify both Bracciano and his mistress. Through her Webster reminds the audience that there are other perspectives on this relationship, which may reflect very ironically on the duke's vow to *protect* the object of his passion (line 270).

As Vittoria has significant involvement in only four scenes, and in each she is presented with different characteristics, she offers a great challenge to both audience and actor. Her next appearance is in the powerful 'arraignment' or 'trial' scene. Webster has carefully manoeuvred audience responses beforehand, as Vittoria has been excluded from the dumb-shows of the two murders, so there is doubt about her involvement. Vittoria has been targeted by her own brother, acting as *pander* (I.ii.227); by the powerful Bracciano, making her an offer she hardly dares refuse; and Francisco and Monticelso have conspired to sacrifice her in their larger game against Bracciano. To them she is expendable: *There's small pity in't* (II.i.393). The brief comedy at the beginning of the trial scene over the Lawyer's use of language suggests that the trial will be a mockery; as with Bracciano's pursuit of Vittoria, the audience can foretell the outcome, but will be absorbed in other considerations.

The trial reveals the vulnerable position of a woman in this society; she is seen simply as a commodity that necessarily belongs to some man or other, as when Monticelso asserts that Camillo *bought you of your father*, insultingly adding that the *ware* he bought was *light* (III.ii.239–243). Webster has positioned the audience to sympathize with Vittoria, and the proceedings support this sympathy (see pages 237–238 below). Sympathy for Vittoria conflicts with the logic of the play; it is clear that she does indeed correspond to the men's definition of a whore, but it is the powerful males who alienate the audience with their perversion of justice, the inequality of treatment they mete out, their hypocrisy and their contempt for their subjects. Vittoria is presented as the helpless, if not innocent, victim.

Perhaps to underline the injustice she is suffering at the hands of corrupt men, Webster involves the audience by giving Vittoria a direct appeal to them. She refuses to accept the use of Latin because *amongst this auditory/Which come to hear my cause, the half or more/May be ignorant in't* (III.ii.16–18). Clearly this refers to the theatre audience, in the Red Bull, as well as the notional audience within the trial scene. Vittoria goes further and makes a direct appeal for a more just verdict than she knows she will receive onstage; all those present should become engaged with the concept of justice: *All this assembly/Shall hear what you can charge me with* (III.ii.20–21).

The audience are aware that while Bracciano is treated courteously, Vittoria must accept her unjust punishment. When in Vittoria's next big scene he turns on her with jealousy, it is no surprise that she should reject her lover. The end of the play is foreshadowed when she adopts a Christian register: *and now I'll go/Weeping to heaven on crutches* (IV.ii.121–122). Despite the outcome of this scene, when she tacitly agrees to elope, Webster has created a moral complexity which makes her character in the last act credible.

Although Vittoria's procession over the stage as a bride and duchess is full of irony, the audience notice at the same time that the ambassadors, who should be models of correctness and morality, willingly attend the wedding of a whore to a murderer; Vittoria is inextricably bound up in this society. The sight of her trampling, with Zanche, on her brother's supposedly dying body in V.vi gives the audience a visual image of women taking revenge for being metaphorically trampled underfoot by powerful and ruthless men. In this moment, when she feels freed at last from dependency on any male figure, do the audience see a different Vittoria?

She reaches tragic status at moments before her death, achieving the self-knowledge essential for a tragic heroine; she fully understands how this society works. On Bracciano's death she is aware that she is *lost forever* (V.iii.34), and more importantly, she understands that this society is *hell* (V.iii.186). By the end of the play she has a clear grasp of the condition in which it leaves its victims:

> O the cursed devil…
> Makes us forsake that which was made for man,
> The world, to sink to that was made for devils,
> Eternal darkness.

> (V.vi.58–64)

The last step in achieving tragic status is the admission of her own culpability: *O my greatest sin lay in my blood;/Now my blood pays for't* (V.vi.242–243).

It has often been said that Webster's characters are to be judged by the way they die; like Flamineo, Vittoria dies a noble death with self-knowledge and untainted honesty. Is this her tragic moment? Webster does not sentimentalize her death, however, as she dies not knowing where her soul, *like to a ship in a black storm* (V.vi.250), is to go after death. In this shipwreck analogy Webster offers a striking image of an individual's life in this society: a lonely, dangerous and directionless one. The cost is both spiritual and physical.

Bracciano

Bracciano is the least complicated of the leading characters, for he is no clever Machiavellian, but his presentation is also ambiguous. Webster uses Lodovico's words in the first scene to convey Bracciano's power, so it is striking that at his first entrance this duke describes himself as *Quite lost, Flamineo* (I.ii.3). Gradually meanings emerge; he is accustomed to Flamineo performing services for him to repay patronage – he is not used to having to ask for favours; and most significantly, these words are prophetic about the passion that will destroy him and many other people. Flamineo is expendable once the duke has Vittoria.

In this scene Bracciano is portrayed as the courtly lover with a grand passion who will do anything for his lady, and whose love will control his life. This is the devoted lover whom the audience will see in the *Barriers* at his wedding in Act V. Webster here offers a vision of a man playing the role of a medieval chivalric knight, in line with his courtly professions of love, made all the more intense by the plot to poison his chivalric armour. Moreover, in contrast to the perverted sexuality of Monticelso (evident in the speech in which he defines 'whore', III.ii.79ff), and to the icy Francisco's apparent lack of sexuality, Webster makes this quality attractive.

The movable face-protector of the chivalric knight's helmet proves
Bracciano's undoing

Yet there are of course contrasts in Bracciano's character. He
is ruthless in his exploitation of personal power, as seen in the
neglect of his son Giovanni, the cruel treatment of Isabella, and
the brazenness of his assumption that his power exceeds that of
State or Church law as he performs his own divorce: *And this
divorce shall be as truly kept, /As if the judge had doomed it*
(II.i.195–196).

Webster underlines his cruelty with the image of Isabella's last
attempt to kiss him (see the stage direction at II.i.162). The image
of the thwarted final kiss recurs throughout the play. Isabella dies
kissing Bracciano's picture, as shown in the dumb-show at
II.ii.23; Giovanni is prevented from kissing his dead mother
(III.ii.336), and finally Bracciano cannot kiss goodbye to Vittoria
for fear of spreading the poison to her (V.iii.26).

The actions of a great man affect all those dependent on him,
and determine the course of history for the State. Webster shows
the audience the very real threat of interstate war, of which

Francisco, Monticelso and Isabella are aware; Francisco details the costs of war at IV.i.5–11.

In the last act Webster tips the balance of sympathy in favour of Bracciano again as he dies a dreadful, drawn-out death, fully aware of the fate of the great man: *horror waits on princes* (V.iii.34). He is also shown to be concerned for Vittoria's and Giovanni's safety. Yet he is allowed no dignity in death. Flamineo, hearing of his death agonies, sees only financial gain from his death (V.iii.84), and the killers taunt him with their parody of religious rites, and gibe at him cruelly. His last words testify to his earthly love as he calls for Vittoria – there is no spiritual dimension.

Webster uses a visual pun to enlist sympathy for the dying man; his killers wear the garments of Capuchin monks, an austere order of Franciscans. They are marked out as Francisco's men, presenting a physical image of his role in Bracciano's death, which has gone far beyond the actions of a 'just' revenger. The audience's final censure is drawn away from Bracciano's black deeds to contemplate the cunning and deadly power of the cold Duke of Florence.

Activity

Consider Webster's presentation of the ironic effects of Bracciano's promise to protect Vittoria in I.ii.270–273.

Discussion

Webster uses irony as a dominant method of creating meanings; he employs different types of irony through language, actions and echoes that reverberate throughout *The White Devil*.

Bracciano promises the yielding Vittoria that she is *lodged within his arms who shall protect you* and that he will *seat you above law and above scandal* (I.ii.270, 273). An attentive audience will question what sort of man the duke is – his arrogance is evident, for is any man above the law? Can society tolerate the wilful actions of a tyrannical ruler who allows himself to be ruled by sexual desire?

Webster repeatedly makes clear the irony of this promise as

subsequent events unfold. A series of murders bring about social anarchy, the end of Bracciano's rule, and death for all those associated with him.

While Webster initially invites sympathy for the lovers by contrast with the foolish husband Camillo, and through the courtly terms in which Bracciano declares his love, nevertheless the duke falls short of his own ideals. He deserts Vittoria three times: almost immediately when he flees from Cornelia's wrath to go *to bed* (I.ii.315); next, at the trial, when he abandons Vittoria to her fate (III.ii.180); finally, in his attack on her integrity at IV.ii.71. He may love her, as his calling for her with his dying words suggests (V.iii.173–4), but Webster makes it plain that such a love could never prosper.

Francisco

Francisco is probably the most deadly of the three powerful men in the play, possessing a sharp mind, an icy callousness and an indifference to anybody of lower status, which includes all women. Webster presents Francisco as the supreme Machiavel, manipulating and corrupting others while keeping his own hands clean. His dramatic role is that of the revenger, but he is noteworthy for his cruelty and his indifference to law and justice.

Webster initially presents Francisco as the wronged brother of Isabella, although his ruthlessness in relation to his own sister is revealed when he states that he would rather have *given/Both her white hands to death* (II.i.63–64) than to an adulterous Bracciano. Is his concern simply social, for the 'honour' of the family name? On the other hand Francisco is shown to be a caring uncle to Giovanni at the beginning of this scene, in contrast to his negligent father. Generally the audience will feel wary of this powerful leader who quickly threatens Bracciano with war (line 72). He regards Vittoria as entirely expendable (lines 393–395) even before his sister's death; when the news of this reaches him, our perspective on Francisco incorporates all that we expect from the genre of revenge tragedy.

During the trial scene (III.ii), Francisco is presented in contrast to Monticelso; he is more silent, controlled and cunning. It is no surprise that he gets rid of the lawyer pleading against Vittoria, as if agreeing to her own request, because that leaves her to the mercy of Monticelso. His comments are terse, giving nothing of himself away when he intervenes briefly to clarify accounts of events. Monticelso plays the dominant role in this first wave of the revenge plot, at this stage the social revenge of shaming; after the trial, Francisco is responsible for the retributory and bloody revenge of Act V.

Monticelso's intemperate rage against Vittoria emphasizes the apparent stillness and quietness of Francisco, and the latter's reception of the news of Isabella's death is similarly misleading. To heighten the pathos, Webster makes the innocent Giovanni the messenger of death, so Francisco's first response is gentle, and even appeals to religion (III.ii.329). Can his quiet, grief-stricken demeanour be genuine?

> **Believe me, I am nothing but her grave,**
> **And I shall keep her blessèd memory**
> **Longer than thousand epitaphs.**

> (III.ii.343–5)

Webster toys with his audience's expectations when the plotters discuss revenge in IV.i. Initially Francisco's calmness is sustained when he rejects the idea of war, but Monticelso's register is heightened into the heroic terms of *th'bloody audit, and the fatal gripe* (IV.i.19). The audience will recognize immediately that this is the language of revenge drama, and there will be some sympathy for Francisco's situation when he responds with *Free me, my innocence, from treacherous acts*. But does he really have a claim to *innocence* at this point? We have seen the way the two men conspired to punish Vittoria. And is it merely the possible retribution for the *treacherous acts* that is feared? The fact that it is not principles that cause him hesitation is made clear with his eagerness to see and use Monticelso's *black book*, and above all with his resolution not to trust Monticelso, but to pursue his own *plots* (IV.i.38–42).

The audience will therefore be attentive to Francisco's great revenge soliloquy (IV.i.74–123, 128–136). Webster presents him in conventional revenger terms, and then undermines this; Francisco coolly examines *a list of murderers,/Agents for any villainy* (lines 86–87). He has no intention of acting himself, but through *Agents*. It is impossible to see this as honourable.

As in other revenge plays including *Hamlet*, the victim's ghost appears to spur on the revenger; but when he sees Isabella's ghost, Francisco does not indulge in metaphysical speculation – he is sure that the apparition comes from the power of his own imagination. For him, there is no world other than his own. Webster completes the distancing that the audience will feel from Francisco when he makes it clear that he is playing a role: *Come, to this weighty business./My tragedy must have some idle mirth in't* (lines 115–116). He goes on to write a letter in the role of Vittoria's lover.

Francisco efficiently manipulates Lodovico into doing his dirty deeds; he flatters his servant profusely, saying *Noble friend, /Our danger shall be 'like in this design* (IV.iii.78–79). Most certainly their danger is not alike.

Webster presents the outcome of his cold and calculating planning in the last act. Perhaps the masterstroke is the chosen disguise as Capuchin Franciscans. The conspirators are visual emblems of Francisco's extreme cunning; they remind the audience that he is the driving force behind the plotting, even though he is likely to go unpunished and, with Bracciano's death, to become more powerful than ever. At the end of the play we are left with the question of how the young and inexperienced Giovanni can have a chance of independence in the face of such masterly control.

Monticelso

Monticelso, the third powerful man of the play, is again presented in an ambiguous way, finally leaving the audience with a puzzle. As pope he becomes leader of the Church; as a man he is seen to be corrupt. Dramatically, he is the second revenger; thematically, through him Webster raises many issues such as the corruption of justice and the relationship between Church and State.

Initially Monticelso is presented as the man of God, counselling Bracciano in Christian terms: *When you awake from this lascivious dream,/Repentance then will follow* (II.i.34–35). Bracciano, listening to him, promises to remain *As silent as i'th' church* (II.i.24). In the same scene he becomes peacemaker, avoiding war between the two dukes; no doubt an audience would approve of this. But this is a long scene, and Webster changes the audience's perceptions when the two plotters are alone onstage. Masks are dropped; Monticelso reveals his cunning in having pre-planned Camillo's commission in order to leave Bracciano exposed to temptation (II.i.374–376). With his naming of Lodovico in the following lines it is as if he foresees the whole revenge conspiracy.

So it seems that Monticelso is cunning, but is he corrupt? In a moment of self-revelation the cardinal admits that his actions may be seen as *dishonourable* (388). Webster makes it plain that while Monticelso is aware of a moral code, he chooses to flout it: *For my revenge I'd stake a brother's life* (390).

Monticelso reveals far more of himself in the trial scene. He has admitted to Francisco in the previous scene (III.i.4–5) that the murder charge against Vittoria is unlikely to succeed, but he introduces it at her trial, evidently in order to make the lesser charge of being a whore seem more convincing. The trial scene reveals his utter contempt for the law as he is both prosecutor and judge; the overblown rhetoric of his speech beginning *Shall I expound whore to you?* (III.ii.79) alienates the audience, insofar as it conflicts with their sympathy for Vittoria, and they reject its misogyny. He further condemns himself when he shows that his concern is for his kinsman's financial loss in marrying Vittoria (III.ii.240–243).

Since the trial scene has revealed that both State law and Church law are corrupt, the audience will be prepared to scrutinize proceedings at the papal election (IV.iii) carefully and critically. Webster uses Lodovico to commentate on the proceedings (which would be exotic and rather suspect to a Protestant English audience) and to play a peripheral role in them; thus a murderer takes part in the election of the head of the Church.

On Monticelso's last appearance in the play, he surprisingly warns Lodovico against *that cruel devil*, revenge (IV.iii.128). He seems perfectly well aware of the conspiracy when he lends the *black book* to Francisco, but perhaps he is similar to Francisco in that he will promote unlawful and sinful revenge, as long as his name is not connected with the scheme. After this, Monticelso is absent from the play.

Or is he? As both cardinal and pope he would wear a crucifix around his neck. On his first public appearance after his election he offers a blessing, during which he would make the sign of the cross over the heads of those present. The crucifix has become a symbol of his identity. Is it possible that, as with Francisco, Webster presents a visual and verbal symbol of his presence as revenge is taken in the final act? Cornelia's broken crucifix (see V.ii.10–13) would make an ideal image of a man of God 'broken' by corruption, as would the crucifix the murderers use in the black parody of religious rites at Bracciano's death (V.iii.136ff), again a most fitting link. Perhaps the presence of the crucifix serves to remind the audience of Monticelso as the second source of power, at the head of the Church.

Giovanni

Like Vittoria, Giovanni has four major scenes and each fulfils different dramatic and thematic functions.

His first appearance is an important moment because of the dramatic context: it is immediately after Bracciano's successful wooing of Vittoria, and prior to his divorce from Isabella (II.i). As an innocent child he is used as a measure of his father's selfishness and lack of responsibility. He is bidden to go away, just like his mother; as a woman she has no rights in the public sphere, but must perform her duties in the domestic and dynastic sphere, and Giovanni's existence shows that she has performed her prime duty in producing a son to guarantee the lineage. When he re-enters this scene, it is as the instrument of peace between the warring dukes.

Giovanni's next appearance is in the first dumb-show, where he witnesses, and expresses sorrow at, his mother's death; he is a visual image of the damage these corrupt great men can inflict on the young and the innocent, qualities that cannot survive in this society.

This is reinforced immediately after the trial scene by highlighting Giovanni's lack of understanding about the *cruel fold of lead* (III.ii.335) and the denial of the farewell kiss for his mother. The pathos of his innocent enquiries about the process of death is used to heighten the horror of the murder. He has to be protected from the truth. When his father is poisoned he is, once more, sent away; thus he is prevented from showing his love for his father, at the same time as being protected from the horrors of the scene (V.iii.15–16).

He appears much more adult when he will not tolerate the offensive comments offered by the cynical Flamineo and tells him: *Study your prayers, sir, and be penitent* (V.iv.23). This Christian register suggests moral probity; importantly this is his last appearance before the conclusion of the play.

His final appearance at the end of V.vi causes dispute. What are Webster's purposes?

The audience has seen only snapshots of the young prince, and he is very young; there is not much evidence for making a judgement about his personality. Flamineo's opinion is that his *talons… will grow out in time* (V.iv.10), and *He hath his uncle's villainous look already* (V.iv.32).

At the end of the play, Giovanni is initially, for the third time, protected from danger and horror as the English Ambassador shields him from the shooting. However, Giovanni sounds stern: *Away with them to prison, and to torture* (V.vi.294). The fact that Lodovico is threatened with this treatment takes us full circle, to the first scene of the play where Gasparo says that Lodovico's banishment by the State is a *gentle penance* (I.i.36). Is Giovanni repudiating this *gentle* treatment for a murderer, and if so does the play support his apparent harshness?

Giovanni continues to speak in a Christian, moral register, invoking *heaven* as well as *justice* (V.vi.295–296). But Webster has shown both concepts to be devalued in the world of the play. There has been no serious contemplation of a Christian scheme of salvation, and the head of the Church has shown himself to be capable of evil. We have seen the rigged 'justice' of the trial, and the violent 'justice' of revenge-gone-mad; murderers have been pardoned, and innocents made to suffer.

On the practical level of administering justice, can we expect Giovanni to take the word of a murderous servant against an uncle whom the audience have seen to be kind to him and to have guided him? In any case, how could Francisco or Monticelso be placed on trial? Who could give evidence against them? Lodovico has admitted Francisco's revenge plot to Monticelso in the form of a religious confession (IV.iii.109–111), which cannot be disclosed, much less used in evidence.

Lodovico

Lodovico is a central commentator who introduces fresh information and perspectives to the audience. In the opening scene, he reveals the corruption in court life and the precarious situation of people without wealth and power in this society. Lodovico has evidently frittered away his family's money (*in three years/Ruined the noblest earldom*, I.i.14–15) and is now powerless. He closes the scene with this *sententia* or moral saying: *Great men sell sheep, thus to be cut in pieces,/When first they have shorn them bare and sold their fleeces* (I.i.61–62). These words encapsulate one of the most important themes of the play.

Commentators generally agree that Lodovico forms a parallel to Flamineo. The two men are in the same social position: intelligent, educated and able, but without a chance of social advancement and useful employment unless they win and retain the patronage of a powerful ruler. Both are therefore forced into the service of a corrupt lord, and are ruthless in the pursuit of self-interest.

There are important differences in the way Webster presents the two characters, however. While Flamineo reveals his past in a dialogue with his mother Cornelia (I.ii.329–339), Webster uses elements of the traditional morality play in the opening scene, as Gasparo and Antonelli act as Good Counsel to Lodovico, recounting his past and offering guidance for the future. While Flamineo enjoys practising *mischief* (I.ii.359), Lodovico seems more violent from the outset and more actively villainous. He threatens to *make Italian cut-works* in the *guts* of his enemies (I.i.51), and regards the murders he has committed as merely *flea-bitings* (I.i.32).

Unlike Flamineo, who is the discontented yet apparently willing servant of Bracciano, Lodovico openly curses his fortune and resolves to try his hand at piracy. Yet once his banishment is revoked he enters the service of Francisco whole-heartedly, appearing to dedicate himself to Francisco's cause, and seemingly careful to protect the latter's reputation and safety. This is evident when he expresses dismay that Francisco, as *a great prince*, might be seen to be personally involved in revenge (IV.iii.75–76), and then when he advises him: *My lord, leave the city, /Or I'll forswear the murder* (V.v.7–8). In his final words, does Lodovico seem to regret having told Giovanni that his uncle gave authority for the murders, and want to take entire responsibility for them himself? Lodovico seems to have strong, if perverse, principles and Webster uses his character alongside that of Flamineo to explore problems of power, patronage and preferment (see page 231). This is most evident in the scene where the two speak of forming an alliance – Marcello advises us to *Mark this strange encounter* (III.iii.67).

Far more than the rather pragmatic Flamineo, Lodovico appears to take an aesthetic delight in plotting and murder, in true Machiavellian style; his final words describe the killlings in artistic terms: *I limn'd this night-piece, and it was my best* (V.vi.300). Structurally, as mentioned above, it is through him that Webster takes the play full circle.

Activity

Compare the three revengers of *The White Devil* – Francisco, Monticelso and Lodovico – and the ways in which Webster presents them.

Discussion

Webster makes clear distinctions between the three revengers, who each represent an essential ingredient of revenge tragedy. Francisco, Monticelso and Lodovico differ in genre, in motive, in action and in outcomes.

Webster prepares the audience for revenge early in the play as he reveals that Francisco's real concern is dynastic, with a fear of Vittoria's *issue* (II.i.352). He is the most deadly and sophisticated of the revengers; although his revenge speech in IV.i links him to traditional revenge drama, Webster presents him with some of the psychological depth of Shakespeare's Hamlet. Yet it is clear that he is not a traditional revenger. He will use *Agents* to carry out his murders (IV.i.87), he rejects the supernatural context of Isabella's ghost (IV.i.99–100), and he goes beyond any revenge that could conceivably be justified in the multiple murders with which the play ends.

Similarly Webster presents Monticelso's as *dishonourable* (II.i.388) rather than a traditional revenger. As a cardinal, his actions are sinful in lending Francisco his *black book* and spurring him on to revenge. On his election as pope, Monticelso seems to have repented (IV.iii.117), but Cornelia's broken crucifix and the corrupt parody of religious rites at Bracciano's death, as we have seen (page 204), symbolically represent his role in the murders.

Lodovico is a different type, as he resembles a feudal knight acting in the service of his lord; hence he takes the *sacrament* (IV.iii.73–74) before committing murder. Nevertheless, his motives are mixed, and he seems to take a delight in plotting and murder, as discussed on page 207.

Isabella

Isabella is both a representative figure and an individual. Like Vittoria she foregrounds the problems women face in this misogynistic and patriarchal society. Her first appearance presents a visual image of the restricted position of women in this society, as she enters with her young son (see pages 204–205 above), and her dignity in a difficult position must arouse the audience's sympathy. However, as always Webster's presentation of her as an individual reveals both her virtues and her flaws.

In her approach to her husband in II.i, either inadvertently or deliberately she seems to be reproaching him at the same time as exalting her own virtuous restraint; she first speaks to him of sin and repentance, by implication comparing his state of sinfulness with her own piety, then she asserts: *I do not come to chide. My jealousy?/I am to learn what that Italian means* (II.i.159–160).

When she decides to role-play the jealous and angry wife, ostensibly in order to protect her husband, it is difficult to believe that her heart isn't in her words as she switches register and launches a violent attack on the *strumpet* and *whore* Vittoria. It seems that she does understand 'jealousy' after all. In Christianity there are seven deadly sins: pride, anger, envy, covetousness, lust, gluttony, and sloth. Isabella freely exhibits the first three of these in her new persona.

Isabella de Medici, in a copy of a portrait by Agnolo Bronzino

Her murder is distanced by being presented in dumb-show, but again there is a suggestion of sinfulness in her behaviour. Isabella *kneels down as to prayers*, and *does three reverences to* her husband's picture, before kissing it three times (II.ii.23ff). Is this idolatry, a sin against the first of the Ten Commandments? Perhaps so, but it is also a graphic image of Isabella's situation; without her marriage to Bracciano she has neither role nor function.

In the divorce scene, and anticipating Vittoria's tactics at her trial, Isabella directly appeals to the audience to think about Bracciano's outrageous assumption of power over State and Church law, as she echoes the words he has used to try to get rid of his wife:

> And this divorce shall be as truly kept,
> As if in throngèd court a thousand ears
> Had heard it
>
> (II.i.254–6)

The *thousand ears* inside the theatre make it resemble a court accommodating a multitude of judges; each member of the audience is asked to consider the tyrannous power of a great duke and the failure of both State and Church law to protect the vulnerable in a corrupt society.

Cornelia

Cornelia, who like Isabella is a mother, has the role of presenting conventional Christian responses to sin, but other dramatic functions are evident in Act V.

On her first appearance she frames the lovers' union with Flamineo, and is the instrument for breaking it up. While his role is that of the bawdy commentator, reminding the audience that however elevated the language, this love scene is based on lust, Cornelia draws attention to the immorality of all three (I.ii.226–230). Then Webster develops her thematic function as she asks: *What? Because we are poor,/Shall we be vicious?* (I.ii.326–327). In the following dialogue it becomes clear that she simply cannot accept Flamineo's solutions to the problems faced by young men such as him; does Webster suggest the failure of conventional religious morality in such a society? Similarly, Cornelia refuses to accept Vittoria's motive of social advancement; she represents those who would simply acquiesce with a pre-determined fate and a pre-ordained position in society.

Later, however, Cornelia's virtuous image is compromised as she attends Bracciano's wedding to Vittoria, physically and verbally attacks Zanche as if she is to blame for bringing corruption into the family (V.i.193), then tries to defend Flamineo after he has killed his brother. It would seem that her struggles to protect her diminished family (her only possible role in this society) have forced her to compromise her principles. Bracciano is evidently moved by her grief (V.ii.52).

With the onset of Cornelia's madness in V.iv, Webster shows that this struggle is too great. Even Francisco feels pity for her plight. Flamineo feels the *Compassion* (V.iv.117) that will help him to achieve some tragic status. Her sad dirge forms an ironic chorus on the evils portrayed onstage.

Zanche

Zanche is another character who illustrates the status of women in this society; she is personally defined primarily by her pursuit first of Flamineo, and then Francisco in his disguise as Mulinassar. She is the victim of trickery in both men; it seems probable that Flamineo has pretended love to win her support in gaining Vittoria's submission to Bracciano – it is she who improvises a bed for them on the floor in I.ii. Afterwards she becomes expendable to Flamineo, but remains a danger because *she knows some of my villainy* (V.i.158). He does defend her, however, when she is attacked by both Cornelia and Marcello; this quarrel leads to the subsequent killing of Marcello, and may suggest that Flamineo has some feelings for her.

Like Vittoria, Zanche becomes freed from dependency on men at the last. She shows resourcefulness in trying to protect herself and Vittoria from Flamineo in V.vi; and she joins in the trampling on his supposedly dying body, suggesting that she is aware of the moral damage inflicted on her. As she faces death she is *proud*, courageous and even witty (V.vi.229–233).

Marcello

In Marcello, Flamineo's younger brother, Webster presents an alternative response to the fate of less privileged young men – he uncomplainingly serves Francisco, apparently without further ambition and while striving to respect the Christian virtues promoted by his mother. He says he is *honoured* to be commanded to search for pirates (II.i.359). The marked contrast between the two brothers is made clear when Flamineo mocks the *poor handful* (III.i.43) a life of service has so far earned him.

But is Webster questioning the quality of his virtue when, with the voice of conventional morality, Marcello expresses fears for his sister in terms of violence against her? He says he wishes that his *dagger's point had cleft her heart* (III.i.34) rather than that she had submitted to Bracciano. This is a callous sort of love. Further, Marcello is shown to be cruel in his attack on Zanche (V.i.198–199), even though he is provoked by Zanche's insults of his mother; and he is hot-headed and foolish in issuing a challenge to his unpredictable brother (V.i.219–220).

Such virtues as Marcello has seem to be ineffectual and go unrecognized in this society, for he is arrested along with his brother after the killing of Camillo and bailed in court (III.ii.253–256), and he does not escape the bloodbath of the last act.

Structure, language and effects

Setting and staging

The Red Bull was probably a typical citizens' theatre with a stage projecting into the audience, surrounded by galleries. The large stage would have had a trapdoor, with entrances on three sides. The curtained back entrance, known as the 'discovery space', was used for episodes such as the dumb-shows; there was a balcony for acting and an upper layer, 'the heavens', supported on posts.

In the original manuscript of *The White Devil* there were no divisions into acts or scenes. Webster later provided divisions for Acts IV and V, and modern editors have deduced the others. This leaves some freedom for directors; sometimes Act III is played as a continuous unit so, for example, the props for the trial scene would be evident throughout, a visual image of the central issues of justice, politics and corruption.

As there was little stage scenery and the audience were very close, staging and the use of spectacle were important. As befitting a play exploring the corruption radiating from the courts of rulers, and whispered dealings conducted behind closed doors, the settings of *The White Devil* are all interior: there are ducal and papal palaces, private houses, an enclosed convent and a courtroom.

Webster uses staging symbolically. The stage could represent zones of power: the margins near the audience would represent public space, with the central area more private. At Vittoria and Camillo's home, attendants with torches could occupy the front of the stage, with her scene of submission to Bracciano either on the main part of the stage or in the discovery space. The 'blocking' of characters – how they are dispersed over the stage – is another important effect. The lovers could occupy the central space, with Flamineo and Cornelia commenting from the front public space, probably from separate sides. The audience, familiar with this usage, would be attending to all three stage areas simultaneously: three different registers and three different perspectives could be presented almost simultaneously.

The audience were also familiar with other types of symbolic staging, for example the three main processions: the ambassadors before the trial (III.i), the papal election (IV.iii), and the wedding (V.i). Ironic effects could be achieved through repeating the route and gestures used by the players.

Johannes de Witt's illustration of the interior of the Swan Theatre
in 1596

Activity

Analyse the effects Webster achieves in the dumb-shows in II.ii.

Discussion

Webster is masterly in his theatrical use of the stage, and the presentations of the dumb-shows are no exception. This scene is carefully framed; it is preceded and succeeded by meetings where the great men are seen plotting revenge and murder, perhaps to create some initial sympathy for Bracciano. But how will he respond? He will call on the devil for help!

How would Webster stage this scene? While the stage directions for the dumb-shows themselves are very precise, a director has some freedom of choice for the staging of the scene as a whole. How would you stage it? The relationship between the characters onstage and the audience should be considered. How far should the audience be distanced? Perhaps because of his power and status, Bracciano should occupy the edge of the stage, nearest to the audience. Slightly further back the Conjurer, with his lavish gestures as a grotesque Master of Ceremonies, might occupy the central stage area, and perhaps the dumb-shows themselves should be played in the discovery space.

This scene has a complicated structure and a complex relationship to the audience; it is a frame within a frame within a frame. The audience watches Bracciano as he watches the Conjurer, and as both watch actions unfold. The two men act as commentators and mediators for the audience, yet at the same time they are being judged. This device is very bold, but not unusual for Webster; most of the unfolding action of *The White Devil* is observed by one or more of the three commentators.

Because of the distancing of the action within dumb-shows Webster creates a sense of unreality, of these events being out of time and out of place, almost dreamlike. This emphasizes the associations with the black arts; the first line of the scene stresses that it is *dead midnight*, the hour when spirits rise and evil things happen. Bracciano is linked to devilry and evil in the Conjurer's comments about those who *make men think* that the devil is *fast and loose* (line 19). He is damned from this point on.

The precision of the stage directions ensures that both dumb-shows are enacted slowly and ritualistically. The first is rather like a pageant, presented with soft music, and probably in dim light; it is feminine in its presentation, with the sensuous references to music, perfumes and kissing. Yet shockingly, the murderers laugh with pleasure at their performance; this is reflected in Bracciano's own shocking reaction. His satisfaction with the scene damns him in the audience's eyes; the casual response of the two commentators to such brutal activities is horrifying.

The second dumb-show is different. The atmosphere is changed with the summoning of *jarring* music, which creates a feeling of unease and reflects the action of Camillo's neck breaking. This time the action is probably well lit; there is vigorous activity and male bonding; the action reflects society as a whole in being masculine, competitive, and threatening. The men drink and dance and whisper. As Bracciano reminds the audience, this is a *far more politic fate* (line 35).

Webster shows the duke's lack of concern over the murders, and his belief that he is above the law. He is interested only in assessing the effectiveness of his agents and in attaining his own desires. Both dumb-shows reveal much about character and are used to develop the plot, while not directly presenting the audience with atrocities at this early point in the play. The enactment of the two dumb-shows should show the audience the true horror of the murders, however.

Webster uses the dumb-shows to reveal Bracciano's inner world; despite his assumed image as a feudal knight devoted to serving his lady, he is utterly ruthless and selfish. His willingness to consort with the devil to get his own way comes back to haunt him at his death. Webster presents us with a tortured man in his death throes, whom the devil apparently comes to claim (V.iii.106).

Linear structure

The linear structure is the construction of the play from the first to the last act, through which the issues of a traditional five-act revenge drama develop. Certain internal divisions cut across this formal division into acts; for example, some commentators consider that the action of the play falls into two halves, the first ending with the trial scene, III.ii. Others find that the play has three stages, which might be called 'The Lovers', 'The Trial' (possibly including the first wave of revenge), and 'The Final Revenge Sequence'. Cutting across these again there is the rise and fall of Flamineo, and the ascendancy of Lodovico, with the change of power relationships at III.ii and III.iii.

Christina Luckyj, in *A Winter's Snake: Dramatic Form in the Tragedies of John Webster* (see Further Reading page 263), argues for a concentric (or circling) structure. This is evident in I.ii: at first Flamineo's gulling of Camillo allows for the lovers' meeting, the central aspect of the scene; then Cornelia parallels Camillo's intrusion in her outburst, and again Flamineo tries to eject the intruder. This structure can be identified in other scenes, and in the play as whole if it is centred on the trial scene; the murders are replaced by revenges, Bracciano's plotting by Francisco's and Monticelso's, and Flamineo is replaced by Lodovico.

The handling of time is uncomplicated in this play, with a time gap of probably about seven years after III.ii, or perhaps Act IV; this would become evident through Giovanni's appearance in the last act.

Spatial structure

Webster also creates a different type of structure that cuts across the linear development of the play, 'freezing' the action at moments to allow the audience to consider the implications of what they are seeing. This is known as spatial structure. For example, the presentation of Vittoria at the trial scene is modified by framing to increase sympathy for her, as discussed above (see page 195). Audience responses are affected by what has happened before, and what happens after the trial.

Webster uses other devices to similar effect, such as repetition and echoes, as in the repetition of the 'kiss' motif (see page 198). The use of echoes and repetition allows Webster to redefine concepts that are important to the play in a sophisticated way – concepts such as justice, honour, politics and goodness. The same applies to words such as 'blood', 'love' and, of course, 'devil'. Each word is continually and ironically redefined, to develop Webster's purposes.

Another example of an echoing motif is that of the bed, associated with Bracciano and Vittoria. Zanche uses a carpet and cushions to make an improvised bed for the lovers at I.ii.214; Bracciano lays out his *rich gown* in order to recline on it at the beginning of the trial of Vittoria (III.ii.3); Vittoria throws herself in anger upon a bed when Bracciano makes jealous accusations against her (IV.ii.127). Finally, Bracciano is wheeled onstage in a bed (V.iii.85) to face his death. Through the repetition of such motifs, Webster creates a chain of events suggesting how the last situation inevitably developed from the first.

Activity

Explore Webster's use of parallels in the structure of *The White Devil*.

Discussion

Webster has crafted a highly symmetrical play: there are two dukes, two servants, two central female protagonists, two dumb-shows, two ghosts, two dreams, and two fables. There are similar symmetries throughout *The White Devil*.

Scenes are presented in parallel to each other; the lovers' meeting in I.ii is paralleled in their quarrel (IV.ii); Isabella in her divorce scene (II.i) foreshadows Vittoria at her trial (III.ii) (see page XXX). There are parallels in the conspiracy scenes (II.i and IV.i); and there are several parallels to the central trial scene (III.ii), with different types of trial being shown in different contexts. For example, look at the links between Vittoria's trial and that of Bracciano by the two great men (II.i); at Bracciano's appraisal of his agents and the two murders in the dumb-shows (II.ii); at his own trial of Vittoria (IV.ii); and at Flamineo's 'trial' of Lodovico (III.iii).

Why does Webster create such a structure? Think about whether the repeated use of the 'trial' theme suggests the lack of trust between all the characters, and the search for truth or meaning in a society devoid of a moral code. Think about how public and private matters are interrelated through these parallels; and compare the last great 'trial' of Bracciano, Vittoria and Flamineo at their respective moments of death (V.iii and V.vi). What is revealed through their self-analysis?

Theatricality

Webster has been accused of 'sensationalism', but the historical events in his source materials (see page 9) were themselves sensational, and provided all the essential ingredients for a Jacobean revenge tragedy.

There are seven murders. The first two are presented as dumb-shows, a device that distances them from the audience. The commentators on the dumb-shows (Bracciano and the Conjurer) undercut the horror further by their approval of the killings and the methods used. The other five murders are accompanied by irony and satire, creating the same distancing effect.

Flamineo's feigned death is the third in a series of scenes showing his ability to trick and humiliate others. He gulls Camillo in I.ii; he teases and gets the better of the Lawyer immediately before the trial in III.i; and parodies his own death in V.vi.

Flamineo's displays of cleverness would appeal to the Red Bull audience, as would the two dumb-shows, with their links to black magic, feeding into the general sense of a wicked society. Similarly, the appearances of the two ghosts (IV.i and V.iv) would be highly dramatic moments, pleasing the audience while at the same time developing character and suggesting a universal frame within which actions are to be judged: *In what place art thou? In yon starry gallery, /Or in the cursèd dungeon?* (V.iv.129–130).

The series of processions across the stage noted above would similarly have pleased the Red Bull audience, both for the visual effects and for the irony triggered. The ambassadors' costumes would be an important point of interest; Flamineo describes them before the trial scene (III.i), and Lodovico does so at the papal election (IV.iii), explaining the symbolic significance of each, much like a TV or radio commentator today. He explains their status and decoration, with Christian iconography such as crosses; the discrepancy between the display of outward grandeur and inner moral decay is suggested through their repeated appearances.

Another procession follows very soon after the wedding procession, where Bracciano enters with the disguised Francisco and revengers symbolically *bearing their swords and helmets* (V.i.44). Time is running out for Bracciano. The staging of the tournament (V.iii) draws upon the nostalgic values of chivalry, and the stage directions call for several combats to be presented. Bracciano's appearance dressed as a medieval knight, along with the disguised conspirators, perhaps appeals to the audience's sympathy immediately before his death, if they admire his courage, virility and dedication to Vittoria. The use of spectacle feeds both the senses and the mind.

Metatheatricality

'Metatheatrical' literally means 'beyond theatre', and refers to those moments when the author reminds the audience that they are watching a play. It is often an invitation to consider what they have seen, and to make judgements.

There are several instances of this technique in *The White Devil*. It can occur when a character seems to draw attention to the fact that there is an audience beyond the stage. Vittoria draws attention to the audience at her trial (see page 195), as does Isabella at her divorce (see page 210).

It can also occur when a character, in collusion with the audience, plays various roles. Francisco plays the role of a Moor and the assassins appear as monks; in his soliloquy at the end of Act I, Flamineo proudly accepts the role of Machiavel, and he later adopts that of madman (III.ii.306–310). The audience are thus warned not to trust anyone onstage, and to carefully weigh the evidence of their own eyes and ears.

Similar effects are created by the use of commentators who offer different interpretations and perspectives on events. And the dumb-shows in II.ii remind the audience that illusions are being created for their benefit.

The use of conventions such as *sententiae* (moral sayings) serves similar purposes. These are usually in the form of a rhyming couplet, and may end a scene or act, for example Flamineo's comment: *But this* [madness] *allows my varying of shapes./Knaves do grow great by being great men's apes* (IV.ii.244–245).

The relation of Vittoria's dream of the yew tree (I.ii.239ff) develops plot, character and ideas, and like Francisco's fable about Phoebus's desired marriage (II.i.333ff) it halts the action temporarily, allowing the audience time to consider and formulate judgements.

Activity

What effects are created by Webster's inclusion of dreams, fables, and *sententiae* in the play?

Discussion

Sometimes commentators regard these elements in *The White Devil* as ornamental or superfluous, but in fact each aspect combines, in the same way as the use of imagery, to develop Webster's purposes.

His drama typically works by displaying the particular and relating this to a general condition; this is how his criticism of society is developed. Francisco's fable of Phoebus's marriage (II.i.333–353) acts as a warning to Camillo, but extends beyond this to make a general statement about the rules of marriage in this society. Similarly, Flamineo's fable of the crocodile and the little bird (IV.ii.220–233), although typically ambiguous, relates initially to the situation of Bracciano and Vittoria, as well as that of Bracciano and Flamineo himself; yet it reveals a general point about the status of women and servants in this society. Webster also uses both fables to reveal character.

Sententiae are moral sayings intended to convey a lesson. They are scattered throughout the play, notably at the ends of scenes in the form of rhyming couplets. Webster uses them to develop his themes, plot and character in the same way as fables and imagery. An example is Lodovico's couplet at the end of the first scene, which relates to one of the main themes of the play and prepares the audience for what is about to happen. Another example is Francisco's comments about Zanche at the end of V.i, which link with other uses of animal imagery in the play and predict the direction of the dénouement for the audience.

The dreams are used in a similar way, and generate many meanings. Vittoria's dream at I.ii.242–265 is revealing about character, plot and the issues that will arise during the course of the play. Zanche's dream at V.iii.230–246, which parallels Vittoria's, tells us more about women of lower as well as higher status in this society, while revealing character and furthering the plot.

The structure of *The White Devil* is not straightforward, and Webster includes diverse elements, yet nothing is superfluous. Every aspect harmonizes to present a coherent and eloquent drama.

Variety of language

Webster uses blank verse in iambic pentameter, the conventional form for tragedy. It is an elegant and flexible form that can encompass great variety, from the courtly language of the lovers, to persuasive and powerful soliloquies, such as Francisco's great revenger speech at the end of IV.i. At times the verse is full of tension and excitement, and it can give staccato effects as speakers cut across each other. For example, see the lovers' quarrel in IV.ii: at its height three characters – Bracciano, Vittoria and Flamineo – rapidly interchange speeches, giving a special pace and mood to the scene.

Webster also uses prose and rhymed couplets to achieve particular effects. In this play prose is the lower order of speech, but it can still create similar effects to poetry.

The sense of language being debased is at times relevant when Flamineo speaks in prose, especially where there is a suggestion of social disorder. When he speaks to Bracciano about Vittoria at I.ii.17–49, his language is informal and even crude; the audience wonders whether the register is appropriate for a servant to his lord. Might it indicate over-confidence in Flamineo? He is discourteous about the ambassadors at the trial (III.i.65–80), and again his judgement might be questioned, especially since his fortune is about to be reversed.

Flamineo speaks disordered prose when feigning madness at the beginning of III.iii; like a madman Flamineo seems to have lost his grip on himself and his place at court. In his prose exchange with the disguised Francisco (V.i.136–146), he fails to penetrate the latter's disguise; later in the same scene his exchanges with Hortensio and Zanche again reveal fatal misjudgements of character – his mistress will betray his trust. His ill-judged comments to Giovanni at the beginning of V.iv result in his expulsion from court.

However, the prose register Flamineo uses to relate the fable of the crocodile and little bird is vivid enough to sound persuasive (IV.ii.220–233). Francisco speaks in verse to tell the fable about Phoebus (II.i.333ff), and sounds like a wise prophet demanding attention from both Camillo and the audience for his *old tale*.

Webster uses puns, sometimes visual (see page 199), at other times verbal (see Activity, page 224). He makes effective use of asides to reveal character and further the plot, and they are often comic, as in I.ii when Flamineo insults Camillo in asides to Vittoria while simultaneously praising him aloud, or when he speaks to the audience directly and wittily, for example at I.ii.50–54.

The legal jargon, rhetoric and Latin tags used in the trial scene provide evidence of Webster's own legal experience. Across the play the register varies from sexual innuendos to scholarly classical references (for example, IV.ii.63–64), biblical references (I.ii.310) and Roman Catholic liturgical register (IV.iii.43–46). All contribute to the audience's acceptance that what is revealed about people and events is truthful and logical; the audience is persuaded that the fiction created onstage is true of life generally, rather than true to life.

The sadness of Cornelia's song, set against the villainy that has caused it, offers music as a comment on human disharmony. And, of course, Webster exploits the poignant effects of silence in the dumb-shows, highlighting the callous cruelty of the watching Bracciano.

The power of silence is immense, and when exploited by the great men it reinforces the impression of their tyranny. Those who have the upper hand do not need to speak in order to assert themselves; in the trial scene Francisco says very little, but when he does speak he is coolly precise (*Why, you understand Latin*, III.ii.15) and authoritative (*pray change your language*, III.ii.22). At times Webster uses Francisco as a commentator for the audience: he says *Now mark each circumstance* (III.ii.119). Monticelso rants and raves, but Francisco remains controlled and seems even more dangerous.

As discussed above (pages 202 and 204), neither of these two powerful men is seen onstage at the end of the play, except symbolically; their silence and invisibility are eloquent as the effects of their power are still keenly felt, and it is evident that both have won the game.

Activity

Analyse Webster's use of language, especially wordplay, in Flamineo's descriptions of Camillo in I.ii.

Discussion

In Webster's hands prose, as well as poetry, becomes a highly flexible and expressive medium, which he puts to many uses. Many of his techniques are evident in this scene. For example, Flamineo's comment that Camillo is *wondrous discontented* provokes Vittoria's suggestive response: *I carved to him at supper-time* (lines 127–129). Flamineo's insults of Camillo are developed through a series of puns, which build up in five stages. The word *capon* (131), as applied by Flamineo to Camillo, not only suggests castration but introduces the language of food and of low-level kitchen staff, a status to which he feels Camillo rightly belongs (lines 133–136); this is linked to a recipe for *calf's brains without any sage* (139), where the wordplay combines the seasoning of food with a lack of wisdom; then the idea of food is repeated in the word *hams* (140), referring to a man's upper legs, but including a pun on sexually transmitted disease; finally, the series is completed with the imagery of the courtier's clothing making Camillo appear as a *maggot* (146).

Webster achieves several effects here: Flamineo is presented as witty and lively, while Vittoria's unequal marriage to Camillo is highlighted. Perhaps Webster is drawing attention to the tyrannical treatment of women in such arranged marriages. The audience may be persuaded to sympathize with the lovers in the wooing scene that develops between Bracciano and Vittoria.

A similar sequence occurs in a verse passage with Webster's use of a sporting analogy at line 64. Trace the movement from the *earnest bowler* to *leans*, to *his bowl run*, to *bowl booty*, to *bias*, and finally to *Jump with my mistress*. Analyse the effects Webster creates through this sequence.

Imagery

A coherent pattern of imagery within *The White Devil* emphasizes the theme of a corrupt and sick society. Most of the central images are established in the opening act of the play.

Lodovico first speaks of Fortune at I.i.4–6, to suggest that an individual cannot control his or her own destiny. Related to images of Fortune and fate are those drawn from astronomy and the natural world; Lodovico is compared to *An idle meteor* (I.i.25), which suggests the futility of human endeavour and at the same time, the folly of ambition as time will reverse all apparent achievements. Images from the natural world are often used to suggest disorder; in this opening scene there are also the references to *thunder* (line 11) and an *earthquake* (line 27), implying that humanity has perverted this world and inhabits a flawed universe.

Closely related to this is the use of imagery connected to poison and physical decay, such as the *mummia* in line 16 – decayed and diseased flesh that makes the consumer vomit. Poison imagery is connected to the shedding of *blood* (line 35) and to *witchcraft* (I.ii.288).

A sixteenth-century illustration of the Wheel of Fortune; some rise, some fall, but nothing lasts

Webster also uses animal imagery to suggest the ways that humanity has ruined its own world, with references to a *wolf* (I.i.8) and *sheep* (I.i.61); when controlled by their lust and other base instincts, human beings – even great leaders – are no better than animals.

Sporting images, as when Camillo refers to Bracciano as *an earnest bowler* (I.ii.64), suggest that powerful men use the less powerful – including women – for their own entertainment, and treat life as a game in which their sole aim is to win power and satisfaction. References to the consumption of *caviare* and *the phoenix* (I.i.21, 23) draw attention to the uncontrollable appetites of those who hold power.

Other imagery is used more obliquely, such as the images of precious stones and metals (for example, I.ii.231ff) and of perfumes (I.ii.161), which suggest the conflict between appearance and reality, and the idea of illusion and delusion. Because of the duplicity and deceit evident in court life, it is impossible for an individual to fathom what his rulers are really doing and what he should value in this society.

Symbolic use of colour, predominantly black, white and scarlet, suggest similar themes of appearance versus reality; Flamineo uses the motif of *black* and *white* in his description of Camillo as a *maggot* (I.ii.144–146), while the power of *scarlet* will be made graphically clear in Vittoria's words at the trial: *O poor charity,/Thou art seldom found in scarlet* (III.ii.71–72). The cardinal is evil beneath the scarlet Church robes. Red is also symbolic of blood: the blood of revenge, of passion and lust, and of hot temper, but also of lineage, and of family.

Near the beginning of the play Bracciano orders his attendants to *put out all your torches* (I.ii.9), and the visual counterpart to the verbal black/white imagery is light and darkness, which alternate throughout the play. Links are made between light/darkness and good/evil, human/animal, and appearance/reality, culminating in the deepening darkness of Act V.

These pairs of concepts develop the ideas contained in the title of the play, *The White Devil*, which also fuses opposing meanings.

Activity

Discuss Webster's use of imagery connected with blood.

Discussion

Webster repeatedly uses imagery of blood, redefining its connotations; with every image a fresh aspect extends the audience's understanding, in a cumulative process.

A clear sequence of imagery can be detected throughout the play, and most of the characters refer to blood in one or more connections.

- Gasparo links the idea of bloodshed with sin in I.i.35
- Monticelso refers to the royal bloodline of rulers in II.i.101
- Flamineo mocks Marcello's blind loyalty in his willingness to shed his lifeblood for his lord in III.i.42
- Vittoria refers proudly to the nobility of her family lineage in III.ii.55
- Francisco suggests the revenge tradition in referring to murder as *The act of blood* (III.ii.190)
- Flamineo aligns himself with the darker forces in his reference to *a witch's congealèd blood* (III.iii.92)
- Lodovico furthers this idea in suggesting that Vittoria's blood should be used to *water a mandrake* (III.iii.116)
- Vittoria crowns the sequence with her exclamation *O my greatest sin lay in my blood;/Now my blood pays for 't* (V.vi.242–243); many meanings are fused here.

Through precisely plotted repetition, meanings expand so that on each new appearance of the word all previous connotations are included and an audience's understanding becomes increasingly complex. In Vittoria's exclamation quoted above, earlier meanings cohere; there is the blood of family, of ambition, and of passion, paired with another set of meanings in the second line. The connotations include blood that is shed in accordance with the revenge tradition; violent death; and the unavoidable consequences of social and moral sins.

Webster uses the same technique with many other concepts and words. It is evident, for example, in allusions to the concepts of loyalty, honour and virtue, and the use of words such as *politic*, *service*, and *jewel*.

Literary interpretations

When you have a firm understanding of *The White Devil* and have formed some independent views on this play, it is helpful to study other readers' interpretations. One of the most interesting areas of discussion is about the title of the play.

Who is 'the White Devil'?

The title is probably drawn from a proverb that would have been well known to Webster: 'The white devil is worse than the black', and also perhaps from this verse of St Paul's in II Corinthians 11:14, on the deceitfulness of evil-doers: 'Satan himself is transformed into an angel of light'. Both of these sayings relate closely to one of the main issues of the play, the contrast between appearance and reality. The world portrayed in it brims with illusion and deceit, just like the art of the *nigromancer* with his *sophistic tricks* ironically described by the Conjurer at II.ii.7–8.

Might Webster imply that any specific character qualifies for the description of 'white devil'? Many commentators consider Vittoria to be the one referred to in the title, and even though Webster creates at least some sympathy for her, she is certainly viewed as a devil in disguise by many of the characters. At her trial, Monticelso more than once describes her as such. He says:

> You see, my lords, what goodly fruit she seems…
> I will but touch her and you straight shall see
> She'll fall to soot and ashes.
>
> (III.ii.64–8)

Later in the scene, he says: *If the devil/Did ever take good shape, behold his picture* (lines 217–218). And Bracciano, in his jealousy, calls her *the devil in crystal* (IV.ii.87).

Vittoria may be dressed in white for her bridal procession across the stage in V.i, and this may form another link with the play's title. The audience is aware of her role-playing behaviour, and recognizes that appearances may be deceptive in this play, and that we cannot know her motives.

But other characters in the play may also be considered as 'white devils', including Flamineo, Lodovico, and the three 'great men'.

Webster creates an understanding between Flamineo and the audience; since he is open and direct in his ambitions, as his powerful exchanges with Cornelia reveal (see page 191), he seems a less likely candidate to be the deceitful devil. Lodovico, meanwhile, has a name that recalls the word *ludo*, Latin for 'I play' – does this suggest that life is just a sinister game to him? But again, he is a Machiavel who is, from the start, very direct about his purposes.

The three powerful men, Bracciano, Francisco and Monticelso, all exhibit 'devilish' characteristics. Bracciano, as discussed above (see page 197), is the least complex character. He admits his infatuation (or perhaps love) for Vittoria openly, and does not take much trouble to hide his motivations even from his enemies. Francisco is more of a mystery, and he admits to deviousness in his 'revenge' soliloquy: *He that deals all by strength, his wit is shallow:/When a man's head goes through, each limb will follow* (IV.i.128–129). This is indeed a suggestion of the subtlety of a 'white devil', and his use of disguise reinforces this. He absents himself from the final massacre, thus 'whitewashing' his character, but he is visually represented by his assassins' disguise as Franciscan monks – possibly white-hooded.

Monticelso, the corrupt churchman who hides his evil schemes and is evidently driven by the accumulation of wealth and power, could be strikingly 'white' when he enters in his papal robes (IV.iii.59). However, he disappears from the play early, and on a baffling note – he advises Lodovico against revenge (see page 204 above). But he too is visually presented in Act V by two crucifixes, one broken and one corrupted by its use in the parody of the last rites offered to the dying Bracciano, as noted above.

In a sense all of the characters in this play are to some extent white devils, even the seemingly virtuous Marcello (with his hot temper and cruelty to Zanche) and Cornelia (who is likewise cruel to Zanche, and finally resorts to lying in order to try to

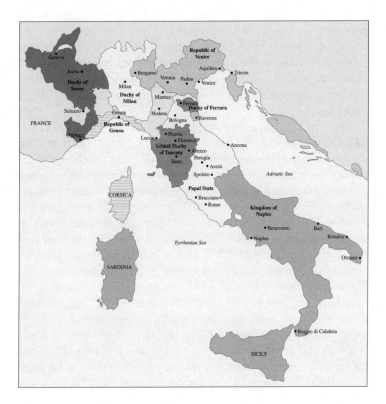

In the sixteenth century, Italy was divided into city states and
territories with competing interests

protect her murderous son). Could it be, therefore, that Webster's play presents a study of the archetypal and universal 'white devil' as a generic type? See page 248 below for a discussion of the frequent use of the word *devil* in the play.

This is the approach taken by J.W. Lever, in *The Tragedy of State* (see Further Reading page 263), who goes so far as to suggest that the 'white devil' is actually the whole of Renaissance Europe. Webster certainly presents biting criticism of contemporary Italy, as exemplified in the powerful men of Bracciano, Florence and Rome, and extended by the presence of the ambassadors of Savoy, France, and Spain. He includes references to Spanish cruelty in the Netherlands (III.ii.87), to Irish savagery (IV.i.134–135), and to France and Poland (III.iii.4–7) and Turkey (II.i.187). As Lever concludes, 'all these are the broken humanity of Renaissance Europe' (page 85). However, Webster excludes his own nation from this indictment, by showing the good judgement of the English Ambassador – see, for example, the comment *True, but the Cardinal's too bitter*, (III.ii.108), and the end of the play. Was he hoping that James I would pay heed to his lesson, protect the spiritual and physical well-being of his own nation, and so avoid the label of 'white devil'?

Problems of power, patronage and preferment

Webster presents several areas of enquiry into the damage that tyrannical rulers inflict on their subjects, and also spiritually and morally upon themselves.

The abuse of power by the three great men is demonstrated throughout the play, as they consult only self-interest. Bracciano flouts the laws of both Church and State in his divorce: *And this divorce shall be as truly kept,/As if the judge had doomed it* (II.i.195–196) – note the irony of the word *doomed*. He arranges the two murders of Isabella and Camillo, pursues Vittoria ruthlessly, and regards Flamineo as expendable.

Francisco shows his willingness to abuse absolute power when he is given Monticelso's *black book*; he relishes the fact that *in so little paper,/Should lie the undoing of so many men* (IV.i.89–90). Francisco is the coldest, possibly the most dangerous of the men in his manipulation of Lodovico to carry out his murderous purposes. His disguise is not penetrated; he is deadly in his pursuit of self-interest.

In his comments on the *black book*, Francisco also condemns Monticelso, who has perverted divine power: *Divinity, wrested by some factious blood,/Draws swords, swells battles, and o'erthrows all good* (IV.i.93–94).

Monticelso's conduct of the trial of Vittoria, and the dubious papal election, suggest that the Church is as corrupt as the State. Absolute power is seen to corrupt absolutely, denying any possibility of the rule of law and morality.

Webster explores the issue of patronage and preferment through his presentation of Flamineo and Lodovico, who represent one of the most serious social problems in the Italian ducal courts. They are victims of a corrupt system of patronage, but they respond in equally corrupt ways. (For consideration of women's responses, see page 238 below.)

These two young men suggest the most serious effects of tyrannical power. Both are of noble status but are poor; both are educated, but neither has a means of making a living other than serving a great man. Flamineo makes clear the penalty of failure to remain in favour, in his reference to *the galleys, or the gallows* (I.ii.328); that is, slave labour or execution. They have no means of rising socially as a reward for merit or hard work, but can prosper only through the favour of a powerful man. Their intelligence and resourcefulness will therefore be placed in the service of, and at the mercy of, a tyrant.

Flamineo is bitterly aware of the implications of his choice of *mischief* (I.ii.359). He adopts and plays out the role of the cynical Machiavel, including murdering Camillo, in the hope that serving Bracciano will bring him rewards. Lodovico, on the other hand, opens the play with the one-word question *Banished?*

Having committed murders, which he regards as trivial *flea-bitings* (I.i.32), he narrowly avoids the gallows and seemingly resolves to turn to the galleys, as he is *rumoured for a pirate* (II.i.377). However, finally he is forced into the same choice as Flamineo, surrendering his independence by obtaining a pension from Isabella and entering into the service of the great duke Francisco, at first apparently innocently *I'th'train of the young prince* (III.iii.65). He is a third revenger, acting to please a powerful duke while also personally motivated by his love (or lust) for Isabella.

At the midpoint of the play Flamineo and Lodovico are in parallel; then the latter ascends as the former declines in influence. Lodovico embraces ducal service in a totally different manner from Flamineo; he has the title of 'Count', presumably deriving from the *earldom* he has *Ruined* (I.i.15), and therefore retains links to feudal power. He seems to adopt the medieval code of chivalry, having an aesthetic regard for his violent work as he savours the thought of fine *Italian cut-works* (I.i.51). When there is such work to be done he is treated honourably by his patron and addressed as *Noble friend* (IV.iii.78); he reciprocates, in the service of his lord, by performing what he calls a *most noble deed* (V.vi.282) in murdering their mutual enemies.

Webster strips the word 'noble' of a moral context; it is connected to the debased and corrupt form of chivalry evident in Bracciano's *Barriers* (V.iii). Religious parody enforces the irony: in the Bible, the disciple Peter denies Jesus three times. Lodovico, in an inversion of the Bible story, three times gives unconditional support to Francisco: he has *ta'en the sacrament to prosecute/Th'intended murder* – the sacrament of communion, as chivalric knights would have done before undertaking dangerous services (IV.iii.73–74); he advises his lord to leave the scene of the final murders, and takes the physical risks upon himself (V.v.1–8); and finally, he takes sole blame for the murders: *I do glory yet,/That I can call this act mine own* (V.vi.296–297). This is honourable behaviour if the concept of 'honour' is stripped, like the word 'noble', of most of its moral implications. Lodovico appears to be courageously reciprocating the trust placed in him, as a knight of old might have done; in truth, he is pursuing a personal vendetta and is as corrupt as Flamineo.

Webster invites his audience to think about how power such as that wielded by the great men in this play might be moderated; where are the wise, impartial advisers and the social institutions necessary to curb excess? Who is protecting the well-being of subjects? Should the individual have any rights? Where should the line be drawn between State and Church? Is it the system of patronage, or the patron himself that is corrupt? Webster also implicitly invites the audience to compare what is depicted onstage with what occurs in their own society. How much better than the Italian leaders is James I in his English rule? Webster clearly takes some risks in raising these issues.

Activity

How does Webster present love in *The White Devil*?

Discussion

Webster presents love as dangerous and deadly; whether heterosexual, familial or sibling love, the outcome seems to be wholly negative.

Webster presents three marital relationships and each ends in murder. The audience see the deaths of Isabella and Camillo in the dumb-shows (II.ii); Isabella dies after kissing her husband's portrait, and Camillo is killed in pursuit of those manly skills he has earlier been mocked for lacking. The merits and demerits of these characters count for nothing in the face of Bracciano's lethal single-mindedness. Despite Bracciano's lavish promises to Vittoria that *you shall to me at once/Be dukedom, health, wife, children, friends and all* (I.ii.277–278), their love and marriage result in his death as well as Vittoria's. Webster shows that in the case of powerful men, such adulterous love brings down an entire political and social system; this society must rest on stability and on marriage within the same class, in order to preserve dynastic rule.

The love between parent and child fares no better in the play. This is evident from the beginning in Flamineo's attack on his mother

(I.ii.320ff), and events connected with the murder of his brother, which drives his mother to madness. However, Webster invites some audience sympathy for Flamineo's complaints by presenting the corruption of court life and the lack of opportunities for capable young men. Giovanni's love for his mother, shown in the first dumb-show and elsewhere, offers a contrasting mother/son relationship, yet this love is ended by Isabella's murder.

Sibling love is dubious; Flamineo feels no qualms in his attempts to prostitute his sister, who in return will not repay him for his services to her husband (V.vi.13–14). Flamineo, of course, murders his brother; and his sister attempts to murder him. Francisco goes to extreme lengths to revenge the murder of his own sister; and Monticelso, already shown to be a sinful conspirator in defiance of his religious role, says he is ready to *stake a brother's life* (II.i.390) for revenge. Webster seems to suggest that no love can prosper in such a corrupt society, as there is simply no place for it to flourish.

Cornelia's death does, however, have some impact on the consciences of Francisco (V.iv.55–65) and Flamineo (V.iv.115–117); and Flamineo claims to love his sister at her death (V.vi.243–244). Perhaps Webster is suggesting there is a spark of love that survives the worst excesses of human nature.

The significance of Vittoria's trial

Webster gave the 'Arraignment of Vittoria' (III.ii) a separate title; it is a significant scene marking the first turning point in *The White Devil*. Dramatically, this is the point where the audience sees the start of Flamineo's decline in contrast to the rise of Lodovico; it also marks the first wave of revenge, which perhaps satisfies Monticelso as he shames Vittoria publicly. Thematically, there are two trials: on the surface, it is Vittoria who is on trial, but it is also evident that this is a trial of justice itself.

The scene displays Webster's consummate skill in controlling an audience's response. Sympathies flow against the logical development of the argument, as the lovers seem to emerge from the public ordeal far better than those who seek to condemn and humiliate them. How does the playwright elicit sympathy for a murderer and a whore, against a grand duke and a cardinal?

As always, Webster's build-up to this scene is important. At the end of II.i, Francisco and Monticelso are revealed to be ruthless in their plans for revenge. The cardinal's godless comment *For my revenge I'd stake a brother's life* (II.i.390) is equalled by Francisco's merciless words: *There's small pity in't* (line 393); we realize at the trial that the motives of both men are related to the pursuit of profit and power, even if this is through Camillo or Giovanni.

In contrast, Bracciano seems to be motivated by a deep love, and Vittoria seems helpless against both the temptations he offers and against her accusers. Although the audience is aware that Bracciano has been responsible for two murders, Webster distances these through the two dumb-shows and the idle banter of the two commentators in II.ii.

The dominant impression from the trial is of the danger Francisco and Monticelso present to those who cross them. The Lawyer is soon dismissed, as foretold by Flamineo's insult: *You are a dull ass* (III.i.19). This removes even the appearance of legal respectability from the trial, and the audience can foresee what will happen in court.

The setting of the scene is formal, with a procession of the play's powerful men and the ambassadors; in the staging, the judge's bench will probably be raised so that Vittoria will stand isolated at a lower level, with Monticelso's massive power as judge and representative of the Church made visually apparent. By contrast with Vittoria, Bracciano is treated courteously (*A chair there for his lordship*, III.ii.4) and can come and go freely. His threatening words *Nemo me impune lacessit* ('No one harms me with impunity', III.ii.180) may remind the court of his power, but they also mark his exit. Vittoria is left behind as the victim of both the State and the Church.

In rejecting the use of Latin, Vittoria represents common sense and the idea of public access to legal proceedings. As noted above (see page 195), she implicitly refers to the whole Red Bull audience, appealing for sympathetic judgement from the widest possible group of witnesses. In a double stroke Webster suggests that proceedings onstage will be unjust while flattering the integrity of his audience. For the first part of the proceedings, only Vittoria works within the legal frame; she maintains her status as the accused throughout while Monticelso pays little regard to legal procedures.

It is clear from all that has been seen in the play so far that the wishes of the great rulers cannot be resisted, so Vittoria has had little real choice within this society. During the trial Monticelso arouses further audience sympathy for her as he reveals his view of women as commodities (*He bought you of your father*, III.ii.239) and heaps insults on her. As a woman she seems to be a victim of all three great men, and of society itself, yet she displays both dignity and intelligence in pointing out the injustice of Monticelso being both *accuser* and *judge* (III.ii.226–227). The ambassadors are neutral witnesses whom Webster uses to sum up the situation in asides that the audience may agree with; the French Ambassador remarks *She hath lived ill*, but the English Ambassador replies: *True, but the Cardinal's too bitter* (III.ii.107–108).

The arguments of the trial swing back and forth, with both sides scoring points (for more on this topic see *Webster: The Tragedies* by Kate Aughterson, from page 54). Webster uses his legal knowledge for the rhetoric in these arguments. Vittoria's speeches are by no means beyond criticism: for example, her quotation of a Latin tag at line 201 makes an unfortunately ambiguous reference to chastity; she seems to suggest blackmail with her *houses*, *Jewels* and *crusadoes* at lines 215–216; and she resorts to cursing Monticelso by the end of the scene. Moreover, it is made clear that she is playing a role, especially in her appeal to the ambassadors:

> Humbly thus,
> Thus low, to the most worthy and respected
> Lieger ambassadors, my modesty
> And womanhood I tender

(III.ii.131–4)

But her apparent openness (*Sum up my faults I pray*, line 208) wins over listeners when compared to the cardinal's rant about *whores* (lines 79–102), his sneers, and his unjust conduct of the trial. The overall impression of the scene is that of an injustice perpetrated by a flawed political and judicial system. The cardinal has been seen to be misogynistic and corrupt, and the law is reduced to an instrument by which the powerful gain their own ends. Vittoria's defeat represents the defeat of her gender, and indeed of all those less powerful than her accusers; this is summed up in her exclamation: *Yes, you have ravished justice* (line 275). The judicial system is shown to be empty and corrupt; more than this, the whole society is seen to be run by powerful men for powerful men, as in the construct of the House of Convertites: *Do the noblemen in Rome/Erect it for their wives…?* (lines 268–269). No wonder that this woman *Must personate masculine virtue* (line 137) to have a chance of survival.

Vittoria reminds the audience of the idolatry and superstition of which the Roman Catholic Church was often accused, with her reference to *painted devils* being used to terrify believers (line 148); references to the devil by both Vittoria and Monticelso (lines 217 and 281), the use of animal imagery (lines 179 and 212) and the image of *darkness* in Vittoria's final couplet (line 295) suggest that this place is equated to hell.

Increasingly, Vittoria seems to be the voice of reason in an unjust system, and her errors seem relatively minor as the central issue of justice is raised. The trial is a major turning point in the play, as the audience will now mistrust every word and action of the great men, and foresee a tragic and violent outcome.

Gender issues

Feminist criticism has often seen the women of Jacobean drama as rather passive victims of a repressive society. More recently, writers such as Dympna Callaghan and Kathleen McLuskie (see Further Reading page 263) perceive the female characters as more active agents in their own destinies. The women in *The White Devil* may be seen at significant points to determine their own futures by undermining or outwitting the representatives of a patriarchal social system.

As already noted (see page 194), the female characters in *The White Devil* initially appear to define themselves through their relationships with men: Isabella through Francisco and Bracciano; Vittoria initially through Camillo and then Bracciano; Zanche through first Flamineo and afterwards the disguised 'Moor'; Cornelia through her two sons. Although excluded from political power, women are nevertheless central to political stability. For example, Isabella through her marriage to Bracciano has cemented his political ties with the Duke of Florence, has produced the essential male heir for the duchy of Bracciano, and perhaps has even been a stabilizing influence on her hot-headed husband. But in contrast to him, Isabella remains relatively unseen, living behind closed doors.

As remarked above (page 208), Webster presents some parallels between Isabella and Vittoria; both appeal to the audience for judgement; both use a legal frame to develop their arguments; both employ rhetorical devices in an attempt to outwit their male adversaries; both are mistreated by men close to them and also by the social system instituted and run by men. Beyond that there are differences: while Isabella was born into a wealthy and powerful noble family and her marriage creates a political union, Vittoria's family – though of some nobility – is poor, and her marriage to the impotent fool Camillo was presumably arranged by that family in pursuit of much-needed cash. Bracciano's infatuation with her therefore presents real temptations. While Isabella's social status protects her from public (though not from private) humiliation, Vittoria is publicly shamed.

Although Isabella is not beyond criticism (see page 209), she emerges strong in will and spirit from the potentially humiliating rejection by her husband. In the divorce scene she finds the strength to determine her own future, and challenges the authority of Bracciano. She openly defies her husband's order to *Take your chamber* (II.i.153). Her main tactic is to turn Bracciano's own words against him in front of his fellow great men. She takes control of events by scornfully repeating and adapting in public Bracciano's private words to her. She has the appearance, at least, of being the decision-maker, and is roundly condemned for this by her brother: *you are a foolish, mad/And jealous woman* (II.i.262–263). Like Vittoria she throws herself into her role-play, taking advantage of her pact with Bracciano to insult his beloved and leave him impotent to either defend Vittoria or determine Isabella's fate. Playing the part of a *mad/And jealous woman*, she relishes language normally forbidden to her in order to vent her feelings, calling Vittoria a *strumpet* with *rotten teeth* (lines 244–246). Remarkably, her prime consideration is political: protecting the peace between Florence and Bracciano (line 215), although a major motive for this would be her concern for the future of her son Giovanni.

Webster makes her suffering evident using the device of the dumb-show that depicts her murder, *The circumstance that breaks your Duchess' heart* (II.ii.23). She is seen to worship her husband, perhaps to excess (see page 210). She is killed by her devotion to her religion and her husband.

Vittoria's is a different case. Although Webster ensures audience sympathy for her, he does not gloss over the true status of her relationships. Her childlessness (V.vi.30) is symbolic of the fact that both her loveless first marriage and her morally dubious second marriage are unfruitful, and offers a contrast to the fertile Isabella. As she is not a mother, Vittoria has no social function beyond her sexual attraction for men, and therefore no other role within this society.

During her trial, however, the English Ambassador comments that *She hath a brave spirit* (III.ii.141), and it is this courage that is inspirational. It is clear that she adopts a courageous stand as her only coping strategy. She is betrayed on all sides: systematically by the custodians of legal, political and religious power, and personally by all the men in her life including her own brother, who is prepared to prostitute her and put her at great risk in order to pander to his master's lust.

At her death she is courageous and stoical (see page 196), leaving us with the sense of a flawed tragic figure who is entrapped in and defeated by a hostile patriarchal system.

Zanche, as a person of the lowest social standing, has even less power than Vittoria. It is clear from the outset that she is being used by Flamineo to further his own interests in the seduction of Vittoria: *I have dealt already with her chambermaid/Zanche the Moor* (I.ii.13–14). Her defiant response to Flamineo's treatment of her, in wooing the disguised Francisco and betraying Flamineo to him, rebounds on all of them. But she has not remained passive – she is, on the contrary, resourceful in her response to threats, as discussed on page 211 – and finally triumphs as she faces death bravely, with the grim stoicism a Jacobean audience would have valued (V.vi.229–233).

Cornelia, as discussed on page 210, seems at first to be the voice of conventional morality as she loudly rebukes the would-be adulterers, and argues with Flamineo about his claim that poverty excuses his immoral behaviour. Through her, Webster opens up the essential issues of the play. However, Cornelia too is overwhelmed by human frailty, and when confronted with grief and the insoluble moral dilemma of defending one of her sons for his murder of the other, her mind gives way and madness comes (V.iv.68ff).

Webster uses Cornelia's plight to great dramatic effect in the last act; it provides a note of pathos in a long, dark movement. Even Bracciano is moved by it, saying, *Have comfort my grieved mother* (V.ii.52), and it is after she sings her dirge that Flamineo admits his feelings of guilt, and that Bracciano's ghost appears (V.iv.120–125). Cornelia's madness makes a sad counterpoint to, and heightens the horrors of, the violence in the play, and it has a positive outcome in Flamineo's admission that he has acted wrongly, and his acceptance of the consequences. In this way Cornelia enables Flamineo to achieve tragic status, even if only briefly.

Activity

By close examination of Vittoria's rejection of Bracciano at IV.ii.101–127, explore the effects Webster creates in his verse.

Discussion

Webster uses the traditional form of verse for tragedy, iambic pentameter, yet his style is original and restless, varying in tone from lofty poetry such as that of Bracciano's professions of love in I.ii, through Flamineo's satirical assault upon society's inequality in the same scene (lines 327–344), to the quickfire ripostes of the warring lovers in IV.ii.128–147. His sustained use of allegory and imagery develops meanings, while (perhaps because of his legal training) Webster shows a keen awareness of the dramatic impact of set-piece speeches.

Vittoria is given no soliloquies, but Webster uses such a set-piece speech to reveal something of her inner world when she responds to Bracciano's unjustified attack in IV.ii. The audience has heard Vittoria's persuasive speeches at her trial, aware that she is playing several roles while acting as her own advocate, but nevertheless her courage and spirit here increase her tragic status.

Webster begins by alienating the audience from Bracciano as he echoes the French Ambassador's words at the trial (*She hath lived ill*, III.ii.107), telling her that *all the world speaks ill of thee* (IV.ii.101). Webster creates a double frame for Vittoria; already unfairly imprisoned in the House of Convertites, an imposition she has accepted humbly, she is now imprisoned emotionally through Bracciano's false charges. Vittoria is subjected to male tyranny inflicted by a murderous Bracciano and his servant, ironically her own brother.

Vittoria completes his line *For all the world speaks ill of thee* with a quiet comment, *No matter*, immediately asserting her authority, if somewhat wearily. Her vow to *make that world recant/And change her speeches* (lines 102–103) gains the sympathy of the audience, and she begins her response to his rant by offering a judgement on her former lover. She defies Bracciano's power by referring to his guilt in murdering his wife (lines 104–105), and goes on to refer to his destruction of her own and her family's reputation.

Opening with a rhetorical question, *What have I gained by thee but infamy?* (line 107), Vittoria continues her main speech here with a sequence of five more rhetorical questions, culminating in the sharp

Is't not you? (line 116). Webster invites his audience to agree with her in answering these questions. In the second half of this speech, Vittoria returns to the imagery of sickness in the first half (lines 110–112) with the added connotation of corruption (lines 120–121), as Webster reminds his audience of the contagion of evil. Bracciano's earlier promises are thrown back in his face, and shown to be empty. The tone changes as, anger exhausted, she explains her decision: *Fare you well, sir* (line 119); she has *cut... off* the *corrupted limb* (lines 120–121), and this will allow her to repent. The enjambment (continuation of a phrase or clause over a line break) in the vivid lines *and now I'll go/Weeping to heaven on crutches* (lines 121–122) reflects the clear continuity of her thought. This image of sickness – the only positive one in the play – suggests a damaged but repentant human being who may now find salvation.

Vittoria externalizes her emotional and intellectual rejection of Bracciano by rejecting the gifts he has given her (line 122–123), and the following lines graphically contrast human salvation with the social world of material rewards and riches; again the audience is invited to sympathize with Vittoria's view.

Webster combines words with actions as Vittoria refers to a desperate wish to *toss myself/Into a grave* (lines 125–126) while the stage directions describe her throwing herself upon a bed. The visual imagery is clear; grave and bed are linked in a dramatic enactment of one of the central issues of *The White Devil*: in this corrupt male-dominated society, a woman claiming sexual freedom will find only death.

Although some critics see Vittoria as merely playing another role in this scene, the dialogue and action bring the audience closer to her than at any other time in the play; perhaps she achieves heroic status here. Certainly this speech prepares the audience for Vittoria's courage at her death. However, it is always clear that this woman, like any woman in such a society, will not be able to oppose the desires of a powerful man.

Religion, the Church and the State

As noted already (see pages 188–189), the characters who represent religious and moral authority are seen to be corrupt in this godless society. Is there any hope of effective leadership from the cardinal who is elected Pope Paul IV?

Webster presents political collaboration between Church and State throughout *The White Devil*. Monticelso and Francisco clearly share a common interest in avoiding war over the breakdown in their alliance with Bracciano. However, they mainly pursue narrow self-interest, with Monticelso concerned more for his relation Camillo's wealth than his honour or safety, while Francisco wishes to protect his dynastic interests as uncle and advisor to Giovanni, the future Duke of Bracciano.

The appearance together of Francisco and Monticelso in II.i sets the tone for their relationship, and poses a series of questions for the audience to consider. What should be the relationship between Church and State? Should the Church be politically engaged? When does Church intervention in political and personal affairs become improper? What is the rightful role of a Church leader, and what qualities are required in a good one? Although Webster offers no answers, the response of an audience must be a rejection of all that is witnessed onstage.

Webster uses the *strange encounter* between Flamineo and Lodovico in III.iii to reveal another instance of corruption, as Francisco has intervened on behalf of the murderer and pirate Lodovico to secure a pardon from a dying pope (III.iii.100–102).

The rigged election of the new pope in IV.iii is another, much more significant instance of corruption at work within the Church. Immediately after the election, Francisco's furtive whispering to the newly elected pope is an obvious sign of underhand collaboration between the two men (IV.iii.61). The priorities of the new Church leader are revealed when he chooses to excommunicate the lovers as his first act after giving the customary blessing. His apparent condemnation of murderous revenge shortly afterwards (lines 117–128) seems unconvincing in the light of all that has gone before.

Sixtus V, pope from 1585–90, is the historical figure on whom
Monticelso is based

Activity
What is the significance of the papal election scene (IV.iii) in the play?

Discussion
Some critics assert that the presentation onstage of the papal election
is at worst a distraction, and at best simply an opportunity for a
sumptuous spectacle to please the Red Bull audience. While Webster
may well have aimed to provide spectacle for his audience, this short
scene serves many other purposes, including the following.

- The theme of corruption is developed, as Francisco seems to know
  beforehand that the process will not take long (lines 39–40).
- There is visual irony when Monticelso appears as Pope Paul IV in
  state, given that the audience has seen his corruption earlier.
- Francisco publicly whispers to the new pope, revealing the
  influence he has over him; this is a visual reminder of the power
  of the conspirators and the vulnerability of Bracciano and
  Vittoria.

- The new pope's first act is the excommunication of the lovers. His priorities seem questionable, to say the least.
- Webster ends this scene on a cliffhanger after the pope warns Lodovico against revenge, then Francisco tricks Lodovico into thinking the pope has later sent him money. Has Monticelso changed his ideas now that he is pope? Will the revenge plot be affected?
- There is irony in the fact that the scene is immediately followed by another procession related to a religious ceremony – this time the wedding of a murderer and a whore.

The ending of the play

In the final act of *The White Devil* Webster offers a true theatrical *tour de force*. This long act represents over one third of the total extent of the play, and Webster skilfully controls the pace, maintains interest and involves the audience throughout. It is worth looking in detail at Webster's use of language and dramatic devices, and the final vision projected at the end of the play.

The setting of this act remains unchanged throughout, but Webster creates alternative 'psychological settings' that correspond with the development of the play. Bracciano appears proudly in his wedding procession (V.i) and armed for the Barriers (V.ii.46, V.iii), a strong and powerful chivalric knight echoing the feudal virtues of honour. He courteously welcomes his guests to his ducal palace (V.i.45). However, all this outward show of courtesy ends with the poisoning of his helmet by those very guests. He next appears wheeled onstage in a bed, to be sneered at by his enemies and eventually strangled. The 'setting' of Bracciano's life therefore becomes progressively restricted as fate closes in on him.

Similarly, Vittoria begins the act by processing grandly as the bride and the new mistress of the ducal palace. Her psychological setting too closes in as, unprotected after Bracciano's death, she sees where she really is: *Oh me! this place is hell* (V.iii.186).

Flamineo's psychological entrapment is more marked; at first he seems relatively at ease in the ducal palace, but his misjudgements soon indicate his loss of control, as first Bracciano is unforgiving about the murder of his brother (V.ii.76–79), then Giovanni bans him from his presence and the centres of palace power (V.iv.34–36). In perhaps the most dramatic entrapment of all, he presents himself finally as if in a chimney, the anteroom to hell, as he pretends to be dying (V.vi.142–143).

Webster maintains pace and interest by dividing the scenes in Act V (with the exception of the fifth) into many smaller movements. A scene that is busy and public can suddenly transform into a private, personal encounter, such as in V.i, which has a five-part structure. Initially Hortensio and Flamineo act as commentators, deepening the audience's feelings of anxiety and curiosity, for example through Hortensio's comment *'Tis strange* (line 25); this is followed by Bracciano's public welcome of the visitors, which gives way to the quiet meeting between the conspirators; next there are the angry exchanges within Flamineo's family and with Zanche. Finally, Zanche and the disguised Francisco are seen to form a new and unlikely alliance. At each transition the staging will reflect the change of mood, as public meetings would occupy the central stage, and private ones the marginal areas. Webster would probably have intended the conversations to overlap slightly, so that the audience's attention is demanded on all parts of the stage.

The sensational elements of this act have been discussed above (page 187), and Webster certainly takes risks, especially in Flamineo's mock death (see page 219). One way in which Webster has prepared his audience for this final act is in Flamineo's words to Bracciano:

As in this world there are degrees of evils,
So in this world there are degrees of devils.
You're a great duke, I your poor secretary.

(IV.ii.57–9)

247

The implications of these words will be realized in a last act where the whole stage seems to be peopled with devils. Webster suggests that this society is hellish through his frequent use of the word *devil*: twice in Act I; once in Act II; nine times in Act III; seven times in Act IV; and a massive 18 times in Act V. All the major characters are called 'devils', and so is a wider section of society, the one that appears in Monticelso's *black book* (IV.i.33–36).

This perception of devils is made more concrete in Act V through Bracciano's vision of the approach of Satan himself (V.iii.101–106), and Flamineo perfects this vision with his own description of the dead Bracciano: *forty devils/Wait on him in his livery of flames* (V.iii.216–217). The audience would recognize this almost biblical account of hell; it is as if the great duke has metaphorically become Satan himself. As noted above, both Vittoria and Flamineo understand that they are moving into a hell on earth, and even Giovanni, as its new ruler, is linked with *the devil* (V.iv.31), and explicitly compared with his devilish fellow rulers. Webster makes the transformation of setting explicit in Vittoria's realization that:

> O the cursed devil...
> Makes us forsake that which was made for man,
> The world, to sink to that was made for devils,
> Eternal darkness.

(V.vi.58–64)

The play ends on a dark and sombre note, apparently denying all hope for redemption or salvation. In the world of the play, society is governed according to the whims of selfish rulers; it is devoid of morality, religion or the rule of law; and all types of love and loyalty have been shown to fail.

Can Giovanni remake this State? This seems unlikely, as he is not old or wise enough to undertake such a task and his inexperience suggests he cannot grasp the nature of the problem. Flamineo, as noted above, has affected audience response to the new duke by linking him to *the devil* and claiming that *He hath his uncle's villainous look already* (V.iv.32), and Giovanni seems to echo his uncle's cruelty when he sentences the assassins not just *to prison*, but *to torture* (V.vi.294).

Giovanni uses two troubling words in these final speeches: *justice* (line 295) and *honoured* (line 301). Webster has redefined both concepts through the words and actions of other characters throughout the play. The audience has seen for itself how justice has operated at Vittoria's trial and in the revengers' self-justifications. The word *honour* has been similarly degraded.

The situation at the end of the play is that the real sources of power lie elsewhere, in the persons of Francisco and Monticelso, who are both safely detached from the slaughter. As noted above (page 206), it is evident that Giovanni has no realistic prospect of establishing justice against these two men, even if he wishes to do so.

Perhaps the play ends with the suggestion that at best a solution might be found in youth, innocence and freshness, but it is not likely in this place or at this time.

Activity

How does Webster's use of the traditions of revenge tragedy and the inclusion of Gothic elements enhance your understanding of *The White Devil*?

Discussion

Revenge tragedy is rooted in Seneca's 'theatre of blood' in ancient Rome, which was characteristically bloody and violent, with supernatural and magical elements. Thomas Kyd updated this tradition in *The Spanish Tragedy* (c. 1587), laying the foundations for revenge tragedy in English Renaissance drama.

In *The White Devil* Webster blends many features of revenge tragedy with elements that were later to be termed Gothic: fables and dreams, ghosts and supernatural apparitions. Music and possibly masque would also be included in the pageantry of the processions, and Webster also uses the tradition of dumb-shows to reveal actions that take place elsewhere. All these theatrical elements blend with a more 'realistic' or 'naturalistic' style that achieves some psychological depth in the characters. Although Webster is sometimes criticized for the way he structures his plays – they have been described as developing in a tapestry effect, or in cycles, echoes, and parallels, rather than sequentially – analysis of *The White Devil* reveals that all elements work together to achieve Webster's purposes (see pages 216–218 above).

To assess the significance of Webster's use of Gothic elements it might be helpful to think about the effects created by the appearance of the two ghosts, of Isabella in IV.i and of Bracciano in V.iv. What is revealed about character and motivation? How is the plot furthered? What issues are raised?

Theatrical interpretations

The White Devil in performance

The White Devil was frequently performed from the time it appeared until Oliver Cromwell ordered the closing of the theatres in 1642. When the theatres reopened there were three listed performances in 1660, and in 1669 the best actors of the period played in it.

In 1707 Nahum Tate 'tidied up' the play for performance, calling his version *Injured Love or The Cruel Husband*.

Richard Cave's *Text and Performance: The White Devil and The Duchess of Malfi* (see Further Reading page 263) gives a useful history of recent performances. These productions can be summarized as follows.

1925   The first modern performance by the Renaissance Theatre Company, London, was faithful to the text.

1935   A performance by the Phoenix Society at St Martin's Theatre, London emphasized the poetry of the play.

1947   Robert Helpmann as Flamineo and Margaret Rawlings as Vittoria appeared in a London production that made the most of the sensationalism and bloodshed.

1955   Jack Landau, at the Phoenix Theater, New York, produced a modern gangster interpretation, again focussing on violence, but with some concern for character.

1969 Frank Dunlop directed at the National Theatre, with Edward Woodward as Flamineo. It was a humanist production exalting the courage of the central protagonists, struggling in an evil world. Woodward played Flamineo as half-innocent, half-corrupt, with an emphasis on theatricality.

1971 At the Citizens' Theatre, Glasgow, Philip Prowse placed a board over the stage trapdoor to emphasize Vittoria's vulnerability as she stood in court; this might also have symbolized the idea of hell.

1975 At the Nottingham Playhouse, Richard Eyre based his political reading on the class struggle.

1976 Michael Lindsay-Hogg at the Old Vic explored the theme of the abuse of power, using a present-day setting. The fine costumes were increasingly ironic as make-up was used to portray the ravages of sin in Bracciano and Francisco. Glenda Jackson played a feminist Vittoria oppressed by a patriarchal society based on cruelty.

1979 Michael Kahn directed The Acting Company, New York, in a novel production with Flamineo dressed like a punk rocker sporting a studded dog collar and spiked hair. At the end of the play Giovanni surveyed the carnage while playing 'I Will Survive' on a ghetto blaster.

1991 Philip Prowse at the National Theatre directed a spectacular production emphasizing the ceremonies and processions, with the stage alternately pierced by shafts of light and plunged in darkness. It was a Gothic presentation in which both Flamineo and Marcello, along with Josette Simon's Vittoria, were played by black actors.

1996 Gale Edwards directed the Royal Shakespeare Company at the Swan Theatre in a stunning production stressing the themes of sexuality, lust and corruption. Both Vittoria and Zanche were naked under gowns that were slit to the waist; Vittoria bared her breast to her brother, suggesting incest.

2008 Jonathan Munby at the Menier Chocolate Factory, London, directed a highly erotic production that spoke to modern audiences. As in the original theatre, the audience surrounded the stage. A narrow table ran the length of the playing area, with the audience on each side, and blood-red curtains hung on both sides of the table. Costumes were in the style of the 'Godfather' films, indicating the balance of power. Flamineo was presented as a clearly bisexual villain, with bright blue eye make-up, who had prospered through gratifying predominantly male sexual desires. Obviously drug-addicted, he controlled the suicide pact with his sister, implying incest as they wore identical earrings and shared embraces.

Josette Simon as Vittoria and Denis Quilley as Bracciano in the 1991 National Theatre production

The next section includes comments on the most significant schools of critical thought; when you attend a production of this play you will be able to assess which views have influenced the director's interpretation.

Critical views

As noted above, *The White Devil* remained popular until the closing of the theatres in 1642. In 1707 an adapted version was produced, which suggests that the contemporary view of the play was that it needed some improvement to an untidy structure and inappropriate use of language.

In the nineteenth century, Webster's reputation as a great dramatist was firmly established. Despite George Bernard Shaw's gibes about awarding him the title 'Tussaud Laureate', presumably because of the bloodshed and sensational elements in his plays, Webster's writing was much appreciated. For example, the eminent critic William Hazlitt compared him to Shakespeare, the poet Algernon Swinburne praised the sense of terror he evoked, and later the early-twentieth-century poet Rupert Brooke approved of the darkness of the play, in which he described the characters as being like maggots writhing in darkness.

More modern criticism has moved into some very interesting areas. Early twentieth-century criticism of Webster is humanist in approach, appreciating his study of human nature in response to tragic circumstances. Webster's plays were seen as a tribute to humankind's ability to endure; tortured and purged by suffering, the heroes were seen to attain a kind of salvation. The first great critics of Webster included T.S. Eliot, in his essay *Four Elizabethan Dramatists* (1924, republished as *Elizabethan Dramatists* in 1963) and M.C. Bradbrook, with *Themes and Conventions of Elizabethan Tragedy* (1935, second edition 1980).

A more modern reading of these issues was offered by Travis Bogard in *The Tragic Satire of John Webster* (1955). Hereward T.

Price explored the text through an analysis of Webster's use of language and devices in his article *The Function of Imagery in Webster* (1955).

An interest in form and genre was evident in all of these works, and this approach was developed by critics such as Ralph Berry in *The Art of John Webster* (1972). This aspect has been studied more recently by writers such as Jacqueline Pearson in *Tragedy and Tragicomedy in the Plays of John Webster* (1980), and Christina Luckyj in *A Winter's Snake: Dramatic Form in the Tragedies of John Webster* (1989).

In the form of criticism known as 'cultural materialist', writers address the context of the plays. The term implies an investigation into the political, social and intellectual background to Webster's drama. M.C. Bradbrook considered the political and intellectual context in *John Webster: Citizen and Dramatist* (1980), while J.W. Lever, in his important text *The Tragedy of State* (1971), addressed the political and social environment suggested within the plays.

'New historicist' critic Jonathan Dollimore revised and extended Lever's reading in *Radical Tragedy: Religion, Ideology and Power in the Drama of Shakespeare and His Contemporaries* (1984, third edition 2004), essential reading for students interested in this area. Frank Whigham, in *Seizures of the Will in Early Modern English Drama* (1996), works with a Marxist subtext, exploring the fact that wealth is inaccessible to the subjects of this society. Despite the suggestion of some social change, characters are seen to be disturbed and powerless, and Whigham explores women's use of sexuality as a means of social advancement.

Feminist and genre studies have been offered by many critics, such as Dympna Callaghan with *Women and Gender in Renaissance Tragedy* (1989), Catherine Belsey with *The Subject of Tragedy: Identity and Difference in Renaissance Drama* (1985), and Kathleen McLuskie in *Renaissance Dramatists* (1989).

Luke Wilson offers an interesting account of the influence of Webster's study of the law in *Theaters of Intention: Drama and the Law in Early Modern England* (2000).

Skull Beneath the Skin: The Achievement of John Webster (1986) is a useful compendium of biographical information and criticism by Charles R. Forker. Compilations of criticism include *John Webster*, edited by G.K. and S.K. Hunter (1969).

See Further Reading page 263 for all the works mentioned here.

Essay Questions

1   To what extent does Webster present Vittoria as a victim?

2   Explore the effectiveness of Webster's use of language effects in *The White Devil*.

3   'A young man deprived of opportunities': to what extent is society responsible for Flamineo's villainy?

4   Discuss Webster's stagecraft and the use of theatricality in *The White Devil*.

5   Which aspects of *The White Devil* are specifically Jacobean?

6   Consider the significance of Monticelso's *black book* (IV.i.33) in the play.

7   Discuss Francisco's presentation as the archetypal Machiavellian.

8   Explore the ways in which Webster uses repetition to develop his ideas in *The White Devil*.

9   How does Webster's use of Gothic elements enhance your understanding of the issues of the play?

10   Consider the significance of the following words in *The White Devil*: 'love'; 'honour'; 'good/goodness'.

11   'The outer violence indicates the inner corruption': how far is this true of *The White Devil*?

12   Explore the functions of the ambassadors in *The White Devil*.

13   Discuss the effects created by Webster's use of metatheatricality in this play.

14   What does Webster suggest about the relationship between Church and State?

15 To what extent is *The White Devil* a warning to contemporary London society? Consider how Webster presents these ideas.

16 In what ways is *The White Devil* still relevant today?

17 Consider the effectiveness of the first scene as an opening to the play.

18 'A character can be judged by the way he/she dies'. With reference to three characters, explore this viewpoint.

19 Compare the ways in which three female characters react to the patriarchal society of *The White Devil*.

20 Is the audience offered any hope for the future of the society in *The White Devil*?

21 What does Webster suggest in *The White Devil* about the role of religion in society?

22 Compare and contrast the dramatic and thematic significance of Flamineo and Marcello.

23 Discuss *The White Devil* as a tragedy.

24 What does Webster have to say about politics in *The White Devil*? Go on to consider how he presents these views.

Chronology

Webster's life

c. 1550   John Webster senior born.

1571   John Webster senior made Freeman of Merchant Taylors' Company.

1578/80   John Webster born.

c. 1587   Webster probably enters the Merchant Taylors' school.

c. 1595   Webster enters New Inn as a preliminary to the study of law.

1598   Webster admitted to the Middle Temple, one of the Inns of Court.

1602   Webster receives an advance from Philip Henslowe as part of a group of writers.

c. 1604   Webster writes for the Earl of Worcester's Men, later Queen Anne's Men on the accession of James I.

1604   Webster revises John Marston's *The Malcontent* for The King's Men.

1604/5   Webster works with Thomas Dekker on *Westward Ho! and Northward Ho!*.

1606   Webster marries Sara Peniall, aged 17, who is seven months pregnant.

1612   *The White Devil* performed unsuccessfully at the Red Bull by Queen Anne's Men.

1614   *The Duchess of Malfi* acted successfully at the Blackfriars and the Globe by The King's Men.

1615   Webster claims his right of entry to the Merchant Taylors' Company.

1619   Webster writes *The Devil's Law-Case*, performed by Queen Anne's Men at the Cockpit.

1623   *The Duchess of Malfi* and *The Devil's Law-Case* published in quarto.

1624   Webster writes the pageant *Monuments of Honour* for the Merchant Taylors' Company.

c. 1634   Webster dies aged about 56.

Historical, literary and social events

1547 Henry VIII dies; accession of Edward VI.

1553 Edward VI dies; accession of Mary I.

1558 Mary I dies; accession of Elizabeth I.

1564 Christopher Marlowe, William Shakespeare born.

1572 Thomas Dekker, Ben Jonson born.

1575 Thomas Heywood, John Marston, Cyril Tourneur born.

1576 'The Theatre' built, the first in London.

1579 John Fletcher born.

1580 Thomas Middleton born.

1586 John Ford born.

c. 1587 Thomas Kyd's *The Spanish Tragedy* acted.

1589 Spanish Armada defeated.

1588/9 Marlowe's *Dr Faustus* probably acted.

1590 High prices cause economic depression especially rurally.

1592 Plague outbreak in London: theatres closed.

1594 Rural poverty worsens because of bad harvests.

1599 Globe Theatre built in Southwark.

1600 Fortune Theatre built in north London.

1601 Duke of Bracciano (son of the duke whose story is told in *The White Devil*) visits London; Earl of Essex's execution for treason.

1603 Elizabeth I dies; accession of James I (James VI of Scotland). Shakespeare's *Hamlet* acted; Raleigh/Cobham rebellion.

1604 Marston's *The Malcontent* acted.

1605 The Gunpowder Plot.
George Chapman, Ben Jonson and John Marston imprisoned when their satire *Eastwood Ho!* offends James I.

1606 Middleton's *The Revenger's Tragedy* acted.

1608 The King's Men established at Blackfriars Theatre.

1611 The Authorized Version of the Bible (King James Bible) published.

1613 The Globe Theatre burns down.

1621 Middleton's *Women Beware Women* acted.

1622 Middleton's *The Changeling* acted.

1623 'First Folio' of Shakespeare's work published.

1625 James I dies; accession of Charles I.

     1628 Duke of Buckingham assassinated.

     1629 Charles I dissolves Parliament and decides to govern without it.

c. 1634 Webster dies.

            Ford's *Tis Pity She's a Whore* acted.

     1642 Civil war; the closing of the theatres.

     1649 Charles I executed; Commonwealth.

     1660 Restoration of Charles II; theatres reopened.

     1665 The Great Plague.

     1666 The Great Fire of London.

Further Reading

Biography

M.C. Bradbrook, *John Webster: Citizen and Dramatist* (Weidenfeld & Nicolson, 1980)

R.A. Foakes (ed.), *Henslowe's Diary* (Cambridge University Press, 1961, second edition 2002)

Critical books and articles

Kate Aughterson, *Webster: The Tragedies* (Palgrave, 2001)

Catherine Belsey, *The Subject of Tragedy: Identity and Difference in Renaissance Drama* (Methuen, 1985)

Ralph Berry, *The Art of John Webster* (Clarendon Press, 1972)

Travis Bogard, *The Tragic Satire of John Webster* (University of California Press, 1955)

M.C. Bradbrook, *Themes and Conventions of Elizabethan Tragedy* (Cambridge University Press 1935, second edition 1980)

Dympna Callaghan, *Women and Gender in Renaissance Tragedy* (Harvester Wheatsheaf, 1989)

Richard Cave, *Text and Performance: The White Devil and The Duchess of Malfi* (Macmillan, 1988)

Jonathan Dollimore, *Radical Tragedy: Religion, Ideology and Power in the Drama of Shakespeare and His Contemporaries* (Prentice Hall/Harvester Wheatsheaf, 1984; Palgrave Macmillan, 2004)

T.S. Eliot, *Elizabethan Essays* (Haskell House, 1964)

Charles R. Forker, *Skull Beneath the Skin: The Achievement of John Webster* (Southern Illinois University Press, 1986)

G.K. and S.K. Hunter (eds.), *John Webster: A Critical Anthology* (Penguin, 1969)

J. W. Lever, *The Tragedy of State* (Methuen & Co, 1971)

Christina Luckyj, *A Winter's Snake: Dramatic Form in the Tragedies of John Webster* (University of Georgia Press, 1989)

Kathleen McLuskie, *Renaissance Dramatists* (Harvester Wheatsheaf, 1989)

Jacqueline Pearson, *Tragedy and Tragicomedy in the Plays of John Webster* (Manchester University Press, 1980)

Hereward T. Price, *The Function of Imagery in Webster* (PMLA Vol. 70, No. 4, September 1955, pages 717–739)

Frank Whigham, *Seizures of the Will in Early Modern English Drama* (Cambridge University Press, 1996)

Luke Wilson, *Theaters of Intention: Drama and the Law in Early Modern England* (University of Stanford Press, 2000) – see Chapter 20, pages 225–237

Websites

For further critical perspectives on performances and productions go to the websites of individual theatres or actors. To find Webster criticism online, use a search engine such as Google.